The Candle of God

Shefa

MAGGID

Adin Steinsaltz

The Candle of God

DISCOURSES ON HASIDIC THOUGHT

EDITED AND TRANSLATED BY

Yehuda Hanegbi

Maggid Books

The Candle of God: Discourses on Ḥasidic Thought

Maggid edition, 2010

Maggid Books
An imprint of Koren Publishers Jerusalem Ltd.

POB 8531, New Milford, CT 06676-8531, USA
POB 2455, London W1A 5WY, England
& POB 4044, Jerusalem 91040, Israel

www.korenpub.com

© Adin Steinsaltz 1999

Published in cooperation with The Shefa Foundation

Edited and translated by Yehuda Hanegbi

ISBN 978 159264 297 7, *hardcover*

A CIP catalogue record for this title is
available from the British Library

Printed and bound in the United States

Contents

IMPLICATIONS OF THE MENORA

Translator's Preface

Like the previously published *Discourses on Ḥasidic Thought* by Rabbi Adin Steinsaltz, this is a selection of talks commenting on the writings of Rabbi Schneur Zalman of Liadi, founder of the Chabad movement, and of his grandson, Rabbi Menaḥem Mendel (Tzemaḥ Tzedek). More than the other collections, however, the present work focuses on certain aspects of Jewish wisdom that have become obscured and gone underground, so to speak, in the modern world.

As with all such genuine assertions of wisdom, all we can do is provide a clue, like the saying, "The soul of man is the candle of God" (Proverbs 20:27), an idea that is often repeated in this book. And then, in making the (manifestly impossible) endeavor to explain what the soul of man consists of, and in grappling with what is meant by "the candle of God," we are brought a little closer to earnest comprehension.

Jewish tradition has preserved the religious insights of the past in a marvelously consistent fashion. Sometimes we may become impatient with seemingly irrelevant details in the Bible, Talmud, Midrash, and Kabbala, but we are grateful for the help of commentators throughout the generations. Even if they don't always agree, they at least elucidate the matter in a deeply satisfying way.

In the following selection of talks excerpted from this tradition, some passages may sound too abstract or even, for many readers, esoteric. This can be attributed to a certain historical neglect in Jewish education. There is a gap between the reasonable and the mythological that need not have come about. Because, in point of fact, the essence of Jewish spirituality is very intimate, existential, personal. So much of it goes back to life and love as it was lived by the people – which is one of the reasons the Kabbala has remained closely connected with ritual, legend, and custom.

Accordingly, in an effort to bridge a certain gap between Jewish wisdom and modern life, the following five series of discourses were chosen for the present book. The titles are my own.

1) "Hidden Aspects of Shabbat" based on *Likkutei Torah* (*Beshallaḥ*) by Rabbi Schneur Zalman of Liadi, does not pretend to exhaust the subject of rest, respite, and passivity. It concentrates rather on the delight inherent in such sanctified rest, the Divine delight providing the Sabbath with a purpose and meaning beyond anything we can reckon.

2) The series on the "The Way of the Soul and Torah" based on *Likkutei Torah* (*Vayikra*) may seem abstract for those unfamiliar with Kabbalistic terminology, but in an inexplicably direct fashion, the lively interaction between the individual Jew and Torah strikes one's intelligence sharply.

3) "Sanctity and Restraint" based on *Likkutei Torah* (*Pekudei*) is a rather unusual argument, with provocative ramifications, in order to explain the superiority of the commandments "not-to-do" over the commandments "to-do." It pursues the Jewish principle that right action is what counts; then it subtly confutes the contention that the highest virtue resides in carrying out the positive commandments "to do." The argument dwells on the spiritual reality behind restraint, on the power that is added to oneself and to the world by deliberately not doing certain things that life seems to call forth. The humanity behind "Thou shalt not" is given its higher dimension.

4) Perhaps most challenging of all are the relatively practical discourses on "The Trials of Life," based on *Derekh mitzvotekha* (p. 370, *Aḥarei*), by Rabbi Menaḥem Mendel (the *Tzemaḥ Tzedek*). We are

drawn to admit that although all men are confronted by trouble and affliction, few know how to engage properly and to emerge more or less unscathed. The old wisdom is here presented with a gentle, if startling, persistence, and one is brought to a strange threshold: Suffering can indeed be emancipatory.

5) Finally, the book dares to touch on some of the ancient and profound "Implications of the Menora," based on *Likkutei Torah* (*Beha'alotekha*). Mostly its fascination lies in the evocation of spiritual emanations in terms of light – light as higher layers of the national consciousness, as a social atmosphere, as knowledge, and as enlightenment.

Not in vain does the present work quote the saying about the soul of man being the candle of God. Once, this was quite self-understood by the Jewish people. Now we need to be reminded and even to have it explained to us. We can only be thankful that there are men like Rabbi Adin around who can do this, naturally and without much fuss. Indeed, what each commentator adds to the traditional wisdom is ascertainable, not only by history but also by a perceptive reader's heart.

Yehuda Hanegbi

Hidden Aspects of Shabbat

Chapter one

Torah and mitzvot are called the way of God, as it is written: "Its ways are the ways of pleasantness and all its paths are peace" (Proverbs 3:17). For the ways of Torah are to keep to the paths of the Lord, to do charity and justice. In another passage, we find a statement to the effect that the Heavenly world and this world are built on two letters of one of the Divine Names – the Heavenly world by the letter *Yod*, and this world by the letter *Heh*.

What does this mean? Why should the letter *Yod*, the smallest and most insignificant of the alphabet, be that which becomes the basis for the most spiritual of worlds? And the answer is that *Yod* is ten; by ten Divine utterances did Creation take place, and thus, according to the ten *Sefirot*, were the worlds formed. To be sure, it has to be remembered that God is not the same as His creation, that there is an unbridgeable gap between the actuality of Divine Being and the actuality of all the worlds, from the most spiritual to the most material. That is to say "for with You is the source of life, and in Your light shall we see light" (Psalms 36:10), meaning that in the next world the souls (of men) enjoy the radiance of the *Shekhina*, Divine presence. This bliss is not other, cannot be more than what a person is capable of grasping. It is not a matter of the mind, obviously; it is a spiritual situation. At the same time, just as with intellectual matters or even physical, the soul has to be able to receive that which is bestowed on it; the bliss is only proportionate to the capacity of the individual to absorb it.

The other side of this concept is that the soul is able to absorb something of the Divine splendor, that the infinite light of the next world is not so far beyond the human that it is inaccessible. It is made available to a person by descending level upon level of purity and light. Ultimately it is available, and it can be experienced as real. To be sure, it is a very much condensed and contracted Divine Joy, as we have said, and for all its being intangible, it is not a nothing; being spiritual, it is a positive existence, a genuine reality. It is a nothing only in the sense that it is not anything that we can identify or grasp, as well as being so greatly contracted, and a something in the sense that it is the source of bliss, "for You are the source of life." Bliss and life are identical here. Since the actuality of the Divine is not given, nor even the possibility of being with Him even when in His presence, we say that we can be in His light. And that is the meaning of the *Yod* as a symbol of the great diminution and contraction, of the available reality of the next world for the soul.

Following upon this is the concept of the extension of reality from the *Yod* through all the letters of the Divine Name, the *Tetragrammaton*, which is the key to the order of Creation. But this is a profound kabbalistic way of interpreting the world of God and man. For our purpose, it is enough to note the significance of a beginning point, a point of departure, so to speak, which is in itself meaningless for all but the One Who is giving. For this One Who wishes to transmit something, it is necessary to extend the initial impulse or inspiration through a number of gradations or channels: thought, speech, and action. The receiver does not have to do more than receive through the channels of transmission and somehow reconstruct the message. An idea is expressed in words; the listener has to interpret the words back to the idea. Sometimes a message is transmitted through electromagnetic waves and it has to be rechanneled through a proper electronic apparatus to be heard. In all cases, from the point of departure the message has to take form and go through a channeling, and then there must be a corresponding instrument to receive and "interpret" it.

Thus, the *Yod* of beginnings is the source of life. It has to extend in all dimensions and contract in terms of Infinite Light in order to become reality. For man, the capacity to "contract" in this way is also the beginning of expression. Without gathering together one's impressions and mental processes, focusing them somehow, nothing significant can be done. Speech needs a prior contraction of thought, just as any transmission requires an ordering of the factors involved.

The "contraction" can take several forms besides that of actual diminution or shrinkage. It can be a concealment or screening process that beclouds the light (like smoked glass), shielding the receiver and making it possible to absorb the rays of the sun or the higher worlds without injury to one's self. Another kind of contraction is by the use of a transmitter. The moon can be safely looked at even though its light is of the sun, because it is an agent, lessening the light by reflecting, by transmitting on a lower key, giving off less than it receives. Thus, the higher light of God can usually be received only through those lights that are able to transmit it to us in safety.

Similarly, the Torah has many degrees of light and transmission.

But to return to the concept that the next world was created by the letter *Yod*. The premise is that this world is the revealed world; the next world is really the source, that from which this world gets its substantiality. The Heavenly world is illumed and infinite; this world below is dark, limited, and material; it is revealed only in the sense that it is a visible portion of reality, like the dry land surrounded by the sea. And of course there is considerable hiddenness also within the revealed, but altogether our world is "this" world, that to which we can point and with which we can interact as part of our existence, the world of good and evil.

This, in turn, brings us to the scriptural commandment to "do it today" (Deuteronomy 7:11). Besides the simple fact that this is always good sense, there is the well-known dilemma of putting off till tomorrow. Both the *tzaddik* and the wicked are constantly provoked by the bad impulse as well as the good. The essential difference between the virtuous person and the sinful one is the difference between the postponement of the good impulse, and its immediate putting into action, today, and whether the bad impulse is deferred or eagerly realized now.

In this way we live on in this world of ours, oscillating between a constant choosing of one thing or another.

Consequently, the world also presents a challenge. We are charged with the task of revealing the Divine, of bringing God out of His concealment by overcoming the obscuring barriers. This does not exist in the next world, where the Divine is available according to one's capacity – where there is no object of desire, no privilege or duty. Everything is given and nothing is left to be yearned for. It is a static non-state in which one performs neither mitzva nor transgression. The next world is complete and infinitely satisfying. This world, in contrast, is marked by the need "to do it this day," for only the present strives for perfection.

All of which is only an introduction to our subject of the Shabbat. The speculations concerning the nature of the next world are based on the insights of the Sages as well as reasonable hypotheses. Our intention is to show that the essence of Shabbat is really a trickle, an infiltration, of the next world into this world. It is a percolation and diffusion of an existing Divine Reality.

Chapter two

How shall the infinite plenty be drawn down from above? To satisfy this urgent need we have learned to do the actions of Torah and mitzvot, to bestir or awaken the upper worlds and induce the desired response. We do not have other ways of drawing upon Divine plenty. Man was put into the Garden of Eden to till and to keep it (Genesis 2:15), as it is written: "To till it" means the 248 positive mitzvot, "to keep it" means the 365 negative mitzvot. Just as the work of the gardener makes the earth give forth greater fruit and abundance, so does man draw forth the utmost joy and goodness from life by proper cultivation of Torah and mitzvot.

This is also the meaning of "All that has breath shall praise God Halleluya" (Psalms 150:6). To praise here is also to laud or acclaim, to glorify and adore, that is, to add light (or provide an enhanced view). The word *hallel* (praise) is close to the Hebrew root word *hela*, that which illuminates. When we worship God we also send light upward, so that the human soul is called the candle of God in the sense that it not only sheds light for itself to illumine its own way, it also serves to draw the Divine light to itself. At the same time, the soul is only a receptacle, or instrument, of light, in the way that the candle is only a means for light to fasten itself. The soul of man is simply a place where the name of God is revealed.

A deeper inquiry may consequently expose the question: why then is the soul unable to draw down Divine light by its own powers of thought and striving? Why the need for mitzvot? The answer given by the Ḥasidic Sage is a rather baffling and profound statement concerning the origin of the mitzvot. The primary root of the mitzvot, he asserts, is of the aspect of the inwardness of the highest delight. The mitzvot come from the inner depths of the *Oneg Elyon*, which is the utmost joy and rapture of being.

It is written in the Scriptures (Proverbs 8:30) that the Torah is the plaything of God, and by plaything is meant that which gives pleasure and gladness. More inwardly it signifies God's playing with Himself; in the sense that the Torah in its essence, in itself, not as that which was given to man – is God's amusement. And what would such a Divine plaything consist of, before there was a world, before existence and reality? It would have to be an all-sufficient delight, the blissfulness of being, the very source of all pleasure, "for with Thee is the source of life" (Psalms 36:9). As the primary source of life, it is equivalent to the origin of the higher delight, the *Oneg Elyon*, and as such is the very beginning of all beginnings. It is that which we may first grasp of the very essence of the Divine.

Even before acknowledging that, however, we are made conscious of the fact that God "sanctifies us with His mitzvot." We recite the words before the doing of the action. Sanctification may here be defined as being allowed to take part in elemental holiness as God's way of playing with man. Torah and mitzvot form the substance of a mutual enjoyment. Indeed, the blessing very specifically denotes that we are performing "His"*mitzvot* (מצוותיו), mitzvot that He gave to us and which sanctify us. We recognize that God is relating to us through something that is His, not ours – ואהיה אצלו שעשועים ("And I shall be unto Him as a plaything"). He is letting us share in His delight, by sanctifying us in His mitzvot. We are granted a gift of Divine joy.

This is possible because God raised us to the level of consciousness in which we can participate in His mitzva and in the accompanying heavenly delight. Such, too, is the meaning of being occupied with

Torah for its own sake. There are those who get involved with Torah in order to imbibe its contents, or to use it for whatever practical or even idealistic purpose they think best. They are not relating to the Torah for its own sake, that is for the love of Torah itself and not for the benefits to be had from it. To be occupied with Torah for its own sake means to relate to Torah, not as a literary work or as moral instruction or even wisdom, but to let the Torah emanate its splendor and joy, to let it serve as a channel for Divine light. One thereby reveals its ever new and vital message as a gratification of unspoken wish; it is a happiness that does not come from anything in the world or in oneself.

Hence it is said that "Her ways are ways of pleasantness and all her paths are peace. She is a tree of life to those who lay hold on her; and happy are those who hold her fast" (Proverbs 3:17). Pleasantness here is a certain sweetness. It is a feeling of sweet delight. And the pleasantness of Torah refers to such a self-sufficient delight in God. For there are all kinds of enjoyments; but the higher enjoyment or Divine delight is the source of them all. As it is written: "For with you is the source of life" (Psalms 36:10).

A passing remark is here in place concerning the use of the plural in the ways of Torah. Isn't it one way and not many? To be sure, there is the kabbalistic definition of "way" as the three *Sefirot*: *Ḥesed*, *Gevura*, and *Tiferet*. These are the three basic lines of existence; they parallel the three fundamentals we have learned from the Sages: Torah, *Avoda* (Divine Worship), and *Gemilut Ḥasadim* (Kindness). With Kindness corresponding to *Ḥesed*, Divine Worship to *Gevura*, and Torah to *Tiferet*, these can be considered the three ways of the Torah; each of them an expression of a different mode and attribute. In addition to all these, however, is the more encompassing view that every mitzva is in itself a separate path or way for the experience of delight in being. This is the meaning of the use of the plural in the Biblical statement, "Her ways are ways of pleasantness." And thus every mitzva is a pathway for holiness and Divine delight to go from level to level of being.

To proceed further into the meaning of "for with You is the source of life," we may inquire into the meaning of the words. "With You" does not signify that the source of life is your very essence and reality, but that this source of life is something that is with you, as an aspect of yourself like your name. This name, which is known elsewhere as "His great name," the first name which God had before there was anything else, is "אור אינסוף," Infinite Light. And, as we say in the prayer book (*Tanna D'vei Eliyahu*), "before there was a world, only He and His name existed." This Divine Name, which is Infinite Light, becomes the source of life in the process of Creation. "With you" therefore denotes not by you or next to you, but from you in the sense that the light of the sun is of the sun and from the sun itself, not something extraneous. So we say He and His name (that comes from Him) are one. His name is the way He becomes known to others, it is the potential of that which acts upon all else, the First Light emanating from Him. As such He is called the source of life, or the source of delight, which is the same thing. For life and joy are part of the One Being.

As it is known in Kabbala, the level of reality called "the inwardness of *Keter*" is the source of delight and is an aspect of Infinite Light. Also called "*Atik yomin*," this level of being is primary, preceding all else and serving as a source for all life and existence, including, of course, the delight of existence. But what do we really mean by this primal delight? Evidently it is not the same thing as the delight that comes from below, from taking pleasure in anything on earth. It is not a matter of the usual subject-object relation of sensation and joyful reaction. Indeed, pleasure or delight is not even of itself, it is derived from something. It does not seem to matter much what it is, whether tasty food for the body or spiritual nourishment for the mind. Joy comes from some other reality; one takes delight in something. Whereas the primal delight from above needs nothing else, it is totally self-sufficient. In terms of the Divine, there is nothing else: He is. He exists in and of Himself, and His Delight does not depend on anything outside of the soul (which mirrors Him).

Since the pleasures of the world are dependent on "a something else," the pleasures that are not so clearly derived are clearly more pure. Just as we may conceive of a reality that exists in its purity as something that stands on its own, without any dependence or support, so does the Rambam speak of the reality of God as that which is the background for all that exists. At the same time, of course, the Divine reality cannot be defined by any other reality, for everything is defined by God – at every level an entity is defined very precisely by the one above it. Hence, too, the Divine delight is totally different; nothing creates it, it is not a delight in anything else but itself.

It can be considered on a higher level even than the Higher Wisdom which is above all other levels of existence. Wisdom, or Ḥokhma, is composed of two aspects: Ḥokhma and the delight in Ḥokhma. This seems to indicate that the delight in Wisdom is not the same thing as the primal delight mentioned above; and that Higher Wisdom, which is connected with this particular delight in wisdom, is also not at the utmost level, not being pure and simply itself. It is Divine delight that is pure and simply itself at the utmost.

The concept of utmost simplicity is borrowed from the Maharal, who said that all the entities in the world are compound, everything is a mixture with something else, and that a simple, independent entity is one that is not mixed with anything else and cannot be separated into parts, and cannot be defined (circumscribed by delimiting forms).

In ordinary terms, simplicity is that which remains after all that is superfluous has been stripped away – the naked quality of a thing. But there is a far more profound meaning; after all there can be no end to the stripping away, in so far as the covering or skin of a plant or animal can be removed. The utmost simplicity is that ultimate which is not clothed, that from which all covering is stripped away – the thing itself. The utmost reality is therefore the basic essence of an entity, but it is more than an abstract uniqueness; it is that which is beyond combination or penetration, inward or outward, beyond definition or grasp. At the same time, it is very real. That which is simple to the utmost can, therefore, not be pinpointed or encompassed. And the higher delight, the primal joy of which we speak, is just such a self-sufficient taking pleasure in delight, simple to the ultimate.

The nature of pleasure in our world is to spread out in length and breadth, more so perhaps than any other quality of the soul. This would indicate that the primal delight, which comes from above, reaches out in all directions and goes to the deepest depths. It branches out in an enormous variety of form and detail. Indeed, there is no other power or quality of the soul that reaches so far in height and depth and breadth, in expansiveness and restriction – that is, in amplitude. For nothing is as broad as pleasure; nothing has such a multiplicity of form and expression.

In all, the object and content is that which gives joy and makes one happy. The hedonistic impulse is behind the action and gives it drive and power and meaning.

As a negative part of this process, perhaps, is its opposite, the play of affliction and suffering – that which man tries to avoid. This becomes the subjective definition of good and evil; good is pleasure-giving and evil is pain-inflicting. Even in the Bible it says: "Behold I have given you today life and good and death and evil…therefore choose life" (Deuteronomy 30:15, 19). The choice here is not between good and evil but between life and death. What is good then becomes more than what is merely pleasurable. The nature of the pleasure, the level of its action on me, becomes a crucial question. Pleasure has to be distinguished from the distortion of soul that may accompany it. What is truly good and what is truly not good? The problem circles around the nature of pleasure. Pleasure is good and life-giving. Also there is the blessing on that which "gives life to every living soul," recited after meals. The meaning of "to give life" does not necessarily refer only to the necessities of life without which one cannot exist. It refers also to the pleasures of life, for this blessing is said not only after drinking water or eating meat but also after eating sweets and other delicacies.

That is to say, the essence of life and the joy or pleasure of life are the two sides of the same thing; they are not separate entities; the essence of life is in pleasure and the primal, basic pleasure is life itself. For this does man toil and labor. He does so to live or, rather, to enjoy life. Just as a person engages in bargaining in order to make a profit, so does man engage in struggle for the sake of the pleasure that life affords. What is paramount here is the fact that joyfulness and the recognition of what constitutes pleasure are not the same for everyone. The person whose chief delight lies in wealth lives in order to make money but, in point of fact, his aim is pleasure and not money. The money is only the means. Similarly, for one who strives to obtain wisdom, the aim is really the inner joy that comes from knowledge and a measure of sagacity. The difference between the two is not a difference in the basic aim; it lies in the mode of feeling about the way to obtain it, in actions that are more preferable, in simple human terms of like and dislike. A person chooses to invest his energies in that which ultimately is most pleasurable to him.

The higher the level of pleasure the more superior the aim of one's life. The extent of one's capacity for joy is the chief instrument for achievement at all levels, higher or lower, and may even be considered the primary root of all action.

This is the vertical line of joy, its height and depth, whereas the breadth and horizontal expanse of joy may be seen as the many-sidedness and broad range of the possibilities of pleasure, in the senses, the feelings, the mind, and the spirit. A whole world of opportunities for pleasure lie in food and drink alone, and not only in taste and smell and in the many social aspects of the table, but also in all that is offered as variety. Taste itself is a pleasure that exceeds very many gastronomical possibilities. One can enjoy such an enormous range of beverages, wines, and drinks, it staggers the imagination. Even in the more subtle sense of smell, the pleasure derived from a vast range of odors and scents is different for each one.

Similarly, there is the delight in speech – in communication, articulation or study of language, logic, grammar, eloquence, and the like. It is not necessarily an intellectual pleasure connected with the meaning of what is said; it can be an esthetic delight in the beauty of speech. In certain countries, it often does not matter what a person is saying but how well he says it. For a rather special pleasure is to be found in the purity of a verbal communication, in the exactitude of grammatical forms or the precision of a sentence. Another sort of pleasure comes from the telling of a joke. And then there is the simple satisfaction in talking – simple conversation or sharing thoughts and feelings, expressing worry and getting rid of a burden on the soul. There may not be a solution to the problem, but the speaking is a release and a pleasure of sorts.

Seeing and hearing are the more obvious and constant sources of delight. Besides the harmony of music or visual beauty, the unimaginable extent of the things enjoyed by the eyes and ears of man cannot be expressed. Besides all this, which we may see as the mechanism of pleasure, we are aware of an inner world of intellectual and spiritual content behind all sensation. These higher delights of the mind appear first as accompaniments to emotion or thought. Thereafter, the nature of mind is such that it expands the pleasure derived from the senses, enhances the delights of the emotion and intellect and as we have said, provides height, depth, and breadth to the pleasurable, transforming it from something tangible and carrying it to another dimension, to that of infinitude. That is to say, every object in the world can be enjoyed and it makes no difference what it is; pleasure can penetrate anything. And beyond the sensual, pleasure has the power of transforming the particularity of a thing into something limitless. Enjoyment, therefore, can proceed beyond the personal which is its essential root and become a general or universal factor taking one out of the specific into the unbounded.

What is implied here is that delight, in all its forms, is more than a particular quality; it belongs to life itself, capable of adhering to anything in the world. It is also far more than any one kind of action or any one aspect of life; it is at the core of all aspiration, purpose, and human direction. The difference between the courses of behavior people choose lies in the pleasure they get (or hope to get) out of their choices.

Moreover, pleasures of whatever variety also serve to educate and nurture pleasures of the same kind. Indeed, all training is based on this principle: listening develops the pleasure of hearing music, observation enhances the powers of vision, and so on. And there are many things that have to be learned in order to be enjoyed, whether in art or technology. To be sure, technical learning does not, in itself, harbor pleasure for everyone; one often misses out on an essential delight by failing to "educate" the capacity to appreciate the enjoyable in something.

We are thus brought to an ascertainment of the fact that there are levels of enjoyment. Every man to his pleasure. One is reminded of the story by Peretz about Bonsha Schweig, a lovable example of one of the wretches of the earth. Upon arriving in Paradise, after his death, he is told that he can ask for anything he likes. "Anything?" he inquires incredulously. "Yes, anything in heaven and in earth," he is reassured. Upon which he thinks for a moment and says he would like a fresh roll with butter. That was the pinnacle of his capacity for enjoyment, a pitiful comment on the inequalities in our society. The Jewish instruction to 'choose life' is a matter of ever-greater refinement of pleasure, of developing the power to discriminate between the crude and the subtle, the higher and the lower. In learning to recognize the good, evil is automatically rejected; for there are the pleasures of the below and the pleasures of the above. Pleasure is the key.

Chapter three

As we have noted, pleasure ranges from the highest to the lowest elements in the human soul. And there is perhaps no other force so all-encompassing, so all-inclusive. But the totality of the many versions of pleasure may be seen as having been derived from the Shattering of the Vessels, which is also the origin of everything else that we consider reality in this world. Those many pleasures are also fragments of the higher substance that, together with the higher lights, fell at the Shattering of the Vessels. They may thus be viewed as "waste" or superfluous matter in so far as concerns the highest joy at its supreme level, when the Godhead was undivided, prior to the creation of heaven and earth and the "separateness" of higher and lower worlds. Creation made the firmament to serve as a barrier between above and below. As a result, the lower waters weep with longing for the King; what is below suffers from the separation, the great distance.

Therefore, all the pleasures of the world, no matter how great or lasting, are relatively worthless in comparison to an hour in the Garden of Eden, when the souls enjoy the radiance of the *Shekhina*. As the Sages say: "One hour of contentment in the next world is more wonderful than all the living in this world" (*Pirkei Avot* 4:17). And this because the nature of the joys of the next world are of another order, infinitely superior to the pleasures of this world. Whatever we experience below is limited by the physical body and by the human mind. Even the mind of man is a biologically based function, very much restricted to life and the brain. The soul, unrestricted by the body, is free to receive far more, to experience exquisite joys, indescribable in our terms.

In other words, there is no way of comparing the pleasures of this world – for all their sweetness, intensity, and variety – with the pleasure of the next world. We have no common denominator. Just as we cannot compare a color, such as blue, with a number. We can have more blueness or less, a larger number or a smaller one; we cannot compare them. All we can say about the joys of the next world is that they are so superior to the joys of this world, that it is worth going through the torments of hell in order to attain them. As it is said, there is a river of fire between the Eden below and the Eden above and the souls have to immerse themselves in this river, called *Dinur*, to forget the pleasures of the lower before reaching the upper Paradise, and to avoid confusion when they get there.

The point of the matter is that when a person has to pass from one level of existence to another, one of the rites of passage is the forgetting of what he knows of the past. If he does not do so, he is liable to get mixed up and his appreciation of the new experience will be weakened, if not distorted, especially if there is some relation between the two levels. As in learning a new language, the old has to be functionally forgotten or discarded; otherwise, there would be a tendency to mix them up. Every experience leaves an impression that has to be wiped out, more or less, in order to proceed to the next experience. Like professional wine testers who have somehow to obliterate the taste of the previous sip in order to evaluate the next and have developed ingenious ways to do so.

So, too, as said, the passage of the soul to the next world involves the crisis of forgetting. There is usually a transition period to enable a development of higher awareness to take place, just as people who move to foreign countries need time because they continue to see things with the eyes of their own past culture. All of which, incidentally, is one of the reasons for the saying that there are several things that can be obtained only by suffering, among them being the Land of Israel (also Torah and the next world). Because these things are of the nature of another realm of being, a better world, that require a certain process of eliminating the previous world. This may also be the meaning of the endless struggle of *tzaddikim*, who move up from one stage to another and have to keep discarding familiar sources of satisfaction and of joy in order to achieve ever-higher levels of experience.

This points to an endless elevation of values and levels of happiness. But our capacity to experience them is limited. We are confined to a certain limited scale of response. Beyond a particular extreme, we cannot appreciate what is happening; just as our vision reacts only to certain wavelengths of light, so that we cannot see the infrared, the ultraviolet, or the x-rays, thus, too, for the most part, we do not enjoy the radiance of the *Shekhina*, the source of all delight. In order to do so we have to reach an equal, or similar, quality of light in ourselves, going through a process of soul purification both in this world and in the next. Herein is the secret of education in general and of the holy name of God in particular. The highest delight, the joy without a cause, comes from life itself, and the source of life is "with" God. "For with You is the source of life" (Psalms 36:10); it is not "You yourself." "With You" implies His Holy Name. The source of life and supernal happiness is thus next to the Divine, that which comes directly from God as His Holy Name. His Being and Essence give rise to the ten *Sefirot*, of course, and these contain their own version of life and joy. But what we experience as joy comes from this other aspect of existence, it comes from being "with" Him.

All of which is intended to explain what is meant by "*Oneg Shabbat*," the joy of the Sabbath. For obviously this joy is not that of gefilte fish or any other delicacy of the table. It is the particular essence of that which the Sabbath is, and it is somehow connected to "will," known in Hebrew as "*Ratzon*," as well as to delight, which is "*Oneg*." The mitzvot are simply God's Will. He wishes it. And in performing the mitzvot, one is acting in obedience to His Will, even if only in its most exterior aspect. For it is not given to us to see His face. And the Divine face is the Divine inwardness. All we know is the heavenly exterior, that which is outside, visible, or graspable. Concerning inwardness, or the "face" of man, for instance, it may be viewed as that part of him in which is to be found his greatest achievement, his essential being. Indeed, everything has its inner essence and its exterior. The revealed aspect comes forth from the inner significance. The external aspect of the mitzvot is that they are commandments. It is God's will that something should be done in a certain way. Thus, their inner aspect and their real meaning lies in the delight of the Supreme One, Blessed be He, which delight is the inwardness of will. Joy is thus the inwardness of will.

With man, too, at the various levels of his being, we find that there are inner and outer aspects. For example, even in the context of the expression, "from my flesh I shall see [God]" (Job 19:26), utmost delight is the main objective and the will follows after the delight, desiring it. That is, man wants something that gives him pleasure and his will is the outer expression of this desire. Delight is thus a matter of one's desire, and it does not matter at what level. When there is a desire for something, it expresses itself as a will – positive or negative, to take and to approach or to reject and push away, depending on the nature of the desire. In further consideration of which, we have the word "taste," which has many ambivalent, multifaceted shades of interpretation. Good taste – *"ta'am"* – may be said to be expressive of aesthetic appreciation. *Ta'am*, in Hebrew, is also a reason for doing things. This odd combination, able to express "taste" as the reason for doing something as well as a source of beauty, implies that there is pleasure involved. It may be spiritual in the noblest sphere or just sensible in the lowest, but the reason is a good one if it is "tasty." The utterance "I want this or that," always has a reason of its own concerning which it is possible to ask, what for? Or in Hebrew, what is the "taste" of it – *"ma ta'am"*?

Of course, there are many reasons (or tastes) for enjoyment, and they can even be arranged in some order of priority; but ultimately, they all get reduced to some form of desire. The will can reach such a level in the general structure of understanding in the soul that the mind follows after the will. And there is a will that follows after the mind, just as there is a will that is subservient to the mind. This latter will is of a lower level and is characteristic of what happens in the *Sefira* of *Da'at* (Knowledge). The mind functions and decides to do something in a certain way, embarking on a course of willed action. But beyond that, there is an original will that compels *Da'at*. A human being, of himself, is so built that the beginning of his conscious knowledge comes from

Hokhma (Wisdom). Although the true beginning is from the *Sefira* of *Keter* (Crown) which is also will; except that one is not conscious of the light of *Keter*, only of will. Therefore, only when one looks at "another" can one see something. One wishes to reach a certain conclusion, so that the mind operates accordingly, distorting and arranging things to get to the desired conclusion. Of course, there are matters that do not touch the will, like mathematics, and the will does not interfere with the logic of its process. The will, in this case, does not compel the mind, and reason functions freely. The answer here is irrelevant for the will. But when the will is restrained by some matter or other, the mind bends accordingly. Everyone knows that if something is really desired, the appropriate reasons will be found, the "taste" – *ta'am* – and rational justification will accompany its substantiation.

For when a person asserts that he wants something, it indicates that there is a desire for the pleasure it offers, a lust for the "taste" of it. And this is one of the best philosophic responses to the question, "Why did God create the world?" The answer, as stated in *Midrash Raba*, was that God desired to have a dwelling place below. And concerning desire, there is no arguing about it. It is perhaps the most inward answer to the existence of the world; although more philosophically profound answers have been offered. As it has been noted, the Divine plays with the world as His Plaything. It is God's Delight in the world that is the basis of all existence. And all the notions about purpose or reason for the world are only subsidiary.

Hence, the will is an aspect of that which is "behind" or external to the higher delight in which it is clothed. As it is said: "And thou shalt see that which is behind Me and not My face" (Exodus 33:23). Thus, the inwardness of delight is revealed only as an aspect of will. One receives the revelation of His will but one does not receive any revelation of the delight He has in it. For delight is inward.

Thus, too, the reward of the mitzva is the joy one gets in the performance of it. The mitzva is also an expression of His will; and accordingly, "Thou shalt see that which is behind Me." This is true even for Moses. One wants something, does something; it is the essence of the pleasure involved that is its inwardness. Just as a person remains veiled and obscured to his fellow except for the aspect of will which reveals his desire and inclination. And, when I tell someone to do something, the matter is revealed as my will. I cannot transmit the delight I take in having the thing done for me.

In conclusion, that which God transmits as reality to the world is His will; His delight in everything remains hidden. And that is also the real reason or cause for existence. When we discover this true taste or *"ta'am"* behind everything, especially the mitzvot, all action becomes pervaded with the sweetness and depth of Divine delight.

Chapter four

W

e have indicated that the mitzvot come from the revealed will of God, but that this will is only an outer aspect of a certain Divine revelation. In its inner (or more intrinsic) aspect, this higher will may be seen as an expression of the Divine delight. Even in human life, will is only the outer mode of expressing desire. For desire cannot by itself accomplish anything. It has to be transformed into some form of will in order to get what it wants. Thus, this level of will is known as the "behind," or outer aspect of reality, while the "face," or inner level of reality, is delight or pleasure. In Torah, too, what is revealed to us is only its outer aspect, or the Divine will. What we do not perceive is the inner delight of God hidden behind this will, which, even in our limited way, we somehow do express by saying, "Who sanctified us with His commandments" – אשר קדשנו במצוותיו. The Hebrew word אשר has been connected with the root letters of אושר, or happiness, thereby intimating that it is happiness or joy that sanctifies us (with His commandments). Because of the many delightful aspects of the actions involved in the performance of mitzvot, we praise and applaud their origin.

It has been noted that one of the differences between front and back, between "the face" and that which is "behind," is that the back is not divided into various organs – it is a whole that entirely covers the rear from head to foot; it is a single entity without tones or gradations of value, without higher or lower. But the front or "face" shows enormous variation of form and feature – eyes to see, ears to hear, etc. What seems to be indicated by this is that the will, or the aspect of the "behind," is a whole and undivided unity, while the delight aspect of the "front" has many "faces" and functions in accordance with the numerous pleasures available through the organs of perception. In terms of higher will then, with its singleness of the rear aspect, there is no division. The will expressed by the mitzvot is one and the same for all. Although it may be said that there are levels of severity in the Divine will, it is not a matter of quality or of deciding which is more important. The commandment is the same for the large or the small mitzva, it does not matter. On Pesah, there is an equivalent injunction to eat matza and to eat *maror* (bitter herbs); the commandment is identical, but the taste of each is very different.

The difference in *ta'am*, or taste, does not appear in terms of will. As far as the Divine will is concerned, it does not matter: a commandment is a commandment; a mitzva is a mitzva. Nevertheless, it is also a wonderful harmony and not a repetitive monotone; for the Divine will is above wisdom or *Hokhma* and constitutes, in its inner aspect, the great delight and joy from which comes all music and harmonious formation.

A Hasidic story relates that once a certain rabbi was visited by the Besht (the *Ba'al Shem Tov*), the great leader of the movement, on the Day of Atonement (Yom Kippur). To his astonishment, the Besht kept singing the awesome prayer of repentance, "*Al Het*," in a clearly happy melody, more like a marching tune than a recital of guilt and remorse, indeed, reflecting the liveliness of transgression more than the sorrow of contrition. The rabbi could not help asking the meaning of such impious singing, and he received the reply: "Anyone who is a genuinely devoted servant of the King will sing whenever he is carrying out the King's orders, whether he comes as a victor in battle, or whether he is cleaning out the filth from the homes. Since the King's instructions for this day are to do repentance, to clean out the filth, I sing as I would at any opportunity to do His Will." That is to say, the performance of any mitzva is a joy, whether it be a likeable task or a disagreeable one, a significant act or something relatively trivial. And all the mitzvot together form a symphonic whole, a single command, a collective summoning of our response.

As for the "*ta'am*," the taste or reason for the mitzvot, each has its own joyous essence, as we have said. Every mitzva is unique in terms of its intention or purpose; it is a world unto itself, with its own external appearance and its own interior meaning, just as the pleasure of seeing differs from the pleasure of hearing or touching. And it is not a difference of size; it is a difference of essence; every mitzva has its special quality. Whereas, as we have mentioned, the will to perform the mitzva is one and undivided; it does not discriminate. So, too, is the spiritual delight in performance of mitzvot a higher pleasure than any particular pleasure of the senses. We can thus understand the enigmatic statement in the Torah (*parashat Yitro*), "And all the people saw the sounds" (Exodus 20:15). To perceive, that is, with the eyes what should be heard with the ears. To confuse the senses here is only a way to describe something that is beyond the senses, or that circumscribes them in an unfathomable way. It is an experience of direct inner perception, without having first experienced it outwardly through the senses.

This brings us back to the insight concerning the primordial origin of all things, which is the Divine delight. And it is observed that this original source is broken down into many kinds of joy and participation through mitzvot. So that the mitzvot are called "the ways of sweet enjoyment," ways, also, of getting from one place to another – from the remote darkness to the joyful luminosity of the Divine Presence. The metaphor that best describes this is that of a great river or lake that is used to irrigate a sown field. Without some controlled channel, these waters can be disastrous; the Divine delight has to be directed along a narrow course, or way, to benefit our own specific circumstances. It's as though we plow or carve a line in life along which the Higher delight can then flow. This line is also a way, as it is written: "And they shall keep the way of the Lord, to do charity and justice" (Genesis 18:19), and it is a way of sweetness and joy.

Why, however, charity and justice? To which the answer is given: It is because charity, or loving-kindness, includes all the mitzvot – a mitzva being no more than a stretching forth of Divine goodness, a form of dissemination, a giving of His plenty from above to below. Since charity is that giving which goes from the one who has to the one who does not have, the mitzva is God's way of giving that gift of reality to the world. God offers it to us. And when we perform a mitzva, we open the way; we only provide the channel along which the Divine essence can flow. The mitzva, in other words, is of another sort of reality; it is not the act itself; it is the flow of Divine delight through the act. The act is a vehicle for the mitzva, a means or vessel for the mitzva to manifest, just as when someone wishes to receive alms, he has to stretch forth his hand. He has to have a hand, or whatever, to receive what is given. So, too, the mitzva is a vessel to absorb the Divine grace (or charity) that flows into the reality of the world.

To penetrate further into the nature of the mitzva, let us admit that any act is also a creative gesture; something new is added to the world. On the other hand, it is not the mitzva or act that creates but the fact that God is prepared, in a certain way, to let His light flow along the channel that was prepared by this act. The act is nothing in itself; it is only a means for giving external expression to God's Bounty. It is like a network of irrigation pipes that depend entirely on a central valve. Opening or closing the valve makes all the difference, creates the reality. A postal box is meaningless without the transfer of letters. The connection with true purpose is what counts. This is the task of mitzvot in life; to serve as a connection, enabling the general and private forces of existence to flow in the right direction. In this manner, it is a gift from on high.

An accepted formula for existence has been "Torah, *Avoda*, and *Gemilut Ḥasadim*" (Torah, worship, and kindness). Torah is considered an essence in itself; *avoda* is, again, the general framework for the inclusive world of aspiration and spiritual endeavor, while *Gemilut Ḥasadim* may be said to contain all the practical mitzvot. As such, the mitzva of charity or *tzedaka* is a specific part of *Gemilut Ḥasadim*; it is a way of transforming Divine plenty from a certain source (in me) to a deserving recipient (who is unknown). But it has to be a real giving of oneself, as well as of impersonal substance, to another.

Of course, it may be argued that any mitzva is a transfer of Divine plenty from its source in the Infinity, *Ein Sof*, to a specific point in time and space. What we have considered is the relation between the mitzva as an act of obedience to Divine will, and the mitzva as an expression of the Higher Delight that is behind this will. And we have hinted at the difficulty in describing the Higher delight; the infinite variety of its forms and vehicles, its interior nature, and its extremely personal quality make each situation wonderful in a unique way.

All of which, in turn, is intended to serve as in introduction to the subject of Shabbat and not as a treatise on hedonism. It is written: "Six days shalt thou work and on the seventh day thou shalt rest, and cease from plowing and harvesting" (Exodus 34:21). Why are plowing and harvesting specifically mentioned? The answer given is that for six days one is to do God's work in the world. This is *avoda*, or the imposed tasks of life which nurture existence outside of the Garden of Eden. It is more than just tilling the soil; it is a labor and an agony, a matter of drawing forth nourishment by the sweat of the brow. But the real work of man is Divine worship, also called *avoda*.

In which category there is, again, plowing and sowing. And then, there is harvesting. Plowing is the first task, a matter of preparing the heart by breaking the hardened crust of the soil around it. And also to make furrows of fresh soil, free of weeds and thorns, capable of serving as a bed for the seed. Because, as is well known, no matter how rich the potential of the seed, it needs a soft and suitable bed of soil in order to sprout. Many people often have spiritual experiences, or receive the grace of genuine wisdom through a written or spoken word, but fail to let it develop into anything productive because the seed falls on uncongenial stony ground.

On the other hand, we can point to numerous instances of individuals whose entire lives were changed because of a single phrase or sentence that pierced them to the core. A person has been known to just open the siddur (prayer book) at random and discover something that nourishes his soul for a lifetime. Often it is the result of seeing something familiar in a sudden illumination.

The work of sowing is connected with the receptivity of the heart; only too often the heart is open and ready to receive something truly significant, and what is absorbed in this readiness is a trivial make-believe of little value. It seems to be a fairly universal error, to catch hold of a cheap trinket in an hour of great emotion – whether of fear, exultation, or love – and to cherish it as though it were a precious jewel. Opening the heart and sowing the proper seed thus require care and discrimination. Thereafter, there is the work of watering the soil, for the rains are not always to be relied upon, and then the task of weeding out the undesirable growths that spring up and threaten to choke the crop. To be sure, in the work of Divine worship, the uprooted weeds and thorns may also be useful in their own way and are not always to be discarded carelessly. Another aspect of sowing is the sorrow of investing labor into an action that has no immediate result, the consequences of which we cannot be certain. The phrase, "Light sown for the righteous" (Psalms 97:11), is not a promise. The following words, "gladness for the upright in heart," merely confirm that the sincere person does what has to be done, he sows the seed. He does not feel the happiness because he can not (as yet) perceive the result of his efforts. Similarly, the drawing down of Higher delight is called "work" because it is a descent and a contraction. Thus, "work" can ultimately be seen as the contraction of the light of spirit or intellect into a specific task, a function, requiring a descent of the light to an inferior level. Indeed, the weekday can be considered the time of such directed labor, the work of contracting the wide and free essence of things into particular objects of use. Where there is no such contraction or reduction of both world (thing) and man (his thoughts, creative efforts) into the circumscribed limits of utility, there is no work.

It is utility that describes the fruit, the crop of multiplied seed, the meaningful result of effort. And the "utility" emanating from the sowing of charity is an increase of blessedness. It is expressed as a drawing down of the higher delight by the words "Blessed art Thou" that introduces every blessing. And not only delight, but also Divine plenty and Divine power are drawn down from above to a particular level of being.

This then is the meaning of doing "work" for six days of the week: to plow and to sow. The weekday is the time to perform mitzvot whose purpose is to fix what is wrong, break up the hard crust around the heart, and plant the seed. Such work is done in the upper worlds as well as in the lower and is essential to the preparation for the Shabbat.

It would appear that Shabbat is, therefore, outside the range of positive commandments. There is nothing to be done. The Shabbat has another quality, outside of "plowing and sowing" even in spiritual terms of *avoda*, and not only in terms of physical work. Its essence is total rest.

Chapter five

We have pointed out that people work in physical and in spiritual ways to repair the reality of the world and that this may be considered the meaning of the weekday. Included in this is the "plowing and sowing and harvesting" of a man's labor on himself. But, on the seventh day, there is a cessation of all work and a heavenly delight is manifested. The week is thus devoted to an awakening process from below; it is as though the Shabbat is the hidden purpose of labor – a purpose that refuses to be revealed except on the seventh day. As it is written: "And it shall come to pass that every new moon and every Shabbat, shall all flesh come to bow down before Me" (Isaiah 66:23).

The cycle that becomes apparent, therefore, is the intrusion of the Heavenly world into what we like to think of as the rights and habits of the world below. How else to explain the fact that the stirring of delight takes place by the month or the week, and the souls of men receive their portion at fixed times. The *Book of Bahir* has a description of a pillar (or tower) on which souls ascend to Paradise every Shabbat. And this is possible because only on that day is the higher delight made manifest and the way opened. On the other days of the week, work has to be done to prepare for this manifestation, which, although it comes with its own regularity, requires an amount of labor that is somehow in proportion to the delight given. Just as the food enjoyed on Shabbat has to be cooked beforehand – it does not just appear out of the sky – Shabbat is the time for enjoying what was prepared during the week. The awakening of delight is the result of the performance of mitzvot during the previous days. The Shabbat is not a free gift.

The conclusion to be drawn from this is that whatever a person is during the week, he is the same on Shabbat. If a man behaves like a dog during the six days, he remains something of a dog on the seventh, except that he is now a Shabbat dog, which, like all else in that category, has something festive about it. On the other hand, the toil and sorrow of the week may be unremitting until the Shabbat and, only then, having cast off the physical outer garments, can a person obtain the results of his inner efforts and enjoy the heavenly delight.

Therefore, too, there is no need for work on the Shabbat. What we do on this day is holy activity, which is of a different essence. During the week, one is engaged in plowing, in breaking the encrusted soil around the heart, freeing the space for seed; we are involved with the tasks of *Tikkun* – repairing the world and sorting out the good, separating out the evil. All of which is only preparation for the gladness of the Shabbat. In one moment, there is a reversal, an overturning of the profane into the holy.

To be more specific about this reversal, one of the ways it can be recognized is that certain actions, which are unqualified and optional on the weekday, become mitzvot on Shabbat – commandments of the Lord. The change is a matter of the very formal nature of the Shabbat. Thus, whereas on ordinary days, one is supposed to eat what is necessary for subsistence, on the Shabbat, eating and the joy of eating are mitzvot; on the weekday, sleep is a matter of choice or necessity; on Shabbat, it becomes part of the mitzva of rest, and so on. Which is to say that during the week one relates to action as a means, a vehicle for life to manifest. One eats in order to live, not as an end in itself; and for many it is simply necessary in order to be able to work or to do whatever one wishes to do. Whereas on Shabbat, when work and action are revoked, eating becomes a mitzva, a kind of sacrament. It is part of the process of raising up all the worlds on this day when the profane is transmuted to holiness. This refers to the truism that the work of the weekday is an extension of the Divine hiddenness; on Shabbat, all action expresses something of Divine revelation. As it is written: "And thou shall call the Shabbat a delight" (Isaiah 58:13).

Which brings us back to the Shabbat blessing with its request to "sanctify us with Your commandments." It is in the present tense (as contrasted with the past tense in the phrase: "who sanctified us with Your commandments" of the weekday blessing). The mitzva has already been performed; what one is asking for is the sense of holiness, the sanctity of all action which belongs to the Shabbat. One aspires to the experience of Shabbat as a consummation of the week's strife and effort. The weekday blessing expresses the fact that one is actively engaged in doing and giving, not in receiving. The Shabbat blessing asks for the sense of sanctity to prevail, and no more. It is said that the talmudic sage Shammai used to save everything good and beautiful that he came across for the Shabbat, as if to say that all truly wonderful things should be reserved for the seventh day. So, too, we say "sanctify us with Your commandments" in the present tense on Shabbat because it is the time for the manifestation of that which was still hidden during the week. Which is another reason for the statement that Shabbat is weighed against all other mitzvot, because in profane times the mitzvot that are performed still retain the hidden light, whereas on Shabbat, the light is revealed. This in turn belongs to our previous declarations concerning this world and the next world, putting Shabbat into the category of the world to come when we no longer have to work and when we collect the results of our labor in this world. Thus, too, are the mitzvot of the weekdays weighed against the Shabbat, which receives and reflects all that preceded it. It is as in the old story about the king who ordered a painting of his palace from four different artists. Each of them was provided with a proper vantage point for painting, and three went about their task with proper diligence and application. The fourth painter seemed to be idle or of a different temperament; he did nothing but walk around and observe. When the time came for showing their work in the appointed chamber, this fourth painter hung up a huge mirror on the wall, which reflected the work of the other painters. By which it is hinted that the Shabbat is only a reflection of the week; in it one perceives the achievements or the failures of the ordinary life that preceded it, and all that is required of the Shabbat is that it be clean. It need only faithfully record the beauty of what came before.

In a roundabout manner, the discussion takes us to a consideration of what we mean by doing God's will, in terms of the esoteric wisdom. *Ratzon* or Will belongs to the *Sefira* of *Keter* (Crown), an aspect of the encompassing Light. *Makom* (Place) is one of the names of God and belongs to the *Sefira* of *Malkhut* (Kingdom). And this points to the world, our world of reality. It is when the Encompassing Light is united with the inner light that God's will is done. Thus, when the Divine Light (of encompassment) comes down into *Malkhut*, which is *Makom* (or place of human existence), and there is some sort of real penetration, God's will prevails. And this is the purpose of Creation – that God's Encompassing Light shall become manifest in *Makom*, the particular place, and dwell therein. This is called doing God's will.

From this it follows that the weekdays are secular, in the sense that God's will is not so evident, while the Shabbat is holy because His will does prevail. Therefore, too, the day can remain passive, so to speak, because the Divine light is already indwelling. In the passage of the week, this light has to be drawn down by the mitzvot, whereas on Shabbat this light comes of itself.

The dialectics of the issue is that Shabbat is the sum or storehouse of the week; but it is also the source of blessing, the fountainhead from which all reality issues. This double function of end and beginning is really a circular process; the week cannot start again without going through the Shabbat. In spite of being a halt and a summation, Shabbat is also a renewal; it provides the energy to continue. In this respect then, the Shabbat is of the next world, with its paradisiacal power to keep supplying the life-replenishing delight of existence.

We may presume that in any process of unification, whether in higher or lower worlds, there has to be something that does the uniting. This applies to disparate entities that by their very nature do not need to fuse and may even find it difficult to do so. The further apart two entities are from each other, the more force and meaning to their union. As for our concept of uniting the upper and lower worlds, there is obviously some sort of amalgamating factor needed. Without it, they do not come together; they cannot even communicate. There has to be a middle realm between the upper and the lower. What is this unifier?

It is prayer. Prayer is the element that binds the two worlds, above and below.

Almost as an aside, this is also the answer to the question one may ask about the connecting factor between the weekdays and Shabbat. Prayer combines them. As it is written, the time of prayer is the Shabbat of the ordinary day. And the day of the Sabbath contains in itself all the prayers, uniting them in its own summing up action. For there has to be a binding element in the soul of man between the profane and the holy, between the weekday and Shabbat. Otherwise, they would continue to be apart within the soul as well as in time. There has to be a transitional force, something to energize the movement of the transformation from level to level. In other terms, we may say that the Shabbat is basically a delight, a state of inner joyousness; the weekday is action. How else can the transition be made from one to the other except by prayer. Even though the prayer of the weekday is explicitly tied to the specific day and its world of action, it is also a force that breaks out of the daily secularity with its own spiritual power. As such, prayer acts as the in-between realm, the connecting link between the working week and *Oneg Shabbat*, the rejoicing of the Shabbat day.

Thus, too, prayer is called a ladder, according to the *Zohar*'s explanation of the statement about Jacob's dream of "a ladder set upon the earth, and the top of it reached to heaven" (Genesis 28:12). Esoteric wisdom also describes many rungs or stages of ascension. Most generally, there are the four levels that correspond to the four primordial worlds of Emanation, Creation, Formation, and Action. Within each of these levels are varied numbers of rungs, according to one's capacity to ascend. Prayer books that designate the appropriate kabbalistic correspondences will often point out the world or level to which each group of prayers belongs. Every siddur will be very specific about the placement of the Kaddish in the liturgy as a sign of transition to a higher level. As in a ladder, there has to be a coming down as well as a going up. In the first part of the morning (Sephardic) service, for example, the prayers up to הודו called קרבנות (sacrifices), correspond to the World of Action; the part up to קריאת שמע, the "Hear, O Israel" declaration, corresponds to the World of Formation, the realm of the angels; from this to the blessing after the שְׁמַע declaration, the prayers correspond to the World of Creation, and thence, the שמונה עשרה, the eighteen benedictions, correspond to the World of Emanation. Following this are the gradual levels of descent.

Prayer, by itself then, may go in any direction. What determines ascension is devotion. For the ladder is made up of rungs and the spaces between. There is a certain emptiness between the rungs which is an integral part of the function of the ladder; they are intervals that have to be overcome. Besides, it is necessary to abandon one's foothold on the rung below in order to climb. Often one gets to a certain height and, feeling a sense of accomplishment, one rests on that rung. Devotion is required to leave this secure hold and stretch out into the emptiness towards the next rung. The higher one reaches, the greater the trepidation about the higher world and the readiness to cling to the familiar world, the rung to which one has already come. A person has to urge himself on, saying "I carry my soul to Thee, Oh Lord; I give up my soul in devotion [to God]" (Psalms 86:4).

To be sure, this is a very dangerous psalm to utter aloud, even when one's intentions are most sincere, because, as many people suspect, it usually cannot be maintained, and one should be careful about making declarations. The space between the rungs seems to become more formidable as one ascends.

What is more, as stated further in the biblical text concerning Jacob's dream about the ladder set on the earth with its top reaching to heaven, "behold the angels of God ascending and descending on it" (Genesis 28:12). The ladder is thus also a connection between the worlds above and the worlds below on which the higher entities can come down and the lower can climb up. It can also be likened to a column holding up the ceiling of a building and, as such, it is a part of a support system between heaven and earth.

Another insight into this image of the ladder may be obtained by comparing it to the spinal column in the human body. Significantly, there are eighteen vertebrae, corresponding, as certain Sages have noted, to the eighteen benedictions of the daily prayer. The spine is that which connects the head to the body, along which neural messages are sent;

thus, the vertebrae may be likened to the rungs of the ladder, along which, in life as in prayer, a person ascends and descends.

In climbing up, it is necessary to let go, to depart from the rung on which one is resting and, for a moment, be without adequate support. In life, this passage from one level to another can sometimes be very painful. True, there are transitions and letting go processes that are easy and natural but, for the most part, moving up involves discomfort, unease, and even anguish. Where fear enters and a person cannot move up or down, one foot dangling in midair so to speak, we have stagnation. In this case, the thrust of aspiration and devotion has to be renewed.

In prayer, more obviously than in life, there is constant aspiration, or ascent; the descending movement is a bringing down of Divine plenty. Prayer can therefore be said to serve a double purpose: to raise one's being to a higher level and to carry something back to the earthly sphere whence one began. The whole process can be traced in the liturgy from the praise passages of the *Pesukei Dezimra* to the eighteen benedictions, where one asks for life, wisdom, knowledge, forgiveness, health, and sustenance, among other things, and from which one carefully descends back to this world.

Therefore, too, has prayer been called "*atara*," the crown, or Diadem, of life. As it is expressed in the Song of Songs (3:11): "Go forth, O daughters of Zion, and behold King Solomon with the crown with which his mother crowned him on this day of his wedding and on the day of the gladness of his heart." His "mother" here is *Knesset Yisrael*, and the diadem, the jeweled crown on the head, is the result of the devotion with which one prays.

To be more specific, the jewels of the diadem are essentially inanimate matter, and placing matter on the head of the order of existence (inanimate substance, life, mind, or speech) as a crown, would be a contradiction. But the jewel is not just a piece of inanimate substance; it is a stone that has been broken and ground, polished and cleaned. And this is what prayer does. It takes the primordial elements of life and makes them into jewels fit to be worn on the top of the head. For prayer is not just repetition of words; it includes *kavana*, the heart's devotion and the mind's intention. Thus, bringing all this sincere hope and anxiety of existence before God, including the request for health and sustenance, breaking it all down before the Divine Presence and delivering it to His Mercy – "carrying one's soul to Thee, O Lord" – transmutes the earthly substance to jewels of the crown.

In such fashion, may prayer be likened to the ladder "set in the earth and the top [head] of it reaching to heaven." The crown on the head is also *Keter*, at the pinnacle of the tree of *Sefirot*, reconnected to *Malkhut* (kingdom), on the bottom.

Chapter six

It has been pointed out that we take matter, the substance of the lower world, and transform it through prayer. We raise it up, because prayer is a ladder, or a column binding the two worlds. True, there are subjects of prayer that are already sublime in themselves, such as the Holy Temple. But when a person asks for a livelihood or just for a potato, the potato will not go up to heaven because of the prayer (even though the prayer may well do so). What is transformed and elevated is the meaning, the essence and purpose of an object; a potato that nourishes the performance of mitzvot, charity, and meritorious action is not the same potato that does no more than feed the hungry.

A certain odd Rabbi, Meir'l of Premishlian, was a great scholar, but his teaching was a peculiar mixture of scriptural passages, unrelated texts, and rather original instructions. When one of the most prodigious writers (of religious tracts) of his time, who wrote nearly three hundred books, delivered his eulogy, he said: "I have had the privilege of seeing him at work, and I realize that only because of the simplicity of the man, his innate humility, has he never been acclaimed according to his real worth." In any case, this Rabbi used to say that if all the prayers of Israel were to be inserted into a cannon and shot off like gunpowder, we would get, maybe, a single gold coin, the essential purpose of the prayers. But if this gold coin were again inserted and shot off, then we would get the practical possibility, the money or the means to do all that Jewish life requires, enough to send the children to school, to perform good deeds, to keep the Sabbath, with dignity.

The purifying power of prayer thus transforms substance, whether one is asking for rain or release from suffering; something in gross matter is made into a diadem. Prayer raises the lower to the higher, as we have explained, and also brings down that which is above. The *Zohar* (*Book of Splendor*) claims that Torah and mitzvot cannot rise without love and fear of God, that *"Dehilu U-rehimu"* (Divine Awe and Compassion) are the wings of piety, without which mitzvot cannot fly. Indeed there are mitzvot whose wings are still those of fledglings, and only when fear and love grow strong enough can they take off. Prayer is the factor that determines this power of flight, giving strength to the wings.

There is also the metaphor of holiness as water that falls upon the ground (getting "soiled" in the process), and then seeps into the depths of the earth through the soil (getting purified in the process). Thus, pure water, found in the wells men dig or just gushing out of the earth in fountains, is called the wellspring of life. It is the same thing as the Light that fell from above at the shattering of the vessels that, in falling, descended deep into the substance of earth and matter, from which it then had to be raised. This, in turn, is the task of man, to dig wells or to find the fountainheads from which to draw forth the purified light and send it up again. Another approach to this is to see the descent of Divine delight (like "water") to the lower worlds and to see prayer (like "work") as the act of recovering this hidden joy and freeing it, letting it soar back to God. In all these ways of viewing the process, prayer is the force for both the going down – working or digging – and the lifting up – flight or releasing action.

Returning, then, to the question of prayer on the Sabbath day, let us recall that most of the commandments for this day are negative mitzvot, specifying the things one is not to do. What are the positive mitzvot, besides the general one to remember the day as a day of rest? How is rest to be defined? It could be seen as refraining from all activity, a confirmation of the negative mitzvot making not-doing into a positive action. In this sense, inhibition of action is a purification of the work done during the week. The purifying elements of the week's Torah, mitzvot, and good deeds flow into the Shabbat.

There is a saying to the effect that were all of Israel to keep two Sabbaths, as prescribed, they would be redeemed. The meaning of "prescribed" is not only "doing" as directed by *halakha* (law) but also "going" from one place to another – from below to above in terms of performing the mitzvot and from above to below in terms of bringing down the Divine delight. That is to say, were the "going" to continue in both directions for two consecutive Sabbaths, assuring a steady flow from this world to the highest, redemption would follow. And as we have already claimed, it is prayer that makes this flow possible – the prayer that unites, that, in itself, acts as a link. Hence, the esoteric books, and even the blessing before prayer, call for this union of higher and lower as their aim.

The double aspect of Shabbat has been diagnosed by certain Ḥasidic Sages in greater detail than we can here summarize. Amongst them, of course, the male and female, active and passive, facets of the holy day. In this view, Shabbat is also a positive affirmative action of the spirit as well as a (feminine) withdrawal of mind and body into privacy, prayer, and non-action. The male *"zakhor,"* "remember the Sabbath to sanctify it," and the female "keep the Sabbath" each have two aspects to them: the holiness of that which is unbridgeably apart and the holiness of certain actions that unite; the holiness that sanctifies the Shabbat by what one brings to it and the holiness that belongs to the day itself, irrespective of anything else. Primarily, as has already been emphasized, there are the two movements, from below to above and from above to below, between heaven and earth, between the week's profane contents and their consummation in the act of offering it all up to the Divine.

However, this interaction between above and below is not automatic, as we may surmise, even though we recognize that one receives what one puts into the Shabbat. It is not a mirror reflection, infallibly reacting without distortion or change; it is more like the reflection of one's relationship to another person who, in reacting to one's love or whatever, returns another love; something is added.

A crucial phrase is here interjected: "till Thy people pass over,

O Lord, till the people pass over whom Thou hast acquired" (Exodus 15:16). What can be the meaning of passing over or transcending (the Divine name)? After all, this name, also called "that which is," includes all of existence. On the other hand, the name only expresses knowable reality and, as such, has its limitations in finitude. As we have said, the Tetragrammaton is both contraction and expansion of Divinity; it begins with an infinite concentration and passes beyond to that which transcends all names. Furthermore, with the *Yod* was the next world created, which is known to us as higher delight, the Divine bliss that is the source of all joy and perfection. Going beyond (the name) may then refer to the act of transcending delight itself, the act of utmost devotion, the soul's offering of self to God.

We may have learned the wondrous beauty of the mitzvot, and even of the love and fear of God. Beyond all these, there is the dedication of the soul in the act of consecration to the Divine. Such a complete devotional attitude partakes of the infinite within a person; it takes him beyond his limits. It is the point where a human being can give more than he has received; utmost devotion makes it possible to exceed oneself. Ordinarily a person is contained within a certain limited world. Yet an action drawn from the soul's surrender and consecration can release him. What is most astonishing is that one can so act for the sake of God at any level, whether it be a trivial testing of moral virtue or a great trial of the spirit. One person overcomes the urge to tell a particular joke; another casts himself into the flames of martyrdom. What is common to all such actions is a certain genuine surrender of one's limitation, whether it be a commonplace deed or a performance that no one else can accomplish. It happens when one says to oneself, "Under no conditions or circumstances can I do this," and then one does it. The smallness or greatness of a person determines the size and nature of his devotion; but it is an action available to all men.

We may allow ourselves to call it "the infinite" – that which awakens in a human being when confronted with an obstacle or impediment, with a boundary or margin of any kind, whether in work, understanding, or feeling. To that which has hitherto in life been an impassable barrier, one says: "Nevertheless – with all my might." An added increment, no matter how small, enters into life and makes the decisive difference. And this "just a little more" is a matter of devotion or soul-offering. At this point, a person transcends himself, that is he goes beyond the limits of his self. And since every person, great or small, has his own limitations, going beyond them is the same as the *Yod* (the smallest letter) by which the future world was created. It is an act of passing over, as said. As some Sage once said, it is leaping (in those realms) where one cannot walk.

The second part of the quotation – "till the people pass over which Thou hast acquired" – denotes a passage from above to below. The Divine name descends and emanates from the hidden; Higher delight becomes manifest. Indeed, such an incredibly remarkable thing does happen that, as an individual breaks out from the frontiers of his existence, so does God emerge from the laws of life and nature. The same defiance of limits, the getting out of one's customary way, is parallel to the passage to the next world, not in the sense of Heaven or Paradise, but in the sense of reaching another world. The ordinary realm of existence is the known world of law, the laws of material reality and of spiritual reality. And, in certain respects, the laws of spiritual or abstract reality are even more harsh and unyielding than the laws of material reality. For instance, it is easier to manipulate or play with nature than with mathematics; one can more easily experiment with individual living things than with the laws of heaven that determined the limits of things. But to return to our quotation from the crossing of the Red Sea – "till the people pass over, whom Thou hast acquired" – we may view it as indicating that God also passes over and breaks His own laws of nature and thereby creates a new world.

This concept of "passing over" may also be applied to the phenomenon of Divine forgiveness and repentance. Incidentally, the root letters of the words Shabbat and *Teshuva* (repentance) are almost identical, even though the words are derived from different sources. In any case, Shabbat itself is a form of repentance (or restoration to equilibrium). For the act of atonement contains *Tikkun* or reparation for wrongdoing, it manifests the fact that God "bears with iniquity and passes over [forgives] transgression" (Micah 7:18). The phrase "passes over transgression" is rather contradictory when it is recalled that sin is the one thing that acts as a barrier between God and man. Thus, the concept of forgiveness is an attempt to explain God's "passing over" transgression.

God goes beyond His own rules; He overcomes the barrier between the sinner and Himself. Eventually, God makes His own (impossible) reality, the reality of the next world, the Heavenly World, where the Infinite exists in everything.

What then is the inner meaning of the statement "Behold God gave you the Shabbat" (Exodus 16:29)? After all, we have claimed that a person makes his own Shabbat, preparing it both by his work during the week and his mitzvot; someone who took no anticipatory trouble would not receive anything. The joy of the Sabbath depends on the work put into the performance of mitzvot for the whole week, which could indicate that the profane as well as the spiritual create the holiness of Shabbat. Its delight rests on material preparations as well as on upright conduct. We could conclude, therefore, that the meaning of the statement lies in the addition of the word *your* Shabbat, pointing out that God gave each his own Shabbat. The day of rest is ours to do with as we like. That is, we may react as we choose to the gracious gifts of Torah and mitzvot, and then, in addition, and in accordance with our choice, we are given a Shabbat of our own making.

In the long run, as we may have already surmised, prayer is sustained by the relation to worldly existence, by our need to overcome pain and suffering. And when the troubles increase, prayer flourishes. There is nothing fragile or delicate about prayer in this respect. It seems to thrive in the most brutal and terrible of circumstances. Except that it does not remain implanted there like a flower; it raises the reality in which it is lodged. Indeed, the higher it lifts the life from which it springs, the higher the prayer's own level of being. And it is said that the highest prayer is uttered when a person does not ask for anything for himself, but when his supplication is for the reality of the world, when he enters into the "secret of the revelation of the *Shekhina*." A person is purified not only by this offering of himself, but also by offering up the substance of the world outside himself.

The ladder of the Shabbat prayer is thus, as we have seen, a ladder set in the earth of the weekday and rising to heaven. And on Shabbat the prayers reach beyond the world of suffering and toil; they leap ahead, even beyond the general bequests for salvation and redemption. What remains is the growth process of memory, which is like the purification process of art by which one thing becomes another. As Rabbi Nachman described it in one of his stories, the melodies of the world are fashioned from the sighs and groans of men. Every song comes from some wailing cry that was transformed into something else; it is no longer a wail.

A similar process takes place on Shabbat. The weariness of the week's physical and spiritual toil undergoes a change. All the elements of existence in the world rise up at least one degree and become another, higher, aspect of the same thing. Objects assume a certain brilliance, so to speak, as if someone had suddenly switched on the electricity, and life itself is lit up and transfused.

A properly ordered Shabbat is not a passive entity, in spite of the absence of doing; it does have a certain action even if not in the creative sense of forming something that did not exist before. It gives light, purifies, and in this sense, a new face is given to the old world. One does the Divine will in its aspect of *Makom* or place; there, where one is, the place is blessed and thereby transformed.

We are thus brought back to the concept of *Oneg Shabbat,* the joy of the Sabbath day, which is a reflection of the higher delight of God. For this higher delight is an aspect of the "hereafter," the coming world. But the next world is apparent in human life in this world when it is illuminated by Divine light. And this is made possible when an individual perceives and reacts with illuminated faculties.

The Way of the Soul
and Torah: Essence
and Structure

Chapter one

As already elucidated in the esoteric tradition, the soul is composed of ten aspects of being corresponding to the (kabbalistic) *Sefirot* of the higher worlds: *Ḥokhma, Bina, Da'at, Ḥesed, Gevura, Tiferet, Netzaḥ, Hod, Yesod,* and *Malkhut.* The essence of the soul in itself, however, lies beyond our powers of description and beyond our very grasp. It eludes us entirely and remains forever unknown. In a certain old-fashioned manner of speaking, it may be likened to the difference between form and content. And form, in this Aristotelian sense, is not necessarily the outer shape of things but their characteristics or qualities: The sharpness of a knife is part of its form, its metallic substance is its content. If one removes all form (or qualifications) from any object, what remains is amorphous matter. It is the raw material, the basis for the characteristics, that give the object form and meaning. Similarly, the essence of the soul, like basic substance, is practically out of our range of observation or understanding; all that we can know is the revealed aspect of the soul, the vessel of its expression, the instrument through which it functions. Just as the brain is the manifest instrument of the otherwise ungraspable mind; or as the mouth is the instrument of speech, the ear the instrument of hearing, and so on. We are able to observe the functional organ, not the sense itself. So, too, with the soul, its essence is beyond us; at best we know its form as revealed by the way the ten *Sefirot* manifest and express themselves in a particular person.

Thus, the conscious aspect of the soul may be considered no more than an instrument, one of the ways of its manifestation. The mind is not the same as the soul; it is only one of its channels of expression, just as are the emotions. After all, the definition of anything in itself is that which does not change; its qualities may vary but the essence remains unchanged. Thus, the mind, which is always undergoing transitions and modifications, cannot be considered anything but a manifestation of soul. That which is essence is not entirely revealed by any of these constant manifestations of consciousness, which are really just so many vibrations and pulsations and not even a constant flow. The mind or intellect is just a mode of the soul's expression; it is not the soul itself.

Nevertheless, it is through this changing aspect of consciousness that we can gain knowledge of the unchanging essence. Just as in scientific investigation, the variations in phenomena are studied carefully to discover the constant factor or basic principle. And it is important to get to some understanding of the unqualified soul, the constant factor in human life, precisely because it is not given to any rational perception. Like the problem of human equality, which, in spite of its being indefinable and not quantitative, has to be dealt with in modern society in clearly functional terms, so, too, we ask: Is the soul determined by the level of intellect; at what point in the depths of a retarded human being can the soul be said to exist?

In the Middle Ages, the problem may have been seen in more simple terms. The Rambam, for instance, preferred a single man of wisdom to a thousand fools. Although he never said so in explicit terms, he did tend to identify the soul with the intellect and made his evaluations accordingly. Even gracious manners or good-heartedness were not considered primary in measuring a person.

The soul is thus not the ten attributes; it is a single aspect from which all else gushes forth. What is more, there are higher powers, beyond the mind, a part of which may be considered Will, which are also only instruments of the soul. They are called *Keter* and are the crowning jewels of life, but are still not the soul itself. In addition, we know that the human infant, born with a soul, has to learn and develop the mind, and this, too, can serve as evidence that the soul is beyond any mental or emotional manifestations.

What then is the soul in itself? It is indefinable in terms of intellect and, for that very reason, more simple in terms of essence. In itself, the soul is a Divine spark, an aspect of Godliness in man.

The Maharal, a Sage who disputed the Rambam's conception of the soul, claimed that there was a Divine essence that was neither mind nor matter, and that the human soul was one such manifestation of this reality. He was also bound to admit that it could not be defined. All we can do is conclude that, just as the *Sefirot* are emanations from the Godhead and not Divine in themselves, so, too, is the soul a source of all human attributes and not to be identified with any of them.

True, man is created in the image of God, but we cannot say more about it. In contrast, Wisdom (*Hokhma*), which is also the creative factor, cannot be identified with God because it is a particular quality and limits the infinitude of the Divine. We can say "Thou art wise," but it is not accurate because it, too, is a delimiting of the infinite, an attempt to bring it down to our human measure.

When God reveals something through *Hokhma*, human wisdom becomes a transparent vessel for Divine light. And the soul from which the *Hokhma* issues may be considered infinite. But *Hokhma*, Wisdom itself, can never assume the dimensions of the soul; there is an unbridgeable gap between them; they exist in two different dimensions.

The Sages of the Kabbala agreed with the Rambam's declaration that He is Knowledge, He is the Knower, and He is the Known. But they differed in regard to the limiting of God as a Knower or in terms of any category. Of course, it is always repeated that He is wise and not with knowable wisdom, that He is powerful and not with any known forcefulness, etc. The statement that He is the Knowledge and the Knower says little more than that; it is a partial truth, valid within a circumscribed area. That is to say, when God reveals Himself in power, we relate primarily to Him, to the Divine reality; we do not relate to the vehicle, the amount or form of power manifested.

To put the matter in its simplest terms, let us take a man who appears sometimes as a father, sometimes as a craftsman, sometimes as a soldier. While he identifies with each function, his self cannot be totally identified with any one role. In each realm of function, he is whole and separate from the others, but at no point can we separate the man from what he is doing. The man exists as himself, beyond any role or function, as a complete oneness. In this sense, God exists beyond any characterization; all categories are ways of His manifestation to us. A person does not dress up to play the role of father or soldier; it is a real aspect of his existence. At the same time, the man is not the same as father or soldier; he remains the self beneath the outer garments, beyond the role or function.

The Sages of the Kabbala thus agreed that God is Knowledge and Knower and Known, but that He is also beyond all these, the inseparable Divine within all these, yet not identified with any of them. It is a one-sided connection, not a two-sided one. God is in the phenomenon, the phenomenon is not in Him, and it is a connection within the World of Emanation; it does not exist beyond that.

God is actually totally other; the realm of the holy is apart from all else. The effort to make contact with this otherness was advanced significantly by the Kabbala of the Ari in a way that can be compared to the difference between the modern physics of Einstein and the physics of Newton. It's not that Newtonian physics is wrong; it has simply been proven to be a description of a particular aspect, and not of the whole, of the physical world. In modern mathematics, too, there are formulae and proofs that are valid for only part of reality. So, too, we may regard the views of such classical Jewish thinkers as the Rambam.

To sum up, the soul, like the Divine of which it is a spark, is beyond all definitions and qualifications. The problem for man is to find a way of connecting with the soul from essence to essence. And this ultimately means: How shall we find the way to God?

Chapter two

I t may be important to pursue our inquiry by a quick probe into the place of *Hokhma* in the framework of the *Sefirot*. As we have already emphasized, *Hokhma* or Wisdom, is an instrument of the soul; it is not of the essence of the soul. To quote the Maharal, it is a mystery of non-physical Being without being spiritual. All the designations of other aspects of body or spirit are unable to contain it because, although like them, it is only an instrument, it is a very special instrument by reason of the infinite light that pervades it. For *Hokhma* is a vessel for the Divine *Shekhina* or indwelling. Concurrently, however, the source of the soul is Higher Wisdom. In other words, we have a seemingly paradoxical situation in which the soul (the spark of God in man) is derived from one of the instruments of the soul which is Wisdom or *Hokhma*.

It may be compared to the original living cell of life in the sperm which contains not only the genes of the source person but also the essence of the entire future person. As a certain Talmudic discussion put it: Is the child born from the parents or are the parents merely an instrument to give life to the child? A blind person does not necessarily have blind children; his essential qualities are not necessarily transferred. The father (who is source) only takes part in a process that is beyond him.

In fact, the soul has a number of levels; it may be seen as a combination of many soul entities, one above the other. Even though a person gets one soul, this soul of his is not necessarily composed of a single formation: It may be a combination of one sort of human soul, another sort of spirit, and a Divine soul of yet another kind. So that if a person reaches a higher level of being, he can change his very essence and not only alter a particular level of his soul's structure. He is able to reach a new and higher dimension of being, such as *Yehida*, which goes beyond *Hokhma*. For there exists in every human soul a certain point linked to higher will that is higher than its source in higher *Hokhma*. This is an aspect of the principle that anything having the ability to nullify itself entirely contains in itself the germ of the infinite. The more specifically defined the vessel, the more restricted the particular contents it can hold. The less defined it is, that is to say the more a vessel nullifies itself, the greater and more varied its contents.

To return to the nature of the soul itself, it has been pointed out that even though the various attributes or *Sefirot* reveal aspects of the soul, the soul cannot be identified with any of them and remains beyond all definition. Just as it cannot be represented by any physical formulation, it cannot be designated by any spiritual formulation. That is, it is already neither intelligence nor emotion nor any combination of the two. The soul is a realm of being in which intellect, understanding, love, power, and all the other attributes are given expression; it is that which gives them life and meaning.

If the soul is investigated from another angle, the phenomenon of martyrdom, the soul's capacity to offer itself to God rises before us. There are varying degrees of such intense soul consecration, the highest being total annihilation of the individual self. This is more than an act of intelligent will or decision; it is an expression of the unknown essence of the soul. It is like the automatic extinguishing of the candle's flame in the presence of the bonfire. The spark returns to the torch; a particular existence is released from its constraints.

To be sure, this is not a common phenomenon. The survival factor, the will to be oneself and to persist in the form in which one lives, is extraordinarily powerful and a known obstacle to the development of the soul. When overcome, a wall of resistance falls and the way to devotion and martyrdom as an ultimate expression of freedom is open. Indeed there are persons who have been so tempted by this release into liberation that they had to be watched over. And it was not the lure of death, of course; it was the utmost consecration of the soul, a clinging to the Divine as supreme happiness.

It was said of Rabbi Elimelech that he would deliberately take out his watch during prayer in order to break the headlong rush of the soul to God – to return to the reality of time. Utmost devotion is thus seen as an intrinsic quality of the soul. And when the scriptural text demands the love of a man "with all thy soul," the intention is total offering of the being, not only the externals of thought, speech, and action. Indeed, there are two meanings to the command "with all thy soul." One refers to all the different parts of the soul; the second requires the whole of oneself, without reserve. The first is a deliberate subservience of the various modes of one's existence to God; the second is complete devotion expressed as an unthinking offering of one's soul.

Since this utmost devotion is beyond the mental, there cannot be a rational reason for it. One is unable even to say why since any sensible cause for action is a product of self-interest. No doubt there are cases of self-sacrifice for the sake of the species, but that can be explained in terms of biological survival on a larger scale. Martyrdom, in the sense of conscious offering of oneself, involves a love that exceeds all self-interest and becomes self-nullification. And there can be no "reason" for it; indeed the great self-giving love is the soul's very essence. It certainly cannot explain itself. *Ḥokhma* is here abrogated, apparently, and much of what was previously declared essential aspects of the soul have no place. That is to say, we are confronted with the problem of knowledge again – God as both Knower and Known.

The Shema declaration at the center of daily prayer demonstrates this rather sudden and seemingly inexplicable switch from utmost devotion, "to love God with all thy heart and with all thy soul and with all thy being," to the rather mundane instruction to "talk of them when thou sittest in thy house, and when thou walkest by the way, and when thou liest down, and when thou risest up" (Deuteronomy 6:7). What is enjoined here is to connect the soul with thought, speech, and action, and to do this through the mitzvot which are commanded by the Lord.

Another rhythm is introduced: logically there is a certain gap, a severance between soul devotion and action in physical reality. It is as though two directions are being given, one is a giving up of life, the other is a restoration or enhancement of life force. How do they merge?

This brings us to the cardinal principle of Torah – that Torah is actually Higher Wisdom, חכמה עילאה, the Divine wisdom in which Infinite Light clothes itself. It is also known as that which precedes the world, primordial in the sense that it is the wisdom of *Atzilut*, חכמה דאצילות (*Atzilut* is the highest of the four worlds.) In turn, this *Ḥokhma* of *Atzilut* descends and clothes itself in the wisdom of the lower worlds, *Bri'a*, *Yetzira*, and *Asiya*. That is to say, it does not make an appearance as itself; it manifests as Torah, in terms that are meaningful in this world.

What is meant by the descriptive phrase "clothes itself?" Essentially it is a descent, a lowering, making a higher entity understood or graspable, so to speak, by existences of another order. It can be a matter of a complicated formula or it can be part of a story about a certain reality or a whole world of realities. The story, or formula, is a cover for something else. The symbol, as in algebra, can stand for anything at all. Similarly the story may mean any number of things. And just as it does not matter whether the x of mathematics relates to the number of stones or birds or people, so, too, the story aspect of wisdom expressed in words and connected sentences of Torah is secondary. The idea is abstract and the meaning can appear on a multiplicity of levels. The contents remain but the very same story changes according to the level of the listener. The higher wisdom of *Atzilut* descends and clothes itself in the wisdom of the lower worlds and manifests as Torah.

Torah, in this sense, is something to be studied as well as being a realm of mystical union with the Divine. And when a person understands a portion of scripture, he is united with God to the extent that the difference between subject and object is obscured. Intellectual and spiritual grasp of a Torah passage becomes a situation in which the learner becomes the object of his learning, and the more complete the understanding, the greater the unification. As one of the Sages remarked: It is like the fusion of two drops of water.

Thus, although we seem to have no control over the essence of the soul, we do have some measure of supervision over the mind. This makes it possible for us to unite with the Divine on His terms. We penetrate the barrier that separates us. We can be united in spite of the extreme difference between us because Torah is that narrow point of contact, just as two liquids can combine if there is even the slightest merging. The "Mind" of God is made available to the human mind. A higher soul union beyond the mental becomes possible, even if (as we have indicated) mind and soul are not identical. To be sure, there can be intellectual understanding without mystical union. Study of Torah does not in itself guarantee anything; one may not even be sure to use Torah to learn what to do. But as a way of connecting with God, it is a point of contact, a powerful union with a current of infinite force. How one reacts is different for each person.

Chapter three

Jewish tradition claims that while studying Torah, the soul can be in union with God. This suggests that mind is a central factor in any genuine connection with the Divine. When a person does not understand or feel anything at all, and the conscious mind is not involved in the connection, the nature of the union becomes a matter for doubt. In this regard, the Torah can be considered the higher supernal temple of God.

Nevertheless, when a person is caught up intellectually in a Talmudic discussion, he may very likely be unaware of his soul's communion with God. He may experience a certain mental and moral exhilaration, and he may even have recited a prayer before his Torah study; but while immersed in the effort to grasp the meaning of a particular text, he is liable to be far from the experience of mystical union. His attention is absorbed in the external aspects of wisdom. What is more, while engaged in Torah study, other factors may enter, such as feelings of self-esteem or a pleasant awareness of one's prowess in grasping the meaning of the text. And clearly, such self-satisfaction and pride tend to lead in the opposite direction to the essential purpose of Torah.

The issue raised here concerns the core of the experience of *Devekut* or Divine union. What are we suggesting when we declare that whenever a person inserts himself (egotistically) into a situation such as Torah study, he invalidates its effectiveness as a genuine mystical experience? As is well known, there are any number of methods, ways, and means, and even traditional techniques for achieving spiritual rapture, and these can produce genuine feelings of transcendental oneness with God and the universe. To what extent is such an experience lasting and existentially valid? And to what degree can it be viewed as no more than a wonderful sensation, a passing delight that allows for all sorts of interpretation? In contrast, we are taking the liberty of presenting Torah study as a more reliable approach to Divine union, in spite of the wrong turns this may take, as we have already shown; that is, in spite of how easily it can become a misappropriation of holiness. Of course, there is a strong correlation between all sorts of genuine religious experience, and one cannot neatly separate them. But there are relatively independent circuits that are considered preferable. One of the most significant of these, we here maintain, is total and pure engagement with Torah.

Indeed, in terms of profundity and power there is very little to equal it. Although the study of Torah may be matter-of-fact and seemingly dry in terms of spiritual delights, it may be the more genuine by virtue of the union created between knower and knowledge. The numerous ideas of the Godhead and the human mind absorb each other, so to speak; they merge like "drops of rain water meeting on the window sill." There may not be a sensational mystical feeling but there is a mystical union.

Do we hereby presume to state that – as the Shema prayer designates – we are filling the command to love God with all our hearts and souls through the intellectual action of "speaking" of Torah? Is there not more to the expression of total devotion? Of course, consecrating oneself does not necessarily require annihilation of one's entire being, but there is an element of self-nullification in the act of becoming absorbed in Torah. And if this absorption in and unification with Torah is also an act of dedication to the Giver of Torah, we can discern how it does serve to fulfill the commandment to love God with all one's being.

In another context, the matter is explained by saying: "All who are thirsty, go to the water" – הוי כל צמא לכו למים (Isaiah 55:1). What is one thirsty for? If it is obvious, why say "go to the water"? The point is that one is thirsty for God. The thirst and the quenching of the thirst are not obviously on the same plane; they have to be placed on that level. Just as in the case of any severe pain or need, there has to be an indication of the nature of the lack before it can be filled. One has to know that the thirst is for God.

Talmud Torah, the study of Scripture, is therefore not a continuing effort to learn something, whether it be information or instruction. All these valuable and useful results are only by-products. The ultimate essence of Talmud Torah is in the interior engagement with it as a Divine message; it is a need to be occupied with Torah as one is occupied with life itself, not as a fragmentary interest but as a framework within which all of mind and heart is involved. Gemara (mishnaic and talmudic elucidations of the Bible), for example, includes a vast range of subjects for the mind to dwell upon: farming know-how about seeds and seasons, legal instruction, religious inspiration, details about the human body, social customs – in fact almost all aspects of living in the world. Thus, in many ways, it appears to be an accumulation of human wisdom and not very heavenly. The point of study is to reveal the Infinite light of God in all this. The effort required is to draw upon and extend this Divine light into the world below.

The Talmud tells us that the angels complained to God about this unfair discrimination: Why give this Divine gift of Torah to man and not to us? The Lord answered saying, The Torah commands: Honor thy father and mother. Thou shalt not steal. Thou shalt not commit adultery. But as for you angels, do you have parents? Do you possess anything? Have you any carnal desires? What then do you need the Torah for? Is it because you have heard that it was a Divine revelation? If so, it is not for celestial beings but for earthly beings, to help them reach beyond their earthbound state.

The Rambam's "Thirteen Articles of Faith" lists the resurrection of the dead last, almost as an afterthought. To be sure, it is conventionally accepted as a basic principle of Jewish belief, but one may be allowed to wonder – what is it good for? The Rambam himself had his reservations about it, his basic approach to the physical life being so ambivalent. One has the feeling that he shrank from all that was humiliating and demeaning about the life of the body. As for the resurrection of the dead, incredibly miraculous though it might be, could it not also be seen as a regression, a sliding back from the upward thrust of the life of the spirit. He describes the days of the Messiah as an opportunity for the world to extricate itself from the wholly unnecessary struggles with matter and come to grips with the real task of humanity. Because, in our world, before the messianic redemption, there is a real question that may be asked: How much of our effort goes into superfluous, meaningless actions that we are compelled to do because of circumstances? Most nations of the world spend vast sums on armaments that do not benefit anyone, simply because there is no alternative. The genuine needs of people are secondary in a society that is based on strife. Whereas in the Messianic age, although the world will not change, there will be a change in priorities and what is really important will come first. Then it will be possible to make progress, for the many false compulsions will be eliminated, whether they be due to the misunderstanding of nature or the pressure of social and psychological conditions that force men to invest most of their energy in artificial struggles. There is general agreement about the waste of human effort; the problem is, where is the end of it?

According to the Ramban the final phase is not just that the pure soul is released from the chains of the body and able at last to devote itself to the great task of humanity. Thus, his description of the world after the resurrection of the dead is not of·persons clinically risen from the grave but of a new material reality. This new material world will be different, a new nature will prevail. Part of what we consider important or necessary will no longer exist; in the new order there will be an entirely different arrangement of things. But there will still be a soul in a body. And it is the souls that will become manifest. The final revelation will be of the body, when the physical will be able to see God. The next world is the spiritual world in which the Divine is made manifest to all. But this is still not the ultimate purpose of Creation. The ultimate purpose is to bring the material world to the state of Divine revelation, in the same degree or even more, than the spiritual world.

We may here digress a little to wonder at the incomprehensible partnership of body and soul. For the most part it is a woeful association. If we were granted only one of the two to live with, life would be much easier. The combination is endlessly problematic; the body is continually struggling with its own needs, its failures to get what it wants, and its troublesome relationship with the soul, while the soul never seems to be thoroughly at ease with the body, and both of them fret at the difficulty of achieving any fruitful interaction or cooperation. If only the body were left alone, without the complications of the soul, how free and unencumbered it could be to enjoy the simple life of its creatureliness. Nevertheless, it cannot be refuted that the very superiority of man over other creatures of the earth is derived precisely from this additional dimension of soul. The advantage is inestimably greater than he can guess, but meanwhile, man is left struggling with the problems – the anguish of his two-sidedness – at least until the Messianic era of the resurrection.

One may intervene here with a note of compassion for man. Why wait? Why this long interval of pain and suffering before the release of the soul into the Infinite Light? Do we have to go through this terrible bother with death and resurrection? The answer, according to the Sages, seems to be that no man has to be prepared. Just as an answer has no meaning without the question. No matter how profound or wise the reply may be, it remains devoid of all meaning without the question to which it supplies the answer. It's a matter of stages in a progression: without first clearly posing a problem, a challenging interrogation, or a contentious doubt, the truth has no possibility of appearing as a statement of any kind, much less as an answer, because there can be no answer to a nonexistent question. The whole structure of the world may thus be seen as a framework for man's response to God. First, man has to learn to listen, then to ask the right question, and finally hear the answer. Only then will the world have meaning.

In order for the Divine to be completely revealed to man, the instrument for receiving such salvation has to be slowly fashioned by time. Just as any radio broadcasting device needs a proper apparatus for its reception. The Torah fills the task of preparing man for this final redemption when the human soul, in its combined totality of matter and spirit, body and soul substance, will unite with the Godhead. To be sure, Torah is no more than an expression of Divine wisdom and Will and in one's engagement with it, one is nullified in it. How does it produce its effect on man?

The answer (put in seemingly negative terms) is hidden in the statement, "And thou shalt not desecrate My holy name" (Leviticus 22:32). Do not make a gap, a vacuum, in the Divine holiness. Wherever God's absolute unity and wholeness is not sensed, a hole is created; one's being becomes a gaping emptiness in the Divine existence. And the more the "I"-ness of oneself asserts itself, the bigger the hole. It's as though every person occupies a certain space – length, breadth, and volume – all his own, and in life, this space grows or diminishes. Indeed, there are individuals of such dominating quality that they seem to push others out of their space. To be sure, all these individual amplitudes exist in God. But very much depends on the relationship between them, and as we know, there are all too many instances where the person does not allow room for God at all and the Divine is pushed out.

There is a rather odd story about a Polish nobleman who went to church, prayed before a crucifix, and finished his plea with a defiant threat: "And besides, remember that you're only a [wretched] Jid and I am a Polish *shlachtchtis* [aristocrat]." But of course, even those who are not Polish noblemen often pray with a rather exaggerated picture of themselves. "Don't you realize that you're being addressed by the distinguished Rabbi of the largest congregation in town?" This self-importance, alas, is not just an anecdote. How much does our prayer or study involve an inflated consciousness of the "me" as performer?

At which point we are plunged into the crucial (kabbalistic) idea expressed at the beginning of the book *Etz Ḥaim* of the Ari: "And it is known that for the worlds to exist, there had to be a space provided, a space free of the Divine." For God to create the world, He had to make room for it, He had to withdraw Himself a little, leaving space for that which is not entirely Divine. It is not an objective space, of course. There is no meaning to such a geometric image; it is a subjective space, a disappearance of the overwhelming Divine light. To provide a crude metaphor, let us say that someone talks about something and then stops for a moment or so, during which interval one continues to think about the subject, and the subject of the conversation proceeds to "exist" in the space. Only the manifestation in words is not articulated. It is the listener who has to fill in when this rises to a certain height; it may be called a mystical stuttering. A person in spiritual ecstasy may be unable to express himself adequately and his words sound like broken speech.

We have then a thin line of light, or Divine consciousness, which pierces the non existence. And it passes from world to world, which worlds are created in turn by the line, and which then obscure the line, making it ever more dim and unclear. Ultimately, the line fades out entirely. To make a modern analogy, it may be likened to a broadcasting apparatus that loses power with distance, with only a smattering of sound reaching beyond a certain area, and eventually vanishing completely. At first there is clear communication; afterwards, less and less; and finally, silence.

Moreover, this "line" does not reach the edge of the worlds. There is something called the *Prasa*, or curtain, beyond which no reception is possible. The worlds do not get anything further, at least not directly. There is a division of the original light. We may imagine, for instance, a room made dark and only a thin line of light remaining. This line reaches a screen and part of it passes through, but it is then no longer itself, having absorbed something of the screen and becoming something of another order: the reality beyond the screen. In brief, the worlds until the World of Emanation or *Atzilut* are transparent. After the World of Emanation, Reality is translucent. Light has gone through but it is not the same light; one can no longer discern what it illuminates. It is called "beyond the veil." Beyond this screen or veil one can only know that something is there, one cannot see what it is. Because of this double obscuring of the Divine light, it is impossible to distinguish its source and therefore, it is easy to err and think that it comes from some other place entirely.

In the time to come, in the next world, the bubble of the universe will burst and the worlds will all be bathed in infinite light. There will no longer be any space, or interval between things. Revelation will be evenly distributed.

To return to the analogy of the darkened room, once the windows are opened and the whole is lit up, there is no difference between being close to the source of light or being removed from it. It may, therefore, be said that for God to develop the photographic film of the world, He had to create a darkroom. And one needs a limited source of light, controlled and restricted, in order to function. Once the desired effect is achieved, the windows can be opened. That is, the development of the world requires darkness, the hiddenness of space and the obscuration of

God Himself. Indeed Divine revelation would most likely consume all of existence. Reality as we know it would cease to be. Thus, it is written, the prophet can hear the song of the celestial beings but he cannot see anything. As it was said to Moses: "For no man shall look upon Me and live." There is this limit beyond which all is made meaningless, burnt out and extinguished. As it is hinted in several sources in the Scriptural texts, any trespass of the permitted range of sanctity is a matter of utmost peril.

This world may thus be viewed as preparation for the next world. Anything or anyone unable to bear the great light of the Messianic Age would be consumed by the lifting of the (protective) screens. The *tzaddikim* have to be given the required strength to bear the rewards of their labors in this world. For a person takes what he is able to give in this world and he gives to the "poor" what he has taken; God then has to compensate him accordingly in the next world. Similarly, the *tzaddik* is compensated. But in this world how can the *tzaddik* bear up under such an immensity of giving! Therefore God has to provide him with the strength to do so. This power of the *tzaddikim* to hold up is actually all that we do in the world. That is, all we are about is to bring the reality in the world to such a stage that it can sustain the Redemption. And this matter of the resurrection of the dead is part of the process of the ever-renewed fashioning of the whole configuration of body and soul in order that it should be able to stand up and hold out in this matter. And until this future revelation – for now, that is – we have to work with the thin line that is revealed to us in the Torah we have, in order to be able, afterwards, to receive the luminosity of infinite light that is beyond this line of our consciousness, beyond the concealment, beyond "space" (or the darkened room provided for this world's existence).

Chapter four

Having examined the nature of the dedication involved in Torah study, it is apparent that mystical union is achieved, not by emotional identification, but intellectual identification with the text. As mentioned, it is a matter of union of thought with thought, human cognition of God's "thinking." And as a result there is a nullification of the soul before the Divine.

But beyond this intellectual integration there is another, more profoundly penetrating riddle. If God is all and possesses all the greatness and the glory, what can one give back to God in gratitude? As it is expressed in the Bible: "From Yours have we given unto Thee" (1 Chronicles 29:14). If one is indeed decent and upright, then one returns to God something of the fruit of the earth that was provided by Divine bounty. What else can one give? What is so worthy in God's eyes that He would receive it with joy?

The answer is one's very self. Not something that belongs to me, but my very self. As long as a person considers himself to be "somebody," he has a self that is independent of God, to a greater or lesser degree, and he owns things that are his and his alone. And, in the ordinary course of life, he may part with these as he sees fit.

But the giving away of that which is one's soul, the self of the self, is an act that exceeds anything that can be done by even the highest celestial beings. The heavenly hosts simply do not have it to give away. Man, however, has a soul, a sense of independent selfhood, which he can offer up to God as a sacrifice. This is the most valuable of all the possible gifts conceivable, in Heaven or on earth.

One may argue that even in the simplest human relationships, when one is listening to someone else with complete attention, there is a similar nullification of self, if even for a short interval of time. While listening, one is not doing something else; there is a complete absorption in a single act of concentration that eliminates thought of oneself. Similarly in Torah study, the self absorption is most often temporary; it cannot be considered total self-nullification. It is only when the Torah is accepted as the word of Divine instruction, when it has the quality of "we shall do and we shall hear" (Exodus 24:7), that it assumes the quality of "sacrifice," obliteration of self.

The fact is that this readiness to obey, as expressed by *"Na'aseh Venishma,"* is not really out of the ordinary. When we are given a new contraption, like a washing machine, the first thing we do is read the instructions, learn them, and comply with what is specified. There is not much of spiritual self-nullification here; there is only a sensible renunciation of willfulness, and a certain attentive attitude. The self-nullification of Torah study, on the other hand, is more than attentiveness to instruction; it is a living relation to the whole situation of Torah, which is revelation of Infinite Light. Something more is demanded of one, a participation that raises and illuminates the soul. It is perhaps like being connected to the electric current of whatever one is learning to operate. One thus connects oneself with Torah and lets its power flow through one in varying intensities and with ever-heightening response. For the connection is voluntary and prayerful. It is a self-consecration.

We are hereby led back to the two levels of devotion and self-nullification. One is to offer up one's soul to the One all-inclusive Divine reality in terms of a total renunciation of this world, of the so-called outer reality. The other is a renunciation of oneself, of one's own existence. That is, the person who is prepared to give up his life in this world for the sake of life in the world to come is achieving a truly magnificent height.

But it is still not the utmost. He is simply prepared to renounce certain things in order to gain something that he deems to be worth more. He is working towards an end, for a permanent peace and heavenly bliss. And it is indeed a peak level of maturity to be able to renounce immediate pleasures for a richer life in the next world. Nevertheless, it is the same principle of reward and punishment, even if, at its highest and noblest degree, it reaches into the realms of holiness. And, to a large extent, education is a crucial factor in supplying the highest and most abstract of ideals as a genuine value. Just as money is only a means to get what one desires; it is not an end in itself; it is an abstraction and therefore higher than the thing it buys. An abstract value is not yet holiness, however, just as honor and the other abstract values of this world are not sacred.

Similarly, the most spiritual and abstract rewards of the next world remain tainted by desire, even if they do achieve holiness. One exchanges a transient world for a permanent world. It is still a good transaction if one can make it: the temporary for the eternal. In other words, the nature of devotion remains at the human level. It is only when one gets to the higher degree of devotion, the renunciation of one's soul – of one's own self and all one's desires for the next world as well as for this world – that one gets beyond one's limited humanity.

The fact that so few people ever achieve such a level of devotion may be due to the resistance of the animal soul, which resistance can be overcome by Torah study. Concentration removes the barriers between the self and the Torah by uniting the heart and mind. The soul can rise more freely and give itself to acts of loving-kindness, to which proper study of Torah inevitably leads. And it is understood that one who does not study for the sake of "doing" Torah is really ignoring the meaning of Torah. Indeed, all Ḥokhma or Wisdom is realized only in the acting out, in acts of loving-kindness. The one who studies and does not do is considered as "one who had better not been born...."

For Torah study is not some wonder device that automatically enables one to attain to Godliness. In fact, there are all sorts of ladders to Heaven; no one of them will, of itself, get one there. Many a person, climbing to the skies and performing one mitzva after another, finds that he is not arriving. And, in the other direction, even without conscious effort to be holy, a Jew will be moving just by performing mitzvot at one level or another. He is seldom, if ever, neutral; the good deed and the right thought are often present, even without piety. In other words, there is the problem of the spiritual power of human action, with or without intention. And it is the same question as that posed by the attempt to explain the difference between religion and magic.

Magic is almost completely mechanical. With all the trimmings, its basis is merely a matter of using the correct formulas and incantations. The result is automatic, irrespective of who performs it, just so long as it is the right combination of forces and formulas. In more than one sense, magic is also like natural science in its dependence on its belief in the proper formulas. And all too often, modern psychologists resort to the use of the appropriate verbal formulae to deal with difficult situations. In certain ways, there is a similarity between the one who rubs the magic lantern to release the demon and the one who pulls the trigger to kill at a distance. The action is effective irrespective of the doer; it is essentially mechanical.

As such it differs from the religious act where everything depends on the relation between the doer, the action, and God. To be sure, there does exist the world of things and essential mechanicalness; the religious is the other side, what we may call the realm of the true nature of life.

Thus, Torah is not a source book of scientific knowledge or magic secrets. A person opening a book of Scripture will not necessarily solve his problem even if he does understand what is written. And, as we have said, in contrast to source books of knowledge, his attitude to Torah must be one of utmost devotion.

This does not diminish the need for understanding, of course. Indeed, the more thoroughly one unites with Torah in depth and intellectual clarity, the greater the mystical union with God. And in this respect, there are levels beyond levels of understanding. What is central, however, is the participation of all of the aspects of the self in this understanding. The contact has to be whole; all the parts of one's being should be touched when one claims to understand, even though, at the same time, there are always levels of understanding and knowledge still unexplored that remain beyond one's grasp.

As we are well aware, much of Torah, especially the oral Torah, is very practical. There are clear instructions about specific actions, times, and objects. The reason, evidently, is to make it possible to do the actions required without necessarily understanding all of whatever is involved. Just as most things are accomplished in the world, even in the scientific laboratories of huge technological contrivances, with each contributing individual comprehending no more than a particular part of the whole process. What is important is that each person should do his own task with maximum understanding. The theory, too, which may be very abstract, is also often broken up into parts, mathematical, physical, atomic, etc.

So, too, it may be said that God's Torah is a complex of such proportions that no one person can know the meaning of it all, for there are worlds upon worlds of reasons and significance. The revealed Torah is only an inner circle in which one can sit and study, speculate and obey without end and with utter sincerity of mind and heart. Even if it is surrounded by other circles, one's wholeness is not impaired thereby. The point is that many students of Torah spend restless days and nights in probing the secrets. Much of it is perhaps mistaken in intent. Because the Torah is as it is given to each person.

All of the above applies to the exoteric Torah which is open and manifest and available. Another situation entirely comes into consideration when the approach is through Kabbala, the esoteric tradition. We are no longer concerned with problems and situations that can be handled by the reasoning intelligence alone. Another factor has entered – the unknown, or at least the worlds beyond ordinary experience, teeming with the "faces" of such unseeable cosmic forces as angels, Paradise, levels of the soul, and the like. One learns, of course, and real knowledge is acquired. But it is not an acquisition in the sense that one can say one "possesses" it; one can, at best, learn how to use it. It is a knowledge in the realm of action, not essentially different from the familiarity with the common objects of the world like a house, a tree, a dog. That is to say, it is possible to understand spiritual matters only with the functional mind. But it is not possible to understand their essence. The values of the esoteric Kabbala are not to be grasped intrinsically in their basic reality or substance.

For instance, let us take the concept of the Garden of Eden. Were we to attempt a quantitative estimate of its area, the number of acres, the nature and names of the trees, and so on, we would very obviously be on the wrong track. To be sure there are halakhic or religious concepts, like the fringes of the prayer shawl or the size of a *sukka* or the time for introducing and parting from the Sabbath, that have reasonable definition in measurable terms. However, most kabbalistic concepts do not have a hold on the senses or the imagination. Names denoting entities of infinite vastness remain abstract: the World of *Atzilut* (Emanation), the World of *Bri'a* (Creation), and others.

Undeniably, abstract notions are very much part of our ordinary culture; but they are not necessarily kabbalistic. In mathematics, for example, we have complex numbers and concepts like the square root of minus one that can never be used for ordinary purposes of life or imagination. They are beyond description, beyond the grasp of mind, even though they can be considered real in terms of mathematical manipulation. With such abstract concepts, the mind is not wholly integrated; not only do they fail to create any experience, there remains something fragmentary about them; there's an edge beyond which one cannot go. The abstractions of the Kabbala, however, are of a far more intimate character; they come from Divine wisdom and speak to the individual soul where life and reality and imagination have their own way of integrating ideas.

As an aside, we could point to the fact that many highly intelligent and creative people have trouble with abstractions as such. One eminent physicist, fully aware of the enormously complicated mathematical steps leading to the identification of certain particles, admitted that he needed to visualize them as pink and round (with color and quality) in order to pursue his studies. One is able to perform with only a minimum of understanding, but to create meaningful contact, some kind of deeper understanding is usually necessary.

When one studies the revealed Torah, therefore, the grasp can be complete; in studying the esoteric Torah, the grasp is necessarily partial. If so, the study of the manifest should come closer to mystical union; the more tangible and actual the Torah is to the one who is engaged in it, the more intellectually meaningful it is, the greater should be the spiritual achievement. Why then bother with the study of the concealed and intangible aspects of Torah? What is the justification for the esoteric

Kabbala – not only in terms of practical usefulness, which we will not here discuss, but in its own terms of spiritual aspiration?

The answer lies in the higher unity that is attainable even when one does not fully understand.

Chapter five

If then the study of Torah is a way of making intellectual connection with the Divine word, the deeper the understanding, it would follow, the greater the union. And according to this principle, all involvement with the Bible and the Talmud and much of the oral tradition demands a maximum effort to achieve clarity and precision. But when we approach the study of Kabbala, the intellectual grasp does not suffice and something of an entirely different order comes into consideration.

Before entering into the problem of the esoteric, however, it is useful to indicate that even the perusal of the Pentateuch demands a unique approach. For the written Torah is equally sacrosanct in all its parts. There are sections that are fairly plain to the understanding and can be translated into action. And there are many statements that, as part of a narrative, would appear to be commonplace prose. "And Joseph was taken to Egypt and was bought by Potiphar" – "ויוסף הורד מצרימה ויקנהו פוטיפר" (Genesis 39:1), or "the name of his wife was Mehitibal" – "ושם אשתו מהיטבאל" (Genesis 36:39), and so many others. Such statements are obviously of another order to the unequivocal "I am the Lord your God" (Exodus 20:2), or "Hear, O Israel." This problem of the difference in the holiness of various parts in the holy Torah cannot be answered simply by any rational scheme of going deeper, or by leaving room for mystery. Admittedly, there is a difference between one sort of statement and another, and in the way one relates and responds. The essential point, however, is that the sacred quality of the Bible lies in the letters themselves. It is in the reading of the text of Scripture that the connection is made, not the studying or explaining. This is in contrast to the oral Torah where the intention is intellectual understanding leading to practical action.

The narrative of Torah, however, does have its own levels of meaning. Besides the overt story, there are multiple contents that have incalculable richness of every sort: literary, descriptive, moral, spiritual, etc.; boxes within boxes. It may be contended that the *Aggada*, the mythical and legendary aspects of oral Torah, also have a many-layered wealth of meaning. In both there are unmanifest contents.

The Bible, however, concentrates on the inner meanings and its study lies in a different direction. The essence of Scripture remains forever beyond one's grasp; and in contrast to the practical and explicit message of the oral Torah, one can never completely grasp its ultimate intent. The holiness of written Torah remains profoundly incommunicable and indivisible, no matter how much one penetrates and explains it. In certain ways, it may be likened to the varying levels of interpreting any formula, mathematical, chemical, or otherwise. At a certain lower level, it is possible to demonstrate the logic with tangible examples. At a higher level, this becomes impossible; the mathematics becomes abstract to the third, fourth, or thousandth degree, utterly beyond the scope of imagination or reason. We are left with a valid equation for which we have no other explanation than itself; it means what it says and the mind cannot grasp more of it than that.

The letters of written Torah are thus components of unfathomable meaning, but they are there to be read, to be used and internalized. In the reading, there is Divine revelation, whether one understands or not. As it has been said, the Torah as a whole, is the name of God. Amongst other things, one calls Him by name when one reads Scripture. The division of the letters into words, sentences, and paragraphs is external and only at times is it what it seems to be; it does not express the innermost content of Torah. Just as people divide the alphabet or the months of the year into rhymed phrases in order to better memorize the sequence. Or else like a code which conceals and deludes as well as reveals. In many instances, what is hidden is like an abstract formula that cannot be grasped by the reasoning faculties. In other words, there is meaning to the seemingly pointless lists of names and repeated narratives, but it remains unmanifest.

The oral Torah, however, is in the world of *Bina* or Understanding, and everything in it is intellectually manifest. The contents are not packaged with many meanings and splendors. At the same time, the *aggadic* or mythological aspects of Talmud are like the written Torah in many ways. In other words, all of Torah may be said to be charged with hidden meaning. And what was said previously about the connection between the mind of the one studying Torah and the thoughts of God have to be modified accordingly. As is always experienced in transmitting knowledge, there is often a need to descend, to bring the material down to the learner's level, and it is often impossible to transmit certain concepts altogether. All one can do is convey whatever one can (even if it is by singing) on various levels of communication. A child, for example, has to be told as much as he is capable of absorbing; at any level, the explanation has to be clear in order to have any value.

We come back to the fact that Torah brings one to a grasp of reality, even if the essence is not grasped. Naturally, there are vast and sublime concepts that are only partly understood and trivial things that can be comprehended with ease. The grasp (and not essence) of reality is a relative thing, therefore. And thus, we are confronted with the problem of the esoteric. Why spend time and energy studying that which only adds to the difficulties of exoteric Torah study, with all its already hidden aspects?

The answer is that there are spiritual contents that cannot be apprehended any other way.

Chapter six

The inner meaning of Torah, as we have seen, remains beyond us; what we do possess is an outer understanding which is also of supreme importance for our souls. But just as salt, in itself, is not food and yet gives food its flavor, so do the concealed aspects of Torah give meaning, purpose, and flavor to the revealed Torah and to life itself. True, there are aspects of a practical nature to the revealed Torah and aspects to which we cannot relate, but even these latter are not the same as the spiritual and transcendental contents. We cannot picture an angel or an altar to the Lord. And we cannot, therefore, be sure of their meaning for us. Our study is an effort to get as close as we can to their reality and, as someone once said, this familiarity with celestial beings may, in the world to come, be of use in recognizing them and feeling at home.

One is reminded of an anecdote told about a not atypical rabbi in Poland of the generation before the war. He was in close touch with his son who had gone to the United States, studied, and become a man of the great world. On a visit home, they conversed, and the son told of a trip he had made in the New York City subway. The father asked for further details, having by himself learned the language and culture of the West. The son told him how he had missed a meeting by taking the wrong train; the Rabbi then told him how he had made the mistake: "You should have changed three stations before...." It turned out that, amongst other things, the Rabbi had once come across a map of the New York's subway system and, just as he remembered everything else, he was able to know how to get around in a city he had never seen.

Meanwhile, for many people the study of esoteric wisdom may be no more than the "salt," or that which gives flavor to life and knowledge. Whatever is grasped, even without mental understanding, goes much deeper than can be recognized; it works on the soul. Like music or art, where the communication is chiefly emotional, there is something transmitted that is of the quality of light. One "knows" without being able to explain what it is that has been learned.

Therefore, as may be conjectured, it is impossible to demand of oneself the same discipline and achievement level as in studies of the manifest. What is involved is in the nature of tones and essences, and what is attained is an enlightenment within. The effect on life is much more profound in terms of detecting sin and knowing goodness. The interior enlightenment may seem small but it is comprehensive. And it is superfluous to inquire into the dimensions of wisdom. "How much" is usually a function of one's particular need as well as capacity. Also there are ever-deeper levels of penetration. As one goes beyond a particular external layer of reality, what was interior becomes exposed, one has grasped another fragment of the hidden, and the process continues.

Nevertheless, this is what the student of Torah, or the Sage, achieves: a certain exterior knowledge. The prophet, however, gets at the thing itself: He can say, "I have seen." The prophetic knowledge is a direct grasp of reality. The Sage learns more about the ways and means of approaching reality; he has heard about the truth like one hears a rumor of distant events. There are those who see the events and those who hear about them. The prophet sees and that is his superiority over other men. At the same time (and this is our point), the prophet is also more limited in his function; he can only use what he is given, and he can go no further than he is allowed. The Sage is not so restricted in his realm of operations; he can go still further into his inquiry and achieve as much as he is capable.

Concerning the relative worth of the invisible and the visible, we can take as a far-fetched metaphor the advances of modern physics that have been able to identify many electromagnetic rays by means of technological devices. The invisible light rays are examined, measured, and even used where possible; no human eye can detect them, or see their color or intensity. Indeed a room full of infrared or any other such ray is in darkness as far we are concerned. But our intellectual knowledge of these unseen rays is real enough and can be extended without limit. In contrast, the prophet does see the color (of the invisible) that he is allowed to see (and that is experience of the unknown); the Sage does not see, but his investigations are not confined. So we can point to a certain advantage of the Sage (or student) over the prophet or Divine "seer." And perhaps it is better for man to have a mental grasp of the larger units of reality than for him to have a spiritual grasp of specific situations and things. He may thus be saved a lot of frustration and be better able to judge the facts of life and the world. The soul thereby dwells in a certain freedom whereas, when understanding is interiorized and reaches to great depths and heights, the facts do not speak to one with the same clarity and significance. They are within a truth too profound for the human mind to grasp. The mathematics of more than a limited dimension is also beyond what the imagination can cope with. What is a pyramid of four dimensions? And yet one is able to build a far bigger and more comprehensive world with higher mathematics. The mind can reach beyond the sensual and be powerful in its own scheme of things. What then is the need for esoteric wisdom and the uncertainties of prophecy?

We are better able to confront this problem by relating it to the practical division of the mitzvot into the positive and the negative. The negative mitzvot are the commandments to refrain from certain actions, in contrast to the positive injunctions to do certain things. And even though there is no definite advantage in the negative mitzvot, they are considered superior. The problem returns to the need or soul wish to go beyond the tangible, beyond the physically sensed things of the revealed world. For there is a recognition in us of another reality and when we praise God, we acknowledge the existence of this greater reality and submit to it (such as when we "perform" the negative mitzva). To be sure, when we bless God, it is for the things we have known and enjoyed or intend to enjoy. Thanksgiving or acknowledgment of God's sublimity is for all that is beyond thought or direct experience. They thus express two different layers of the soul: the exterior that blesses, and the interior that, in acknowledging the unknown, rises higher than itself.

Another illustration of the urge toward the realm of the esoteric is in the two ways of response to the father image and to the spiritual teacher who has also given us life. The father (or mother) gives of himself in the creation of the original germ that is the core of a person; it is a giving of the essence of one's being. What the teacher gives is something of another order; it is a part of his accumulated personality and knowledge, not his essence. The teacher can transmit something of what he has attained, he cannot plant his spiritual attainments in another. It is a relatively external transmission then of a reflection of the essence of his wisdom. So, even though, in the Jewish tradition, the spiritual teacher is more honored than a parent because of the special quality of what he offers, the connection with the parent remains more interior and decisive.

We have here given three examples of the two different kinds of soul connection: (1) the positive mitzvot to do something definite, and the negative mitzvot to refrain from a certain action or to avoid something without necessarily knowing why; (2) the significant difference between a blessing for a specific enjoyment or experience, and the prayer of acknowledgment of the Divine power and glory, without any knowable basis for thanksgiving; and (3) the positive relation to a teacher out of gratitude for what is consciously transmitted and the unconditional relation to a parent irrespective of what happens in life. The difference between the two kinds of connection may be explained by likening it to the two kinds of agreement. The just, positive, rational, and revealed agreement is basically a contract; the two sides consent to certain stipulations on which mutuality is based, and the failure of either side to live up to these conditions breaks the contract, leaving the other side free to do as he sees fit. The second is a covenant, which stipulates the basis for an unbreakable bond between the two participants, and although there may be specifications and provisos, they do not constitute conditions; the covenant is a pledge of consistent allegiance in spite of any failure to comply with the terms of agreement. Abraham's covenant with God is valid for all time. And even if Israel, "My servant, whom I have glorified," should sin and betray the Torah, the covenant cannot be broken. That is, man continues to have the freedom to think and do as he chooses. This is part of the extraordinary emotional substance of a covenant. The connection is indissoluble and yet bears heavily on those who make promises that cannot always be fulfilled. It is indeed an irrational sort of agreement, binding one into an unforeseeable future. The attitude to it is therefore crucial; the inner relation of the soul is what gives the covenant power and meaning.

In the Talmud, there is a passage in which certain Sages say that, after death, the human soul is "questioned" in the next world. After being interrogated about his social and religious conduct, the person is asked about his fear of God. For everything else is inconsequential if there is no Divine fear. All virtues and righteousness are as nothing without fear of God.

Indeed, Divine "awe" or fear is not just another part of one's attitude and behavior; it supplies everything else in life with significance and value. Like salt that gives flavor, preserves meat, and has ritual meaning in sacrifice, this relation of the student to the Giver of the Law is crucial. Not in vain has salt been considered a symbol of the covenant: it does not become corrupted with time, and it is a vital ingredient in the preparation, enjoyment, and preservation of food. The fear of God (which is an acceptance of the unknown with trust) gives meaning to all of life in a profoundly inward soul connection. There is a stable power here upon which all the other parts of Torah and human behavior can be said to rest.

Sanctity and Restraint

Chapter one

The Hebrew word משכן, translated as the Tabernacle, has the root letters of to "dwell" in some place; and, as it has been said in the Scriptures, God did indeed require the construction of the Tabernacle in the desert, and later, the Holy Temple at Jerusalem, to serve Him as a dwelling place below. It is presumed that God lives in the heavens; nevertheless, it seems He wanted a home to be built for Him on earth as well. At the same time, we believe that "I fill the earth and the heavens" (Jeremiah 23:24). The Divine is everywhere. The matter of making available a dwelling place below should therefore be interpreted as God's wish to be revealed on earth. And this is the difference between the Tabernacle and the rest of all space, above or below. It is the place where the One who is beyond time and space takes up His dwelling and reveals His presence.

True, it is that "He is the place of the world, and the world is not His place" (*Bereshit Raba* 68a). One cannot really speak of the Divine as being present in any place above or below, and this not only because of His infinitude, but also because there isn't even any above or below as far as He is concerned. There are levels in the vast gap between man and God, and in this framework, we may view states as higher or lower.

And in this respect, too, we can speak of the Divine wish to manifest at a lower level, at the very lowest level of existence. It is His express desire, not to live in Paradise, above or below, but precisely at the utmost end of the emanation of the reality of worlds; there, where the descent of spirit can proceed no further into the depths. Indeed, God has to contract himself and conceal Himself as much as possible in order to penetrate this furthest and lowest of His worlds. His Light is barely visible here, and it is perhaps because of this prevalent darkness or ignorance that Divine revelation is necessary. Thus, His desire to dwell in some particular place below is consequent upon the revelation of His Torah; for it is necessary to have a center of illumination. As it is written: "Better an hour of repentance and good deeds in this world than all of life in the next world" (*Pirkei Avot* 4:17).

This indicates that the light of Torah and mitzvot is so great that it illuminates the whole of this world, and it does so with an intensity so meaningful it can be considered "better" than the light of higher worlds. And this is possible because when man does it, it subdues the *Sitra Aḥra*, which is the evil impulse in man. To be sure, the two are not identical: the *Sitra Aḥra*, the Other Side, is a cosmic concept, which only in its human aspect is called the evil impulse. Our wicked inclinations and urges are merely local agents or deputies of the universal *Sitra Aḥra* factor. And when the *Sitra Aḥra*, in whatever form or degree, is overcome, the glory of God is lifted up into prominence above all else, as it is said in the *Zohar*, above the praises sung to Him or the deeds done for Him. For the final subjugation of the *Sitra Aḥra* is the overturning of darkness into light. It involves the transmutation of all five senses: one ceases to see and hear evil and one becomes aware of the holiness of the good.

The light of mitzvot serves to transform the soul according to the formula, קדש עצמך במותר לך – "Sanctify yourself with what is permitted unto you" (BT *Yevamot* 20a). For we may easily observe how the "permitted" – the carrying out of mitzvot according to rule – may also lead one astray. A person might eat only the most kosher food with all the appropriate blessings and rituals yet still conduct himself with greed and gluttony. Hence the need for sanctification as well as for keeping within the confines of the permitted. As some of the Ḥasidim used to say: What is prohibited is prohibited; as for what is permitted, don't be so quick and eager. Indeed, every blessing before eating may be viewed as a part of this restraint, this need to subdue the evil impulse that tends to grasp at things. In the wake of this initial victory, small and yet not at all insignificant, the aspect of overcoming manifests itself in the functioning of all the five senses and the mind. The purpose of the mitzva is to make Israel a holy Temple of God. The individual person himself has to become such a receptacle, full of a certain light that transforms him into a living Temple of the Lord, a dwelling place below for the Divine.

It has been said that when the declaration of thrice holy is pronounced in prayer, there is a corresponding response as in the verse (Jeremiah 7:4), as though indeed the speaker is a Temple of the Lord. And why three times? Because of the three expressions of the soul: thought, speech, and deed. A mitzva composed of all these three forms of expression enables a person to reach a level of sanctification. And thus each individual can be a holy Temple.

Nevertheless, there is a profound contradiction hidden away in the statements we have made. If man is able to be a Temple where God can dwell, then the evil impulse is a negligible factor, like a house lizard that creeps in. Indeed, evil is only a parasite, subsisting on the leavings of the good. Only if the *Sitra Aḥra* is great and powerful can we maintain that overcoming it exalts the glory of God. Otherwise, the mitzva is not the significant thing we have made it out to be. Chasing away a house lizard is hardly the same as killing a dragon.

There are two aspects, therefore, to the *Mishkan*, or Tabernacle: to depart from evil and to do good. It is where God is present, both within and beyond, and it is where Israel is sanctified to the point where every Jew is made holy unto himself. We are not confronted with a simple problem of good and evil; what we have is a situation where either one can be so great that the other is made negligible.

The matter may be better understood if we recognize the difference between the two categories of mitzvot: the positive and the negative; the commandments to do, or perform, certain actions and the commandments to refrain from doing certain things. The Sages have given much thought to the question of their relative worth and the conclusion reached was that the negative mitzvot, the commandments not to do, were more important than the positive mitzvot, the commandments to perform certain actions, rituals, prayers, feelings or whatever. For example: It is prescribed that if one has transgressed and failed to do a certain mitzva, one must stop and move no further until one is forgiven. Whereas concerning a failure to follow a negative mitzva, it is said that the repentance is suspended and only on the Day of Atonement can one atone or be absolved. From which it may be gathered that the importance of the negative mitzva is of a higher and clearer order than the positive mitzva. For the positive mitzva is quite apparent in its performance and its relation to holiness fairly obvious, bringing down something of Divine light as a result of definite physical action. Whereas the negative mitzva is not only a refraining from transgression in spite of opportunity or temptation. It is a state of restraint and control, of sufficiency with God and, in its higher stages, an absence of conflict. The desert, with its lack of objects of desire and temptation, fits the state of mind of the negative mitzva more than the seething city and its conflicts. When a person is at peace with himself in the prolonged state of keeping the negative mitzvot, he is at a higher level of being.

One of the ways to comprehend this matter more clearly is to recognize that the physical body, which has been called the dwelling place of the soul, is far more than a house or structural containment. Every organ in the body is a vehicle for or manifestation of a specific "corresponding" aspect of the soul. Just as the mental intelligence is lodged in the head and the manipulative facility in the hands, every organ has its soul function. The correspondence goes far beyond any outer characteristic, such as the material substance or biological function of an organ. A physical organ is a vehicle or means of manifesting something quite specific in the spiritual being. The vital core of an organ, irrespective of its function, relates in some profound manner with a soul quality. And, in terms of Torah, it is said that each of the 248 mitzvot corresponds to one of the *Ramah* organs in the body. To be sure, there are far more organs or parts to the human organism, but the Hebrew word ever refers only to those parts that have bone, flesh, and sinew. As we know, too, this correspondence of an organ to a spiritual reality and to one of the *Ramah* mitzvot is rather "technical," in a manner of speaking, because, in truth, the spiritual cannot really be divided. Something of soul is manifested in every part of the being equally, and every mitzva has its own integral holiness. The soul "consciousness" which is centered in the brain and heart extends to all the organs and provides vital force and functional perfection to each. We do not say that the legs walk or the lips talk; it is the person who does these things. If any one organ should be allowed to separate itself from the whole, we consider it an ailment. The person is sick. If anyone person of the body of Israel should begin to act separately, we relate to him as though he were ill.

In short, the soul illuminates each organ, giving it its own vital force and meaning. When this central line is shut off, the whole physical system ceases to function; the organs have no capacity to even exist without the spiritual factor. Complementary to which, the soul cannot act without the organs, it cannot manipulate things without the hands, or speak without lips. Indeed, the spiritual element is itself only the means for Divine action. God uses Ḥesed or Grace to get certain things accomplished, although He Himself cannot be said to be Ḥesed. Just as electricity is only the energy that makes certain appliances provide cold or heat, without in any way becoming a refrigerator or stove, the soul, too, does not embrace or injure anyone; it is that which makes it possible to do so.

What is more, the Divine Life–giving Power does not only provide the basic energy for proper functioning, it also provides each thing or organ or organism with its uniqueness, its being what it is and its way of acting or reacting. Which is to say that both the substance and the content of any entity are the product of the same Divine or spiritual Source. So, too, are all our organs connected in their functioning (or in some other way) with a mitzva, which, in turn, is a manifestation of Divine Reality in the world. And this is true, not only in the external functioning of visible organs in the body; it holds for the most subtle operation of the most detailed elements within the organs – all are sustained by the powers of the soul. In the same way, the mitzva, even though it is only a fraction of the general essence of holiness, serves, in practice, as a light that manifests an aspect of the highest essence of the whole.

Chapter two

In brief, what we have said concerning the positive mitzva, the performance of that which was enjoined by Torah to "do," is that it acts like an organ of the human body, as a vehicle of higher will. Each one of the *Ramaḥ* (248) organs is a means which the soul uses to manifest itself in action. That is to say, the soul is a general life force behind the particular life force evident in the individual act. And there is a relation between the two, the general and the particular, between the above and the below, and this may be seen as a model of the relation between God and the world.

This is so because what we have called the "above" consists also of the ten *Sefirot*, which are Divine modes of manifestation. Moreover, as the Sages have taught us, they are not qualities of God, they are aspects of Divine unity, not to be separated from Him. In the existence below, the qualities or functional instruments of an acting force are seen as something apart from that to which they refer. (To say that a man is tall or hungry does not tell us much about the essence of the man.) The attributes are external and often alien to the thing itself. The *Sefirot*, however, can be seen as being manifestations of the Divine unity and not only as vehicles or instruments of His will.

To be more specific, let us see what happens when a certain aspect of Infinite Light clothes itself in the *Sefira* of *Ḥesed*. In the *Tikkunei Zohar*, *Ḥesed* is called "arm," that is, an organ and a vessel for the grasping and distribution of Light. The ray of Infinite Light (which is "clothed" in it) is not a particular light, it is a general light, but in the *Sefira*, it takes on the particular quality and tone of the *Sefira*. As some ancient texts have described it, the situation may be likened to pure water that assumes the color of the glass receptacle into which it has been poured, so that one sees green water, red water, or whatever, without there having been any change in the composition of the water; the water remains clear and colorless. So it is with the Infinite Light that vivifies one *Sefira* or another; it does not become something else, it is still of Divine and unqualified essence even when it assumes the particular "color" or quality of a *Sefira*.

Thus the mitzva of charity and loving-kindness is an expression or irradiation of the *Sefira* of *Ḥesed*, bringing Divine Light down into the world. When one fulfills this mitzva of charity, the hand that offers the free gift is the hand of God. It is God who is bringing down loving-kindness through the agency of the human hand. Just as, in our daily prayers, we repeat the supplication phrase to God, "who brings down the rain," and at the same time, realize that it is not a miraculous intervention in nature but that clouds and wind and temperature are conjoined to act as agents for the blessed downpour. In this sense, incidentally, Divine *Ḥesed* is often depicted as rain, with a particular person – like a wind-borne cloud – acting as His instrument.

The element of self-nullification is here very important, because the act of giving charity is valid only when a person is connected to a source (when he does not feel himself as the doer), when he feels that his hand is an implement of a Divine wish, and he himself is in some way or other eliminated. He has become an indirect instrument of something else and has somehow been separated from the act. The hand that gives charity is not his. At the same time, when he is connected with God, he is conscious of what is happening, he takes part in the loving-kindness behind this giving of charity, paying proper attention to the one who is in need of it.

Whatever the circumstances, when *Ḥesed*, Divine Grace, is asked for, it is somehow obvious that it will be vouchsafed through some earthly agent, if for no other reason than that it should be possible to receive it. Otherwise, the grace is liable to be too much for us; we need the restricting power of *Gevura* to limit it to suit our needs. Our prayer for rain belongs to the second, the *Gevura* aspect of the benedictions, because it might easily become a flood if not contained, limited, and kept within bonds. For we cannot bear too much *Ḥesed* and goodness, or *Gevura*, for that matter, or excess of any kind; we live within a very circumscribed range of conditions: temperature and atmospheric pressure, human pity, and power. Too much of anything is disastrous, and therefore, *Ḥesed* and *Gevura* have always to be mixed and merged. Love has to know its limits, strength has to be permeated with compassion.

As it is written: "Who is the hero – he who conquers his impulse" (*Pirkei Avot* 4:1). Our prayers have this quality of *Gevura*, of offering ourselves up instead of making sacrifices in the Holy Temple. But actually, it is easier to get hold of some animal, to bind and slaughter it, than to catch hold of one's own inner drives and impulses. And when a person does this offering up of himself in an act of overcoming his impulse, breaking his wild spirit, so to speak, it belongs to *Gevura*.

There are two levels of organs in the body, the outer and the inner organs. The outer organs do not include all the organs of the body, but only those that belong somehow to the outer frame or skeleton. The inner organs, such as the heart, brain, liver, and kidneys, are not included in the list of *Ramaḥ* organs. And, of course, there is more significant life force in the inner organs.

Thus, too, in the rules of *kashrut*, or ritual purity of edible food, if an inner organ of a slaughtered animal is damaged, the flesh is considered unclean, unfit for eating; whereas only a very serious injury to the outer organs of an animal makes it impure. Why? Uncleanness in ritual terms defines something that undermines life; whereas an outer injury, even the severance of a limb, does not render an animal non-kosher, or impure. The inner organs, therefore, are those that have more influence on the sustenance of life itself. Ritual precedence is determined by this principle of the spiritual reality beyond the physical. The Divine has no body or image. And the Torah always harks back to the idea that man was made in God's image. That is, the human structure is modeled on some Divine structure.

Thus, even though the Divine structure cannot be determined from below from the human form, we are able to learn something of the relation of the parts; the relation, for instance, of the upper and lower organs to each other. We then take the core of this principle as a pattern of higher reality.

Thus, too, when the Torah tells of a Divine manifestation, the description takes on a human aspect, not in specific form, but in essence. When the prophet is vouchsafed a vision of God, he says that he sees an image like unto a man (Ezekiel 1:26). And this image, like unto a man, can take many forms. Sometimes, too, the image is very far from the specifically human. Just as in mathematics, the algebraic formula of a geometric design does not look like a circle or a parabola, although it can easily be interpreted as such. In this sense, the human image is only a basic formula that can take on a variety of forms. So that, in spite of the principal concept of the Divine as absolutely beyond form or body, we can still speak of certain aspects and qualities of God.

It has thus been possible to gain considerable insight into the internal and external aspects of Divinity. Much of this has centered around the mitzva to study Torah, to occupy oneself with Torah, which mitzva is concerned with the internal organs. To illustrate the connection, there is an anecdote from the Talmud about Rabbi Abahu whose face was one day radiant with a strange yellowish-red glow. The students went to Rabbi Yoḥanan (their teacher) and told him that Rabbi Abahu had apparently found a treasure since his face was so radiant. Upon which Rabbi Yoḥanan called for Rabbi Abahu and asked him what he had discovered in their studies to make his face glow so visibly, there being nothing else, certainly not any earthly treasure, that could cause such profound inner excitement. And Rabbi Abahu told him that he had indeed found a new Tosefta (fragments of old commentary on the Mishna), which made him extremely joyful. In other words, the light of wisdom is not only an intellectual illumination, it influences the entire human being and even lights up his body. The blessing: "May the Lord shine His countenance upon thee" (Numbers 6:25) is thus a very real inner sensation. The shining of Divine Light can be so profoundly experienced within a person that it radiates from him externally.

As the Sages have said: Everyone who reads and studies (Torah), the Holy One, Blessed be He, reads and studies in correlation with him. Reading and studying "against" one is an aspect of a manifestation of infinite light through Higher wisdom (חכמה עילאה). The mind is made a vehicle of Divine revelation.

Just as it is asserted (in Kabbalistic lore) that the right hand is of the aspect of *Ḥesed*, so, too, may the brain be considered to represent the aspect of *Hokhma*. Nevertheless, the hand and brain are not of the same order; the brain is not one of the *Ramaḥ* organs of the body which, as said, belong to the external framework. The brain is obviously one of the inner organs, and although it is not identical with the soul, just as the hand isn't, it does respond to far more subtle stimuli. The hand can be utilized by a certain stimulation from the soul and its manipulative facilities used accordingly. The brain can receive a far higher range of stimuli from the soul, but it remains an instrument. When the Supreme Light of Wisdom strikes the brain (or any internal organ), the illumination lights it up and there is a radiance within, an inner illumination.

The above helps to explain the repeated declaration in prayer, "…because in the light of Your countenance You gave us the Law." The light of "Your countenance" is the gift of Torah to mankind, and this is also known as Wisdom Revealed. For the study of Torah, is, on the whole, a matter of uncovering the Divine Wisdom in reality.

To be sure, the performance of mitzvot is an extension (of Torah) into the aspect of the external organs. Just as loving-kindness is the expression of *Ḥesed* and is performed with the right hand, etc., that is, even when an action is external, if performed as mitzva, it is illuminated by Divine Light. Hence the statement that Talmud Torah is weighed against all (the mitzvot) is based on the fact that the Torah is the internal light, the "brain" behind the mitzvot.

For the brain is not only another organ, no matter how complex, related to function; it is also the center of the particular forces of all the other organs. So too the Torah is the rationale of all the mitzvot, the mind of their body. The mitzvot have a certain theoretical basis which is Torah. And just as mind has a double connection, to physical function and to "abstract" principles unconnected to the physical, so too does Torah have its double connection, to the specific mitzvot of action and to the mind behind or spiritual source of the specific mitzva, which is of God. Concerning which there are two parts: the revealed and the hidden. The hidden are the two first letters; the revealed, the two final letters (of the Divine Name). And in prayer it is often expressed in the preliminary invocation: to unite the Holy One and His *Shekhina*. This union is the merging of the hidden and the revealed, the non-manifest and the manifest, because we ourselves are so thoroughly engaged only in the manifest; we are cut off from the hidden.

Concerning the (rich and many-faceted) aspects of the Divine Name, we may relate here to the statement, "This is always My name and My remembrance from generation to generation" (Exodus 3:15). The words "my remembrance" – (זכרי) – when combined in gematria with the letters *Vav* and *Heh* add up to *Ramah* (248), the number and wholeness of the positive mitzvot. And this combination of letters of the Divine Name has its origins in ancient times, when the name of God was not pronounced and the word Lord was substituted. This name was called *Adnut*, from the word Lord (*Adonai*).

The difference between "My name" and "My remembrance" is thus this difference between the Tetragrammaton and the pronounced name of *Adnut* (Lord). The word "remembrance" points to the fact that the real name is only "remembered" in silence, not uttered aloud as a "reminder," and is expressed in the *Ramah* mitzvot.

Keeping the mitzvot is an assumption of a "yoke," the voluntary acceptance of a certain responsibility and burden. It is the relation of service to a Lord, hence the name *Adnut* is appropriate to this relation to God and to the view of Him not only as Creator, Sustainer, and Life-giver, but also as the Sovereign Power and Ruler.

This revelation of God in the mitzvot is represented also in the combination of the two names in writing, including the name *Adonai* in the Tetragrammaton. One may still find it in certain prayer books. It is a holy form of the Divine Name and proper meditation on it is a way to *Yihud* (Divine Union) or greater spiritual integration. For the essence of *Yihud* is to combine something of Infinite Light and Power with a particular place (person or situation), which in turn is an aspect of *Adnut* or the Holy Temple. It is the way God's Presence in the Holy Temple is made known, and it can be experienced, to whatever degree, as the holiness of action in performing a positive mitzva.

The word זכר, root of the words "my remembrance," is also the word for masculine, or male. And indeed most of the positive mitzvot are designed for man and not for woman, whereas in the negative mitzvot there is practically no difference at all. This indicates that the positive mitzvot, the injunctions to do certain things, are of an active nature, imposing something on the world. The negative mitzvot have a different form, and do not create by doing. What they produce is not the result of a deed of definable objectivity. They create reality by refraining from action. Their significance lies in non-action. Where the positive mitzvot change something in the world by means of an active intervention, the negative mitzvot are basically passive. One may view them, in this respect at least, as masculine and feminine counterparts.

As has been explained, these 248 positive *Ramah* mitzvot correspond to the *Ramah* organs of the body, which are extensions of the Infinite light of the ten *Sefirot* from on high to the lower dimensions. To be sure, all the mitzvot, positive and negative, can be said to correspond to the parts of the human body. And immersion in Torah can be seen as related to the inner organs. This may point to the meaning of the truth concerning the "outer" organs as corresponding to the positive mitzvot of action, and "inner" organs as corresponding to the negative mitzvot of non-action. In this sense the positive mitzvot are certainly more impressive; they seem to express acts of strength and determination, while the fulfillment of the negative mitzvot is scarcely visible on the surface; they are performed unobtrusively, quietly, with what appears to be passivity.

We are hereby brought to another level of discernment between the level of that which is manifest and the level of hidden truth. The positive mitzvot belong to the manifest, to the level of revealed facts and relationships. The negative mitzvot belong to the hidden order of Divine reality, which is beyond our grasp. We can, however, gain some insight into this hidden Divine Order from observing what we know of the *Sefirot*.

Wisdom, the *Sefira* of *Ḥokhma*, is the beginning of the process of Divine Manifestation in Creation (the World). But it is not a firm and stable elevation, it is still too sensitively responsive to Infinite Light and serves more as a center or vehicle of reception, an intake point. It is the *Sefira* of *Bina* (understanding) that corresponds to our highest known level of being, the capacity to grasp something of the Divine with our understanding. This is the level of the next world, where the saints dwell in the radiance of the *Shekhina*. After all, in order to enjoy this Divine radiance, some minimal level of understanding is required; without being able to grasp the meaning of the *Shekhina*, it is hardly possible to be in heaven. To be sure, the level of this understanding, at best, is fragmentary, even if it is crucial, and the Sages have written extensively on the problem of how much time one should devote to it, and whether it should be at the expense of a more useful mastery of lower level knowledge.

In any case, one of the ways of conceiving the next world, or Paradise, is as an aspect of *Bina*, the existential level of creation from nothing. Because *Ḥokhma* itself is still the essence of nothing; it is only the beginning of that which is. Actual existence comes only with *Bina*, which is the intelligent mind, able to discriminate and comprehend. Consciousness has to be able to recognize what it is aware of before the various aspects of intelligence can produce concepts and ideas, making perception meaningful. *Ḥokhma* is still intuitive, a mere flash of truth, the first glimpse of a concept as a total unity. *Bina* takes the intuitive insight and by means of proper mental analysis, discrimination, and the use of language, converts it into something that can be handled. Almost everyone has experienced such a flash of wisdom or insight, whether it is of a greater or lesser idea, at some time or other. But if the person does not know what it is that he has glimpsed, it passes him by, leaving him unilluminated by it. Such an occurrence may be a sad or grievous event; it can also be rather ridiculous, as when a person becomes elated with something wonderful that he can't explain and has to let it elude him. It is only when *Bina* has been able to give form and character to an insight that it can be useful or meaningful; and then it can be developed.

One of the images frequently used in describing this process is the flash or spark of light. It has been likened to the striking of stones to produce a spark, which, if caught, can start a fire. In life there can be a whole pile of "sparks" and there can be brilliant people who are always full of "sparks," but if the sparks do not manage to ignite anything, there is no fire. And indeed there are always groups of sparkling people and truly brilliant individuals who never produce anything. On the other hand, when the smallest spark does somehow get a grip on something flammable, a small fire can be started which grows quickly and can easily become a conflagration. The spark, in itself, is nothing; it is only the agent of fire; it is generated from stone, or the inert substance which is not flammable. For such is Ḥokhma; it is like the unseen light. Buried in the stone, it is caught when, and if, like flint, it happens to be struck. In terms of energy it is almost imperceptible. Thus, the spark remains practically nothing for the short duration of its bright existence; to fulfill itself it has to rise and "become" fire by igniting another inert substance of suitable composition.

The significance of this process, in terms of the mind, is that Bina, Understanding, can do nothing without Ḥokhma. A person can build impressively great structures of Bina, but without the spark of Ḥokhma to ignite them, they will remain inert and useless. Indeed Bina and Ḥokhma are constantly interacting, the flash of Wisdom continually igniting accumulated knowledge and reason and thereby initiating creative thinking. Wisdom is always hungry for combustible intelligence.

Indeed, the need for interaction between men and women, between the Sefirot and between people of different cultures, is fairly obvious. Creation is almost always the result of mixture, the compounding of Ḥokhma and Bina and, thereafter, with other Sefirot as well. Ḥokhma only grasps something, as a glimpse or insight. Bina understands this more completely as a process, as one thing following upon another which enables one to build further, to expand and create. Except that Bina has to have something to work upon; the mind needs to be illumined in order to act. On the other hand, the man of Wisdom may be able to see the wholeness (vista) of an unfoldment but be unable to understand one thing from another; and he can thus remain stuck in his wisdom, unable to progress.

As it is esoterically interpreted, the name Garden of Eden can be interpreted either as a place ("and a river came forth out of Eden to water the garden" (Genesis 2:10), or it can be a state of being, the beatitude (Eden – עֵדֶן), or a state of complete bliss that no eye can see.

The Saints sit in Paradise (Garden of Eden) with diadems on their heads; they do not sit in the bliss; they sit in the Eden from which the river goes forth. And this river, with all its various waterways from Eden, is Bina. The esoteric literature calls this river course the channel through which the waters of understanding flow and eventually disseminate. The original fountain of Wisdom becomes a great river with tributaries that flow through broadly irrigated lands. Hence is it said that the Saints sit in the garden, and the Eden aspect of it is the "Nothing" – that which the eye does not see. The completeness of the next world, of Paradise, thus resides in its not being existentially something or other; it is the perfection of the not-yet-grasped.

After all, our lives are always full of something or other; the ultimate future, or that which is aspired to, is the achievement that is beyond any objective "something" – the obtaining of the thing in itself is only a reflection of a yet higher aspiration. Not the garden (place) but the Eden (bliss). It is like the wine sealed in the grapes. We have wine in the bottle and there is the wine that has not yet emerged from the grape; and it is this latter wine, still locked in its source, that is the Nothing. And this wine that comes forth from the grape, the juice that we get when the fruit is pressed to its fullness, is the heady drink of our life.

Chapter three

Wisdom and Understanding are essentially part of the hidden or esoteric aspect of existence. True, this may be said of the Divine altogether. After all, what does manifest openly to our senses? At best, we may perceive something of the lower *Sefirot*, like *Hesed*, *Gevura*, and the like, as they become revealed through certain events and phenomena. The Divine Rationale, the thought of God behind it all, remains forever beyond us. That is to say, we can observe and grasp reality only from below a certain level. Beyond that level, even in the range of wisdom (*Hokhma*) and understanding (*Bina*) we are already at a loss, unable to grasp what's happening to us, In nearly all inter-human relations this is poignantly evident; we perceive only the external signs of our reactions to one another, not that which lies below the surface in the depths of our own humanity. It is in this sense that Wisdom and Understanding belong to the Divine Hiddenness. We have no direct communication with the deeper layers of creative thought; we draw from it but cannot quite fathom what it is, how it works.

This realm beyond our grasp is called the depths – "from the depths have I called you O Lord" (Psalms 130:1). Or as it is written elsewhere, "How very deep are Your thoughts" (Psalms 92:6). What is implied is that the essence of mind is bottomlessly profound, linked, on one hand, to the hidden and, on the other, to the revealed truth. For *Ḥokhma* is called truth – *Emet* – which is considered the seal of God. To be sure, the problem of truth is usually considered a philosophical problem, within the scope of *Bina*; but the understanding that is *Bina* only confirms or proves a truth; it is wisdom that "sees" truth in an instantaneous flash. Indeed, distinguishing between right and wrong, truth and untruth, is, in a certain way, a matter that cannot be entirely rational; it is almost always a point of sudden confrontation and reso-lution. Afterwards, the development of this intuitive insight may take considerable analysis, experimentation, and logic; there is the need to overcome contradictions and doubts. At times, as in modern nuclear physics, enormous machines and systems have to be set up in order to prove, or disprove, by way of *Bina* or intellectual reasoning, that which Wisdom, in a flash, had felt was true.

Thus Wisdom, as we have said, is a fountain or source, rather than a river. Moreover the difference between the first two letters of the Divine Name and the final letters of the Tetragrammaton hold the secret of the difference between thought and action. *Yod* and *Heh* represent *Ḥokhma* and *Bina*, the final two letters represent the other *Sefirot*, includ-ing *Malkhut*, or the world. What is desired is a proper unification of the two parts. As the blessing for any action puts it, may the two names, or parts, of the Divine be made one; we call for the union of God (as truth) and His *Shekhina* (as world). The positive mitzva is a fulfillment pro-cess, a carrying out of a "contemplated" action; it is a revelation of light.

The negative mitzva is almost entirely a matter of refraining from action. It consists of a proscription, an injunction to avoid doing something. (Most of the Ten Commandments, for instance, are nega-tive mitzvot.) Why should it be considered to be on a higher level than the positive mitzva? The answer lies in this hidden aspect of *Ḥokhma* and *Bina*. Indeed, it is only through the power and insight of the deeper Wisdom that we can prohibit any thought or action.

What is hidden remains hidden; vast realms of the unknown are forever inscrutable and no amount of intellectual effort to penetrate them avails. Even when Wisdom does cast light on some area of darkness, the essence of that which we can observe is never quite grasped. We see only the externals of things. And yet, we do manage somehow to penetrate into the realm of the esoteric. We pierce through the darkness of the concealed by way of negation. The Sages called it "grasping by rejection," for there is a comprehensive grasp through positive confirmation and there is a comprehension through negation or reduction, by recognizing what it is not. Still, there cannot be a grasp of essence; intelligence is unable to penetrate into the inner nature of things. All we can do is get closer to the truth by way of negation, by saying what it is not.

For all its inadequacies, this approaching ever closer to the thing itself by way of negation, which is the closest we can get to its essence, also defines the frontiers of the thing. This definition of borders is a positive knowledge and, in many realms of science, is often the only knowledge we can have of the object of investigation.

Thus knowledge by negation may include getting to learn an object's range of existence in space and time, its variety of reaction patterns, what it can and cannot do. We are able to measure and stipulate a large number of qualities merely by external examination, without getting to observe the thing in itself. Such clear definition of the externals, and elimination of that which it is not, certainly reduces speculation and sheds light on the unknown. And, in sub-atomic physics, the Heisenberg Principle has made a system out of uncertainty itself.

To be sure, often a descriptive word suffices instead of an explanation, and we think we understand without really comprehending. Like the European doctor who discovered hypnotism in the last century and called it life magnetism; his successes were no less impressive in spite of the fact that they had nothing to do with his explanations. Today the phenomenon is still largely esoteric, in that we simply do not know what it is, but we have learned what it can and cannot do; we have defined its frontiers, and it has become a useful tool. In other words, the ability to define the limits of what we do not know enables us to build a positive edifice for what we do know. It is comprehension by way of negation.

As the Rambam ruminated in *Hilkhot Teshuva*, how can we speak of God's knowing? The paradox of our existence lies in the fact that our mental comprehension of what a thing is and our consciousness that the thing exists are two separate realms of awareness, so that we only grasp things from outside. We obviously do not have God's knowledge of a thing itself. For He and His knowledge are one and unchanging. To which another Sage, the Ravad, responded by asking why bring up the problem if there is no answer.

The philosophic issue here was already familiar in Rambam's time. As some medieval scholars put it: Were I able to know Him I would be God. My lack of knowledge is not the result of insufficient learning or inadequate effort, it is the intrinsic inability of man to really know. Nevertheless, my intellectual efforts make it possible for me to grasp the limits of my knowledge of God and give me a "negative" understanding of the Divine. The human intellect cannot do more; it cannot create anything, it can only make tools to grasp what is given. Wisdom, however, which is Divine, can create – it forms something out of nothing. And this, of course, cannot be understood, it can only be concluded by way of elimination.

Such a way of negation to ascertain the truths of existence has any number of levels. At the highest level, we approach the unknowable by admitting the existence of worlds above, that of *Asiya, Yetzira, Bri'a, Atzilut*. At the other end of the way of negation, we come to ever more subtle distinctions and levels. We can become involved with ever more exacting degrees of quality or accuracy. And we are still in the realm of the negative. What we know is still in the nature of an elimination process. It is like an ever more precise choice of the object of observation; it is not even the creation of an object. In art, the picture is a matter of having a frame that eliminates everything else (negates) and fills in somehow, again, with chosen spaces, forms, and color. In music, the unheard intervals, the control of rhythm and use of silence is crucial to the final effect. Indeed, at the highest level, works of art often cannot be expressed by a positive statement but by a negative declaration, by a suggestion of much that it is not possible to express; it is not a zero that is thus affirmed but a greater something that is apprehended with much that is superfluous eliminated. In all human creation, one draws upon the nothing, one takes from that which is not. We bring light to darkness; that is to say, we have the darkness to begin with and when we light a match, we have used the great nothingness of the dark to make a little something of a light. In the act of writing, a letter is formed by eliminating the blankness of the page with a mark. The white space around the black outlines of a written letter is as important (necessary) as the mark made by the pen. The nothingness of the page has been defined with lines and borders.

Symbolically, too, the letters carved on the Tablets of the Law are hollow spaces. They are the emptiness in the stone, as though to show that the Torah as a whole is a "nothing" that emerges from the densest materiality and becomes the highest and most sublime "something." For it is the Creator Himself who made this seal by impressing His Mark as hollow spaces in the stone. That which is not in the stone as a negation, is, in this sense, a Divine Affirmation and is expressed largely by a series of negative commandments: "Thou shalt not." Indeed all the negative mitzvot are commandments that could not be expressed any other way. They draw upon the Highest Will as that which can only be defined in negative terms.

As said, there are innumerable degrees of refinement in the negative way of grasping reality, just as there are many variations in the nature of light and so-called darkness according to the size of the wavelengths involved. We know by means of certain instruments that these energy forms exist, but we have no concept of what they look like or what they can do.

The negative mitzvot are an aspect of this negative way of understanding. Since so much of essential knowledge is hidden from us, we are granted the partial enlightenment of a silence in doing, a refraining from action. In the positive mitzva, the object that is blessed becomes the instrument for enlightenment. In the negative mitzva, there is no such direct manifestation of holiness. There is no way of being devout in terms of careful performance or diligence. All one can do is to be conscious of the barrier to holiness in the thing or action to be avoided. There is a process involved, like safety gadgets or the hidden electric currents in an elevator, for instance, that maintain security. One may be unaware of the complexity of the factors involved, but one can be protected nevertheless.

The negative mitzva may thus be said to constitute part of a complete circle of security; to break this circle, even without knowing why or where, is not only dangerous, it severs the essential harmony or unity of a certain esoteric system. In other words, it is not only a matter of obedience or disobedience to Divine will, it is a matter of a spoilation factor, a poison or disturbance in existence, the crucial aspect of which is our human inability to know the esoteric truth that the negative mitzva points to and "defines" (by way of reduction). Nevertheless, the negative mitzva does act, in its own way, to bring an enlightenment into the darkness of our incomprehension. It says: Let there not be a veil between myself and this aspect of reality that I cannot bless or deal with directly; let my not doing be an inspirational act of self-nullification. Let it be an aspect of Ḥokhma, or *Koaḥ-ma*, the potential behind action and the core of truth. Just as the wrong doing of that which is prohibited prevents Divine revelation, so, too, the right refraining from doing the prohibited becomes a revelation. There is no way of knowing how this occurs. One can only be sure of the form and be exacting about it. One cannot be certain of that which is hidden, unperceived, and yet definitely there, that which the negative mitzva has prescribed as forbidden yet has been confronted and somehow overcome in the non-doing. In not breaking the circle or the flow of harmony, one somehow gains from it.

The commandment "Thou shalt not" is a clear instruction to avoid damaging or interfering with the order of things, the Divine holiness. And if I adhere to this commandment, I let some of this holiness and light, even if unperceived, come upon me. There are very many degrees of this light from the dark: there are "candles" that splutter in blackness, and there are imperceptible rays that, even if unseen, are absorbed into the being; they penetrate the unconscious and illumine the heart.

We have the intriguing story of Balaam's ass to hint at a possible insight into the dynamics of the unseen. Balaam does not perceive the threatening angel; the ass does see and is unable to proceed. Balaam would need an extraordinary capacity for discernment to be able to see that which the lowly ass can see because ordinarily man is not able to see angels and demons. And this is so precisely because of his greater responsiveness, because he relates and could be destroyed by what he perceives. At a lower level, the danger is minimal; the less one feels, the less the danger in such an encounter. In short, men are unable to sensually detect higher forces because they cannot internalize them adequately.

The positive mitzvot occupy the realm of the apprehensible; they can be grasped and understood, on a human level at least. The negative mitzvot are only partly knowable, and that only as an interdiction, a ban on action or thought. They are clear only in what they disallow; there is no hint at the possible damage or perils involved in doing the wrong thing. It may be compared to the instructions given to someone who is blind. One can explain that it is dangerous to walk past the curb; one cannot show the blind man the passing vehicles that make it dangerous. Words of warning are almost always bigger than our capacity to absorb them, so that we have to leave a certain space, a negative absence of comprehension. Thus the negative mitzvot are powerful in what they leave unsaid; they are on a higher level than the positive mitzvot because they are closer to the realm of the hidden and the holy.

Chapter four

We have pointed out that the negative commandments are simply injunctions against particular actions, instructions to refrain from doing. The positive mitzvot, which are actually considered to be on a lower level, are defined in straightforward, clear terms. It appears that precisely because of their superiority, the negative mitzvot cannot be so plainly defined. We do not have the means to understand them properly and cannot be quite so explicit. We can however reach them by a negative route, through a process of elimination – by knowing what is prohibited.

This definition through negation is of course very partial and unsatisfactory. It offers no more than a general concept of what the situation requires; it provides the framework without which action is either possible or impossible. But altogether, a positive definition is often unavailable and a negative definition is often more feasible as, for example, when trying to define a state of war or peace (peace is when there is no war and visa versa). And there are qualifications that are certainly positive but we do not quite know exactly what they mean, such as eternity, and the like. The negative definition may thus prove an advantage in many cases.

What we are given as a negative mitzva is a statement of boundaries within which we can or cannot act; it does not provide anything that we can be absolutely sure of. Just as in the biblical phrase describing the wilderness as a land not sown (Jeremiah 2:2), what is implied is not a negative action but a statement to the effect that the land was sown with nothing. This follows the pattern of Creation, that in the beginning there was darkness and then light, that chaos precedes form. It is the concept maintaining that there has to be a compression, an abatement of infinitude, a *tzimtzum*, for anything to exist – that light is a contraction of darkness. It's as though the darkness is squeezed until light comes out of it. Creation precedes formation. In our daily prayers, we say: "(He who) forms light and creates darkness." Light is one of the formations that comes out of the dark, just as a potter shapes a particular form (light) out of the amorphous clay, which is darkness.

In short, certain conceptions can only be explained by saying what they are not. Many electromagnetic waves pass us by without our being able to distinguish them; they are darkness. Still, the limited range of such waves that we see as light (and can even distinguish as color) is enough to prove to us that, beside the fact that there is something there, much of what is there is beyond our grasp. We are aware of little more than a tiny sliver of reality. So, too, concerning the mitzvot to do and not to do, the darkness of the unknown in abstinence may contain something more profoundly meaningful than we are able to guess. We can do little more than fulfill such a mitzva as a conscious act of restraint or withdrawal, or at least respond with an unqualified "no" to a life question.

There are also mitzvot that are not clearly defined as either positive or negative; they are more in the category of levels of spiritual awareness, as for instance, the inability or inner incapacity to participate in an act of idolatry, *avoda zara*. Among these we may include the positive mitzvot to rest on the Sabbath or on holy days. All the *halakhic* rulings on the subject of cessation from work are positive in this sense of being clear about a particular area of action; what they omit is the other, subjective side of the non-action.

To be more specific about the Sabbath ruling let us concentrate on the term "rest." This may be seen simply as a negation of work, of course. In addition, however, it is obviously something more than not-doing; it is something one can feel in very physical and emotional terms, even if it has no describable image. It is one of the instances of being able to feel the mitzva of not-to-do in one's being, especially if one fulfills it in a way that is more than just refraining from certain actions.

In addition, there are any number of mitzvot specifying what not-to-do that one performs in the most simple and natural manner – as, for instance, when we go through the supermarket without thinking of pocketing anything. One is carrying out the mitzva unthinkingly; it becomes a consciously performed mitzva when and if there is a temptation of any sort and an overcoming of that temptation.

Even in Jerusalem there are plenty of opportunities to be led astray into idolatry. But most people overcome the impulse without thinking about *avoda zara*. There is no clear-cut definition of what it is. True, there is the saying that the one who openly denies idolatry is like one who keeps the whole Torah. Thus, to be a conscious dissident of this sort, disavowing idol worship as a strong positive act based on an irresistible illumination, is obviously more than what is casually carried out in the category of negative mitzvot (not pilfering in the supermarket).

We are led to consider the fact that there is a Jerusalem above and a Jerusalem below. To be sure, the Jerusalem below is also the place of the Holy Temple and therefore not to be compared to any other place on earth. And the Jerusalem above is sublime beyond words.

But we are concerned with the fact that both the upper and the lower Jerusalems are otherworldly in some definite way. What this amounts to can only be described by saying that Jerusalem is a city of awe, where the Divine Presence has been made manifest. It is the city of the lower fear of God and of the highest fear. Jerusalem is also the city of peace. The combination is expressed by the statement that "Jerusalem is joined together" (Psalms 122:3). It is made up of different parts, a blending of higher and lower that results in a spiritual reality to which people "go up" in pilgrimage and worship. The lower Jerusalem is thus also a center of transcendental higher unity, where the Holy One, blessed be He, and his *Shekhina* are united.

To what extent can we accept this as an article of faith? *Halakhic* thinking is sharply rational and sensible, sometimes to an exaggerated degree – as, for example, in the reluctance to base judgment on circumstantial evidence alone and in the insistence on the testimony of a witness. What is self-evident does not require a witness; whereas the essence of the hidden and the obscure do need to be attested to by living testimony. A Jewish court of law cannot rely on theory or conjecture. It needs the spoken word of a witness. Only concerning that which is absolutely obvious to all can living witnesses be dispensed with.

From which it may be gathered that Jerusalem below does not require much testimonial; it is the Jerusalem above that stands in need of witnesses. To be sure, there is sufficient evidence for this in kabbalistic thought, not only in the very letters of the different names of God but in the need for a source from which the lower worlds emanate. Nevertheless, the Tzemaḥ Tzedek, grandson of the Ba'al HaTanya, felt that the problem of faith did need to be dealt with in a more convincing manner. For if one does not believe, there is no significance to the mitzva to believe. He concluded that the mitzva did not require one to believe in some Divine Force that penetrated the world as a spiritual vitalizing factor, but that it was a matter of "seeing" (the unseen), of believing in that which is transcendental, in that which is not manifest. The mitzva is not to have faith in God as an idea but to experience the hidden essence of things. And therefore there is no need for witnesses (or logical argument).

Nevertheless, as we have said, the problem remains. The self-evident needs no witness because we grasp the essence of it. That which we cannot so grasp, that of which we only know the boundaries and not the essence, needs some evidence. That is, we have to learn about it, be informed about it, and thereby reach a state of conviction similar to our relation to what we can sense or experience directly. As in mathematics, we can have an equation that contains an unknown and yet be able to deal with it and even to solve it. The unknown factor is, as the Sage puts it, the unsown land, where the indeterminate rules. The point is to avoid the obscurantism of making a mystery out of the unknown and thereby (as many scholars do) pretending to a wisdom one does not possess. At the same time, of course, there is a mystery in the commandment not to do; but it is something we can investigate, learn about, and come to understand better, even if partially.

We may compare it to a shadow play of the kind no longer in existence. We do not see three dimensional figures; all that we see are shadows, the dark images cast by the light when it is obstructed by the figures. Whereas the positive mitzvot are plainly discernible in their substantiality (although they too have a shadow, when one does not do what is enjoined), the shadows cast by the negative mitzvot constitute the mitzvot themselves. And this is what is meant by the phrase "witness of Israel." The carrying out of mitzvot to abstain from an action or thought are statements that cannot be said any other way.

To better comprehend this, let us examine the Biblical passage: "And from my flesh I shall behold God" – "ומבשרי אחזה אלוה" (Job 19:26). The intention, apparently, is to convey the actuality of a certain perception that is not necessarily sensual, like the certainty of one's self, one's unquestionable sense of existence that cannot really be seen with the eye or touched with the hand. So, too, is the experience of God a certainty "of the flesh," like the feeling of one's own self beyond the apparent and sensual knowledge of the body. Although theologians have attempted in vain to explain this philosophically, it is quite apparent to any honest self-observer that the "I" includes the body but is not identical with the body; that the real self is beyond the external, "bigger" than anything one can sense. When one says "with my flesh shall I behold God," it is an aspect of the Kabbalistic concept of the Divine as filling all worlds – a vision of God intrinsic to the reality of the world. Whereas when one says, I believe in God, it is of the aspect of the Divine as encompassing all worlds.

In addition it is written, "know therefore this day and consider it in your heart that the Lord is God" (Deuteronomy 4:39). The instruction to "know" is intended to convey that one should bring faith to knowledge, to make it a passage of internalization as well as of conceptualization. It is an instruction to make this transition from the intimate personal grasp of the Divine as "filling all worlds" to the sublime concept of the Divine as "encompassing all worlds," as that which is beyond existence. "Know this day" implies getting hold of a certainty, a positive conviction and awareness of God as definite reality, which, in turn, is what is described as the "witness" for Israel – the "witness" being that which is direct knowledge and not transmitted from one source to another in time.

Of course, most of what men "know" is not necessarily personally attained knowledge; it is built on the testimony of others, on authorities, books, and the like. As in a court of law when a person has to give testimony and is asked to tell only what he, himself, has witnessed, it often turns out that he really knows very little, that most of his knowledge is supposition or hearsay or just guesswork based on fragmentary information. Thus, when speaking of real knowledge, it is important to recognize that it is a gradually growing thing, a combination of direct personal experience and of that which comes from critical reading and study as well as hearsay and the word of authority. A witness is one upon whose testimony we can rely; he has knowledge that combines the certainty of direct experience with substantiated learning.

As an example of such witnessing, let us take a simple phenomenon in nature familiar to all, the ordinary iron magnet. We may be totally unable to grasp the meaning of it and to hear about it second hand – of one thing pulling another by some mysterious unseen cord or psychic influence – may lead to an odd distortion of images. But once the little magnet is seen for what it is, and we observe the way it attracts or repels, the mystery is resolved. We may not understand more, but we can bear witness that such a thing exists. So, too, is it maintained that Israel bears witness. The Jews can enter into Jerusalem below and know its many-sided beauty. And although no one can go to the Jerusalem above and report back on its glory, the tribes of Israel are said to be reliable witnesses, for they have knowledge from their direct experience of the lower Jerusalem.

Chapter five

Faith begins where knowledge leaves off, where knowledge cannot go. If one can know something properly, there is no need to exercise faith (although what is apparent to one person may not be so to another who will have to exercise faith in order to reach the same conviction). As Rabbi Nachman of Bratslav is reputed to have said concerning the verse, "For I know that the Lord is great" (Psalms 135:5), the emphasis is on "my" knowing, on "my" being absolutely sure, and yet unable to convey this certainty. This difference is perhaps true for all men, as implicit in the declaration "know this day and consider it in your heart." What is prescribed here is a progression from faith to knowledge; that which one accepts as an emotionally vivid belief in the Divine has to become an intellectually clear conviction. It is a matter of making one's faith ever more lucid and unequivocal, getting rid of the obfuscations. Knowledge requires clarity.

As we have mentioned, almost all knowledge is quite naturally a combination of that which is sensorially perceived by oneself and of credible information received from others. Just as on hearing a report from a traveler returning from an unknown country, one allows oneself to believe in the plausible and to entertain doubt about the rest. The difference lies in the degree of clarity and coherence of the information, which depends also on the scope of one's previous knowledge. But, ultimately, there always remains a certain amount of the unknown, the "mysterious." And it is this that requires penetration and inquiry until it becomes acceptable, credible, so to speak, and is resolved into the certainty of which it is written, "And you shall know this day...." But the witness cannot be dispensed with; we have to receive the testimony of someone who has been there. The mitzvot thus serve as witnesses; they come from the higher worlds; they are projections of higher worlds upon this world of ours. Yet still they remain no more than witnesses or rather "something else" that has penetrated to our being here in this world.

Thus, the Torah itself may be seen as witness. Indeed, it has been called the testimony or Testament of God revealed "to us and our children forever." At the same time, the hidden secrets of God are part of the Torah, secrets that are forever beyond us. Nevertheless, the Torah serves as the witness "for" Israel, as well as, in the previous sense, serving to make Israel witness to the world.

The problem is that the light that comes from such a high level cannot be received on the lower level of our humanity; it has to be reduced. It is not a matter of any difficulty in passage – the Higher Light can penetrate anything; it simply has no meaning for us at its own level. Reception requires diminution of its too-penetrating power and intensity.

Such witnessing, therefore, provides indirect experience, a reflection of the Original Light. One does not confront the essence itself, one accepts what one is told about it. Whereupon the very authenticity of the whole process of relying on witnesses becomes open to question. After all, there has to be a certain strong correlation at least between testimony and truth.

The problem may be made more malleable by resorting to the Kabbalistic *Sefira* of knowledge which is *Da'at*. As is true of all the other *Sefirot*, *Da'at* is a definite realm of being in itself, but it is also, and perhaps primarily, a conjunction, a point of meeting and passage. It is that force in the human soul that translates thought to emotion. Because, in itself, thought is not emotional; the mind is principally unmodified by feelings. The higher the mental powers, the purer they are of prejudice, of feeling for or against the matter held up for judgment. Thought is at its best when, untainted by personal likes and dislikes, it is able to absorb phenomena, understand them, and convey their meaning to others. The emotions, of course, are very different, full of judgments and compulsively in favor of or against whatever comes up.

The difficult passage from knowledge to an emotion is made by means of *Da'at*. For there is a point in the function of the mind when thought no longer suffices with defining aspects of consciousness but begins to take sides, for or against. When one perceives something there is seemingly immediate recognition. But if we slow down the whole process and become aware of each phase, we may better comprehend it. Thus when awakening from anesthesia, or drug-induced stupor, it is possible to observe the slow passage back to normal consciousness. At first, one sees forms, colors, without any identifiable meaning; it is really an objective observation unprejudiced by memory. One does not see the chair or person at whom the gaze is directed; one sees a configuration of form and texture, line and color, the objectively pure information that a set of well-adjusted instruments could transmit. Afterwards, one enters into the level of *Da'at*, or Knowledge, where identification takes place and meaning accompanies observation. In other words, the perception of the senses, which is primary, is still not knowledge; one hears the sound of a human voice – only thereafter, recognizing whose voice it is and what it is saying to me, can there be any movement, from ignorance to knowledge, from meaninglessness to significant action. *Da'at* is that which effects the passage from *Ḥokhma* to *Bina*, from all the attributes to their concrete manifestations in the world of *malkhut*.

In certain ways *Da'at* acts as a witness, or at least serves an identical purpose (transforming what is perceived into knowledge by identifying it). In terms of "faith," the people of Israel feel the Divine Presence (just as everyone does perhaps), but because Israel recognizes the voice as the voice of God, it becomes a "witness." This task of Israel in the world is often mentioned in scripture. As, for instance, in the Book of Isaiah, "You are my witnesses, saith the Lord, and I am God" (Isaiah 43:12). Similar passages in the Bible and in the Talmud repeat this astonishing concept that I am God and when you do not bear testimony, when you are not my witness, I am not God.

This view of Israel as God's witness in the world, making Israel responsible for the Divine, has had many repercussions. There is the burden it sets on the Jews, and the aura of chosenness attached to this people. It has also been one of the reasons for hatred of Israel and anti-Semitism of all sorts on the part of those who wish to get rid of God: only by eliminating the Jews can they eliminate God, they argue.

A further insight into the profound relations of the Jewish people to God has been offered by the persistence of the idea that the people of Israel are His children. For, in addition to all else, God is always Father to His people, in scripture, in folklore, in language and life.

Most dramatically significant of all the ways Jews relate to the Divine is the fact of martyrdom. It has been observed that many Jews who have been rather indifferent to their religious duties, and have not given much thought to their God, when faced with the ultimate choice, death or denial of the Jewishness by which they act as witnesses of God, will choose death. When a certain point in the Jewish soul is touched, a great light or passion is kindled and martyrdom seems to be natural. In other words, revelation of Divine reality seems never to be far removed from the Jewish consciousness, whether brought to surface awareness or not. Amongst other things, the mitzvot are conspicuous testimony to this.

The positive mitzvot are more obviously so. They are visible actions, straightforward and complete, with a very definite blessing accompanying each performance. One blesses the specific action or thing that is involved, and the mitzva becomes a sanctification of the tangible.

The negative mitzvot, the injunctions to abstain from certain actions, are less obviously witnesses of faith, but they are more profoundly effective in terms of the life of the spirit. They serve to acknowledge the power and reality of a living God Who is not revealed. One is compelled and made to accede, renouncing oneself. In acknowledging Divine Supremacy, one relinquishes one's own will and keeps the *mitzvot lo ta'aseh*, the commandments to refrain from doing, even though one does not fully grasp the entire meaning of the prohibition.

Significantly, too, the negative mitzvot do not have an obligatory preparatory blessing; it is scarcely possible to bestow a benediction on a non-action. And yet, precisely for this reason, because of the impalpable and imperceptible aspects of these mitzvot, they can be incredibly powerful. How is this so?

Their reality is the reality of hidden truth. They are mitzvot that cannot be expressed by action or speech or even thought. They can be manifested only by a definite negation of a certain kind of doing. This non-doing involves overcoming the *Sitra Aḥra* (the Other Side), which is clumsily called "the evil impulse," and this overcoming may be considered an exaltation of the Divine Name.

It is not a digression to inquire: If, as mentioned elsewhere, the *Sitra Aḥra* is not really that important, if it has no substance to speak of, why should conquering it be such a God-exalting achievement?

Conquest here is not merely an outer deed. That which one does not say, does not see, does not do, has inner aspects which are part of a person's struggle with himself. There isn't much outer victory. What is important is the identity of the enemy, the "Other Side" who blocks the light of Divine glory. Fulfilling a negative mitzva lifts one by freeing the way, removing an obstruction or hindrance to God. It is not a direct battle with some adversary or a positive action; it is a matter of the way in which one says "no" and creates a "land not sown," that may or may not exist. The not-doing becomes a creative act, releasing higher forces.

The concept of the *Sitra Aḥra* does not relate to a reality that confronts one. It relates to the shadow of things; the "Other Side" is a figment of reality. So that when a person pierces and overcomes this shadow, he reaches a certain state known as "dwelling within the hidden" (Psalms 91:1). The struggle against these shadows is a war against that which is basically unreal.

Indeed the adversary has no substance of its own; it can even be said to be neutral or directionless. The horror stems from the combination of evil that has no reality with a self that determines reality. And the only way to overcome it is to overcome the self, to overcome the terror of the self's own making. For there is no fearsome reality outside; it vanishes as soon as one ceases to nurture its shadow with the force of one's own dread. And when a person does manage to cross over the barrier of not knowing what's there on the other side, he is overcoming the *Sitra Aḥra*. Very often it is only as a commandment to avoid doing something that the crossover point exists. When one carries out this "*mitzva lo ta'aseh*," negation of an action, one is vanquishing the foe and passing on to a higher level of being, a level that is made up of things unfamiliar to one, unknown territory, a land not sown.

The matter may be compared to a device that makes a person struggle with an imaginary opponent in order to stimulate greater efforts in the long and wearisome climb of life. The shadow assailant is of really no importance; what counts is the progress made in overcoming and rising to a higher level.

The ordinary human path is, at first, marked by definable facts and fairly positive actions. At higher ranges of life's climb, circumstances tend to become less clearly definable as coordinates of progress. One is no longer so sure exactly where one is or where one is going. In order to find oneself, an imaginary system of coordinates often has to be introduced, and one then proceeds to go from one point to another, surmounting the difficulties and making progress. Otherwise, without such a device, one would be brought to a halt, unable to go on along a pathless way. An intimation of certainty, or at least a positive sign to hold on to, anything to reassure one's groping, is necessary at certain stages. At other stages one may need an imaginary adversary, even an inimical one, to make one fight harder against the inner foe. All of which is ultimately of no importance; what counts is the progress made in the spiritual life where the course is not clearly marked out.

Thus, the positive mitzvot are within a framework of definite actions that are accompanied by the appropriate blessings. The negative mitzvot, constituting that which is not to be done, are outside any such framework of reality and do not have any blessings to help one perform them. Nevertheless one can acknowledge that one is doing the mitzvot even without knowing or understanding.

Chapter six

It is written: "These are the appointments of the Tabernacle, the Tabernacle of the Testimony, as they were counted according to the commandment of Moses" Exodus (38:21). The double mention of the word "tabernacle" alludes to the two aspects of this most sacred location: the Jerusalem above and the Jerusalem below, heavenly Jerusalem and earthly Jerusalem, "the city that was bound together" (Psalms 122:3). There are two tabernacles, corresponding to the two planes of being: above and below. Holiness descends from the higher to the lower, and the resulting union is the manifestation of the *Shekhina* in the world, otherwise known as the *Sefira* of *Malkhut*.

The Tabernacle is thus the specific location of the union with the life-giving force which is Divine. It is specific in the sense that it is not only there where the *Shekhina* exists (as it exists everywhere); it is there where the *Shekhina* is revealed, where it comes as an inspiration. When we say that the *Shekhina* rests or shines on someone, it is indeed special. True, the *Shekhina* is universally present, even in sin – which is why the Ḥasidim say that sin is a shameful disgrace; whenever one does something abhorrent, even in the greatest secrecy, the *Shekhina*, being with the sinner, feels mortified and hurt. Beyond the fact of transgression, crime, or even simple abuse of decency, there is the inevitable accompaniment of shame, which reflects the presence of the *Shekhina*.

The revelation of the *Shekhina*, when it is said to come to rest on someone or something, is different in the sense that the Ever-Present Light begins to light up that upon which it rests. It may be likened to a neon lamp, which contains gas all the time, but only lights up when switched on. Nothing new has been added; it's merely that the same particles begin to radiate. The holiness thus manifesting in the *Shekhina* is called revelation or inspiration. But there is an even higher level in the Tabernacle of Testimony.

The Tabernacle of Testimony is called such because it is the place to which the tribes of Israel came and then bore witness. This witnessing, as we have mentioned, is expressed as a totality of living. By living as Jews, they bear witness to the source of holiness. So that in addition to the tabernacle as sanctuary, the place where the Godhead is present, we have the tabernacle as the place where holiness is revealed; and then we have the tabernacle of witness where the holiness is not openly manifest, where sanctification does not occur of itself, so to speak, but in the secret depths of being, requiring a certain "witnessing" to become permanently lodged in oneself. This third aspect of the sanctuary, the Tabernacle of Testimony, is an aspect of a negative commandment, the commandment to refrain from action.

More precisely, we may state that beyond the aspect of revelation in the holy sanctuary, there is an aspect of concealment, which is so much higher it is made known only through "witness" – because it touches on the greater and more profound reality beyond anything that can be manifested. Therefore it is called the Tabernacle of Testimony.

In the human soul, too, one may discern some such distinctions. A person who is in a state of emotional agitation or inner excitement of any kind will be inclined to speak and express something of what is happening to him whether it be distressful or joyous. It's a bubbling, spontaneous action and reveals the person's state of mind in a manner that exceeds the customary modes of expression. But there are emotional and spiritual states in which a person feels so strongly that he is unable to speak at all. It is an inability to utter the fullness, no matter of what nature, and there is silence. So long as an agitated person can speak, we may be able to detect something of his state, and there is a revelation of sorts into his soul. But when someone is voiceless from an excess of feeling, we can relate to the silence as a revelation of another level of reaction, a more intense and powerful emotion making it inexpressible. Such a situation may help to indicate the kind of distinction between the manifest and unmanifest light, between the positive mitzva to do and the negative mitzva to abstain from doing.

Venturing further into the issue arising from our investigation of the quotation "And these are the appointments of the Tabernacle" (Exodus 38:21), we may look for assistance in another biblical statement: "Raise up your eyes on high and behold Who created these" (Isaiah 40:26). The word "these" in both instances points to a certain revelation; it is used as an epithet for something visible and apparent. It is not a pronoun in the sense of "him" or "them," it is simply a plural form of that which confronts one. On the other hand, we have the word "who" (created these), pointing to something unknown, an unrevealed factor.

Concerning this verbal form of questioning, we can make the distinction between "who" and "what." One of the ways this distinction is explained is by saying that "what" comes from Hokhma (Wisdom) and "who" is a product of Bina (understanding). While "who" certainly relates to the unknown – one is inquiring "who is it" – nevertheless, it assumes a known "it;" someone and not something is there. Whereas the "what" does not know anything at all and the question relates to a fundamental ignorance of what is there, whether a person or the wind or my imagination. In other words, "what" precedes "who" in terms of knowledge. "Who" is an inquiry into the particulars of an essence.

"Who created these" would, therefore, be of the aspect of Bina, and "these" would point to the offspring of Bina, the Mother. These offspring are the six attributes following Hokhma, Bina, and Da'at on the kabbalistic chart of the Sefirot. In the order of their place on the diagrammatic representation of the Sefirot, these six attributes are: Hesed, Gevura, Tiferet, Netzah, Hod, Yesod. In the book of the Zohar, they are known as Zeir Anpin, the Little Face. (The "Long Face" is Keter, Father is Hokhma, and Mother is Bina, while "Nukva" is the name given to Malkhut, the tenth Sefira.) Without going into detail, we may mention that there are many correspondences to these six primary attributes, from the letter

Vav in the Tetragrammaton to the six days of Creation (Sunday is *Ḥesed*; Monday is *Gevura*; Tuesday is *Tiferet*; Wednesday is *Netzaḥ*; Thursday is *Hod*; and Friday is *Yesod*).

But to return to the word "these," it becomes evident that it refers to that which is revealed in the cosmos in terms of the humanly lived attributes in all their aspects. It points to God's great mercy and power; it does not indicate His hidden wisdom and understanding. As human beings we can grasp the Divine compassion as it comes to us, or His severity, power, and beauty. But we cannot grasp the rationale, the Divine reasons behind these attributes. We know the manifest revelation; we do not know "Who created these."

Thus, there is the well-known Biblical declaration repeated in the daily prayer: "Thine, O Lord, is the greatness and the power and the glory and the victory and the majesty: for all that is in heaven and on earth is Thine; Thine is the kingdom, O Lord" (1 Chronicles 29:11). This points to the six attributes as belonging to God, as "Thine" – לך. The gematria of the word "Thine" – לך is fifty, which is the same as the word "who" – מי. And since it is acknowledged that there are fifty gates to *Bina* (Understanding), there seems to be meaning in the use of the word "who" – מי.

Another aspect which, although only peripherally related, may cast additional insight is the place of Jacob at the center of the chart of *Sefirot*, as *Tiferet* (Beauty, Compassion). Leah is *Bina* and Rachel is *Malkhut*; they correspond to the first *Heh* and the second *Heh* of the Tetragrammaton. Leah and Rachel also symbolize different mother qualities, each with a specific orientation. For example, the Midnight Vigil of the devout is divided into two parts: *Tikkun* (reparation) of Leah and *Tikkun* of Rachel. *Tikkun Leah* is on a higher level of spiritual offering, being a service of joy, "the gladness of the mother of the children" the six attributes and *Malkhut*, the daughter. *Tikkun Rachel* is based on the motif of the mother who weeps over her lost children.

There are also six orders of the Mishna, with all that this signifies in terms of the Talmud and the categories of Jewish study. But it is important to recognize that the orders are not at all defined along rigid lines; there are central themes but they tend to include a great deal of varied and far-reaching subjects that may extend into unrelated matters. The Order *Zera'im*, for example, includes inquiry and laws on holidays, marriage, sacrifices, and more, in spite of the fact that its central theme is "Seeds," laws of tilling the soil and the products of the land.

The idea behind all this apparent looseness and inclusiveness, the flexibility and responsiveness of the "six" orders, the totality of the *Sefirot*, the Days of Creation, and the like is that this inclusiveness signifies the essence of holiness. The world of the sacred, and in particular the world of *Tikkun*, is not built along specific points and lines of reference, on clearly defined forms. Wherever there is a fixed or predetermined design that cannot contain something else, we may justifiably suspect that it does not belong to the holy. The holy includes everything else; in every part there is the whole. That which seems to be especially pure and inviolable, self-contained, and perfect may well be an artificial creation. The genuine thing is inclusive and has more in it than itself; there are a number of other essences contained within it. This is true of the Divine Attributes as well as the sacred formations in tradition.

All of which is related to the almost universal fact that those creatures who do not mix or combine or feed their young are sterile. Propagation requires connection and coupling. There has to be association with that which is other. Even creatures who contain the other sex within themselves still require contact with another of the species in order to multiply.

The point is that this is true of the spiritual as well as the physical aspects of existence. A primary quality of the sacred is the capacity to combine and to be fertile. That which is so clean and pure and solitary and has no need of anything else, is very likely to be barren and unable to bear fruit. And this is also one of the signs of the *Sitra Aḥra*, the inability to produce something new, to give birth to life.

Following the significant use of the word "These" (are the appointments of the Tabernacle of the Testimony), we have the word "appointments," which has varying shades of meaning. One of them is the allusion to the appointed times of sexual contact and of the female cycle. And if it is recalled that the Tabernacle is itself a life-giving connection, a union between the Godhead and His *Shekhina*, the connection with intimacy is apparent. True, the Tabernacle is built with walls, curtains, partitions, veils, and enclosures of all sorts, but the intention is to create a secret inner place, secluded and private, appropriate to holy union.

In the wider sense, the Tabernacle is therefore the place where the people of Israel unite with the Divine Presence. It is the place of meeting below. It is also the witness, the Tabernacle of Testimony, for the Heavenly Jerusalem, for the existence of a higher essence. To be sure, this higher essence is hidden; nevertheless, it becomes known through the meeting of what has become symbolically referred to as Leah (or *Bina*) with Israel on one level, or on another level, of the earthly encounter between Rachel (or *Malkhut*) with Jacob. Israel and Jacob are thus different entities, or at least different symbols, of the spiritual devotion demanded of the people, a higher and a lower, denoting two aspects of Divine union.

Without trying to enter into the enormous amount of thought and contemplation on this matter which is so central to Hasidism, we may turn to some of the concluding remarks made by Rabbi Schneur Zalman. As he sees it, the inner life may be likened to a growing plant. The source of all growth is the little seed, the hard nucleus that has to perish by rotting in the soil; that is, the seed has to nullify itself by giving itself up to the power of germination. And this power is the central power of growth. So long as the seed remains a clean and wholesome self, not spoiled by contact with the dark, engulfing soil, it can remain a correct and meticulous specimen of its kind. Only by surrendering its continued restricted being as a seed and totally subordinating itself to the infinite power of growth in the earth can the plant begin to emerge from it. The critical point of transformation is immersion, when there is a genuine contact with the soil, when there is such union with the earth that the seed can relinquish what it contains and all that it is, and from the resulting essence begin to be what it was intended to be.

To a large extent, this curiously uneven procedure is true of human relations as well. A person tends to be himself, tries to preserve his sense of pride and personality and to expand from a more or less well-defined or imagined self-image or central being. An individual is a rather closed unit. Clearly, however, such a closed unit cannot easily create contact with another person. A certain opening has to be made, larger or smaller, for giving and taking. And indeed, even for giving one has to make a crack, some fissure in oneself, almost as great as that required for receiving from another. Ultimately, in order for the process of exchange to have meaning, there has to be more and more release, and then, renunciation of self.

Of course there is resistance. One wishes to keep the secret and not to share it with someone else. The mind holds on tightly to intimate thoughts of self, tries to keep the surface clean. But modifications have to be made if one seeks to relate. And if the relation should develop, the secret has to be shattered, the hard crust has to be relinquished, and eventually, the seed-self nullifies itself in love.

This touches on the general, more philosophical problem of change that so occupied the ancient Greek thinkers. How can one kind of existence become another? There is an aspect of surprise, of the unsuspected, in any transition from one existence to another; how much more so in the growth process. The change from one substantiality to something different, whether it is in the nature of material objects or states of being, happens by going through a neutral phase. And this phase is a nothingness, a wiping out of the previous existence and the emergence of a possibility, a not-yet reality of the new potential. Indeed, the greater the change, the more dependence on the quality and quantity of the intermediate, non-being phase. The smaller the change, the less prominent this phase of nothingness. When a silversmith wishes to make a candlestick out of a cup, he has to melt the object down to a total shapelessness (and the cup has to "participate" in this ceasing to be what it was and to be nothing before becoming a candlestick). Every change has to involve some such process of extinction before the creative aspect can manifest. A different dimension must intervene, whether it be the paradox of stillness in movement or disintegration in growth. And the more substantial the nature of that which is undergoing change, the more resistance it offers and the greater the degree of decomposition required.

As an aside, and not entirely inappropriately, the situation of the Children of Israel in Egypt may be brought up as a further illustration of this course of change. Their bondage, physical and spiritual, was a necessary stage in order to break out of a previous pattern and emerge into the entirely new and sublime aspect as a people of God. A descent into the lower depths of this world and contact with the awfulness of the World of Chaos seems to have been an essential part of their redemption.

It involved a deep crisis, a tearing away from accepted ways and habits, as well as from the sources of physical sustenance. And only then, completely cut off and separated from the Egypt of slavery, could they receive the crown of their true inheritance, the "crown of King Solomon, with which his mother crowned him on the day of his wedding and on the day of the gladness of his heart" (Song of Songs 3:11). The crown is a circular diadem on the head, a (halo) covering or an encompassing feature representing the unknown within and above the self.

And here, too, we are confronted with another sign of the sanctity of the negative mitzvot, the commandments to abstain from doing. From them, as from the jeweled crown, there radiate hidden lights, just as the earthly Tabernacle of Testimony radiates that which acts as a witness for the Heavenly Tabernacle, which is hidden from our perception.

Chapter seven

When the prayer declares "All will praise Thee, forever" – "הכל ירוממוך סלה," the meaning would seem to be that there is no end to the levels of cognition of the Divine and that, at the same time, the apperception of God is always from below, lifting up the Divine Name, to a level beyond what was previously apprehended. What, however, is the meaning of the word *Selah*? One of the explanations is that it stands for eternity: everyone will keep on raising You up, forever.

This brings us back to the use of the two words, *Adi Adaim*, in a different vocalization, which indicate both the jeweled diadem of the Crown and the "witnessing" aspect of the timelessness of that which is so adorned. Whether it is profoundly rooted in significance or not, the word "*Ed* – עד" – witness or adornment – also means forever, or "until," in terms of continuity up to a future point in time. In other words, a certain ultimate is indicated.

We are reminded of the previously raised question: "Who has created these? – מי ברא את אלה" (Isaiah 40:26), which, as we have already observed, is not really answerable; it points to the same ultimate. Thus, there are questions that are not raised because the answer is obvious, and there are questions that do not get asked because no query can get to the question itself. Such may be the aspect of the word *Ad* as used in describing the Tabernacle of Testimony. In modern Hebrew, the word *Mishkan* (Tabernacle) also indicates a certain limit or pledge, that which is not to be overstepped.

But if the expression *"Adi Adaim"* seems to relate to a knowable limit, it is certainly not an ultimate one; there is always another "until" – *"עַד"* – this point, and then another, forever. We are confronted with a limitless frontier, a horizon, a never-attainable edge. This leads us to the other, more commonly used expression for the Tabernacle, the Holy of Holies.

In some of the kabbalistic writings, the phrase Holy of Holies is identified with *Ḥokhma* and *Bina* and their relation to the primary *Sefira*, which is *Keter* (crown). In these esoteric writings, the *Sefira* of *Keter* or the crown is often written in various modes of the question, "who or where art Thou" – and the answer is "I am that I am." This serves to bring us back to the multiple concept of *Adi Adaim*, the double diadem (crown) on the head, above the mind. From this fountainhead, the *Sefira* of *Da'at* (knowledge) makes it possible for all the lower *Sefirot* to receive the sacred influence, making them attributes or vehicles of Divine manifestation: love, strength, beauty, etc.

What is being indicated here is that man is made up of two layers of being: a mental (and/or spiritual) consciousness and a whole series of attributes or impulses that are derived from this consciousness. That is to say, consciousness determines the objects (of thought and action), the aims of ambition, and the direction of emotion, as though all these were a further development of that which is already there (in the mind). Consciousness here is more related to the *Sefira* of *Da'at*, in the kabbalistic sense of that which discriminates between good and bad, desirable or undesirable. Before *Da'at* there is no such concept of personally preferred positive and negative; the basic distinction is between true and false, between that which is a genuine, harmonious reality and that which is unreal, chaotic, and formless. This also refers to the basic difference between *Ḥokhma* and *Bina*. In higher consciousness, one defines a thing – a lamb or a tiger – without giving it any emotional value; as in mathematics, there is no place for subjective evaluation or preference. The "pure mind" (above *Da'at*) recognizes emotions but does not put them into any kind of preferential order. *Da'at* takes this intellectual knowledge – the ability to define things for what they are and makes it into a matter of distinguishing good and bad.

The Gaon of Vilna, in his commentary on the Book of Proverbs, depicts *Da'at* as the basic, most important factor in life. As it is written in the Midrash, "If you have procured knowledge (*Da'at*), you will lack nothing" – "דעת קנית מה חסרת" (*Vayikra Raba* 1). One can have great learning and even much understanding, but it is *Da'at* that is decisive in determining one's scale of values. In other words, *Da'at* is something more than what is ordinarily considered knowledge. It involves the significant transition from things as objects to things that are objects that have a direction, that one can control or sort out. A lack of such knowledge, which is *Da'at*, can be considered a flaw in the personality, not in the intellect. Even a *talmid ḥakham*, a scholar, can lack *Da'at*. A person can be wise and well informed and still fail to be a genuine human being. And it is *Da'at* that, in many ways, makes the difference; it is fundamentally a moral essence. That is, without *Da'at*, existence remains amoral. *Ḥokhma* and *Bina* are ultimately a reliable base only for knowing what is true or false; they cannot discriminate between the varying kinds of truth and falsehood. As higher intellect, *Ḥokhma* and *Bina* only distinguish essences, they do not necessarily distinguish values; they define what is real without giving it a place on a scale of merit.

It may be concluded, then, that *Da'at* determines relationships, whether it be in terms of food and drink or in terms of politics and human affairs. After thus determining the framework for relationships, it is possible to establish order in human attributes and the emotions that are derived from them. The emotions then function like *Da'at*, with meaning and relevance, with their own value system and on their own principles. And although they are not rational, they are built into the hierarchical structure of the *Sefirot*.

The most important and decisive component at the top is the mental aspect; *Ḥokhma, Bina, Da'at*. They are the factors behind the human experience that provide direction and meaning. The other *Sefirot* following *Da'at*, and so largely determined by *Da'at*, are the attributes and emotions, from Love, Strength, and Splendor to ambition, endurance, passion, and all the rest. What is puzzling is the paradox that these emotional forces of life are far more powerful in life, or at least they seem to have much more influence than the higher factors of the mind. Notwithstanding, the hierarchical order of the *Sefirot* remains. At the same time, it would appear that above the mental there is a layer of impulses, drives, and emotional forces that, although they get their rationale or significance from *Da'at*, dominate the action of mind.

This is connected to the animal factor, or emotional consciousness of man in contrast to his mental consciousness. But as a higher animal consciousness, above the mental, it seems to direct the mind and make conscious a highly volatile construction, with levels, rises, and falls. A person can reach a height above the mental, a level of higher emotion beyond the ordinary emotions of life, and the mind thus becomes a channel connecting the higher animal (or creaturely) consciousness with the ordinary animal consciousness of life.

This level, sometimes called "*Behema Raba*" or higher creatureliness, is a level of emotion above the mind, which, as we have said, to a large degree directs the mind. This would indicate that the mind acts as a channel at times, rising and falling accordingly. In this way, too, a person is often able to reach a level which is higher than the mind, experiencing heights of emotion that are not ordinarily known, but which are basic and primary to the essence of a person. In this respect, the mind is seen as a channel that links the superconscious feelings of higher creatureliness and the conscious feeling of individual, personal existence. This would indicate that *Da'at* is also that which connects *Keter*, of the upper spheres, with all the lower levels.

Consequently, the "*Adi Adaim*," the double diadem, receives such a meaning: There are attributes above the mental that clothe themselves with the attributes below the mental and they become jewels, "*Adi Adaim*." These attributes are basically two, because the attributes, after being broken down into detail, are built, essentially, on the basis of positive and negative, attraction and repulsion. All the other subtle aspects of attributes, emotions, and impulses are variations on this theme of love-hate, attraction-repulsion. This duality flows into *Da'at* and creates its own kind of "*Adi Adaim*," building it into a many-layered spiritual structure.

To return to the Tabernacle of Testimony, it may be said that it is the hidden center of the world, and, being hidden, needs the testimony provided by the double diadem and the regular appointments of the Divine service.

What is symbolically being referred to here is the difference between praise and blessing. Blessing ברכה is an extension of the manifest sanctity; praise הגיאה is acknowledgment of that which one may or may not agree to or understand, but which one accepts wholly as right and admirable, and before which one abdicates. A person blesses because of something that is manifest to him. Praise, as הודאה, comes as a result of some deeper compulsion, beyond cognition, which is in the nature of a revelation and bears witness to the otherwise concealed. It goes beyond one's own realm of knowledge or mental awareness and points to a certain nullification of self. One of its outer signs is the act of bowing or prostration, as in the genuflecting ritual on Yom Kippur.

There are also fixed prayers of praise that express many aspects of this need to go beyond the scope of one's own moral and intellectual being; the phrase that seems to formulate this most succinctly is "We thank Thee that we praise Thee," where the same word – *modeh* (which is also related to witnessing) – is used for thanksgiving, acknowledgment, and praise. It is not even an expression of gratitude for life, goodness, or grace. It is simply acknowledgment of gratitude for being able to give thanks, for the privilege of praising Him, for having the strength to do so. All the other details of these prayers are variations of this feeling of self-abnegation. To be sure, in the synagogue today there are only minimal bowings; whereas in the Talmud, we have references to complete prostration on the ground. As for ritual bowing, it is a very complex and subtle physical act, little known and seldom practiced.

It is written that Moses fell on his face before God when the party of Koraḥ accused him of inventing the laws. This action is more than a prayer; it is the complete annihilation of the leader as person, making him only a messenger. Thereafter, the messenger has to be treated with the respect due to the one who sent him, although an insult is certainly felt as such by the messenger, whether it comes from the people or from the Divine. Nevertheless, when God refuses him, Moses falls on his face, as though to emphasize that he is not personally affronted at all. And thus, too, the Tabernacle of Testimony can only be appointed by Moses himself. For he is the perfect vessel, absolutely receptive. Indeed, only someone who is completely selfless can enter the sanctuary. There is no other way of reaching the secret place of the Tabernacle of Testimony. It is such a level of selflessness that what remains is of the utmost purity, beyond all measure of attainment.

This brings us back to the negative mitzvot, מצוות לא תעשה, whose chief quality is an injunction to refrain from action, to extinguish the desire to do something. The common denominator is a certain silence.

The Tabernacle of Testimony is thus the sanctuary of the "witness" factor – עד – in its three (Hebraic) meanings: as a form of corroboration, as the double diadem of the crown, and as eternal and timeless continuity. All of them integrate into one supernal essence, as a result of which it is called the Holy of Holies. The Sages have explained that this means the holy that is above the ordinarily sanctified, like the expression "King of Kings." It represents the level of the hidden and unknowable. An example of this idea is to be found in the matza, the unleavened bread, of Pesaḥ. The difference between bread and matza is that between being and nullification of being; matza is the saltless and yeastless simplicity of the bread substance, without size or taste. It is as though the King of Kings had appeared to halt the dough in its becoming, keeping it at its humblest, lowest possible state (of human nourishment). We are enjoined to eat matza for all the seven days of Pesaḥ – "*Matzot* shall feed the seven days." This rather surprising formulation may be explained by realizing that what is meant are the seven lower attributes: *Ḥesed, Gevura, Tiferet, Netzaḥ, Hod, Yesod,* and *Malkhut.* The love from the highest feeds the life of the lower. For He renews, in His Goodness, the act of Creation each day. And as we have said concerning the question "who has created these?" the "these" refers to the seven attributes, and the source, "*Mi*," is *Bina* (Understanding and contemplation).

The renewal of Creation each day is the continuity of Divine Love, and it is that which brings the contemplative person to a level of love and fear of God appropriate to his state of mind and soul. But another, more profound, problem, lies in the repudiation of the world before God. In His Light, all the worlds are nullified. And from the human aspect, love for the Divine does not leave room for anything else. This love, called "*Adi Adaim*," the "jewels" of the crown, is the ultimate relation with God.

In order for man to reach a higher stage of being, leading to the *Adi Adaim* of the Crown, he has to nourish and sustain himself by actions of renunciation, work in the realm of ביטול or nullification that is available to him. This involves doing things that are outside reason, above the mind. Because the higher essence cannot be reached by mental efforts, only by the movement of שיויתי – *Shiviti* and דוממתי – *Domamti*-contemplation of God's presence in stillness. It means to be (from the Hebrew word שוה, *shaveh*), spiritually equal and spread out above and below, morally and emotionally, beyond any defined state of happiness or unhappiness, willing, knowing, or feeling.

And this is the same quality of being that is demanded of a person in fulfilling the negative commandment, the *mitzva lo-ta'aseh*, the mitzva to abstain from action. There is a silence surrounding it, a deep and full stillness, full of the unspoken self-repudiation that leads to realization of Divine love. Then it is possible for the higher attributes of *Keter* that do not ordinarily come into direct expression to manifest themselves and become part of conscious life.

One of the most conspicuous examples of this form of Divine service is Yom Kippur, the annual ritual of the Day of Atonement. There is a rather special abrogation of self operating on this day; nothing whatsoever is done, one is altogether passive insofar as the world of action is concerned. It is a state of inner subservience, expressed only partly by a certain bending and bowing of the body. The day is characterized by an emptying of self to become an instrument, a vessel for spiritual force to move into and through until it fills one's entire being.

Another side of this (penitential) process, very different in tone and direction, is the ritual of the *sukka*, at the Feast of Booths. One enters into the *sukka*, goes into the mitzva; that is, the mitzva is not performed, the mitzva is not in the building of the booth, but in sitting within it, surrounded by it. And by inference, one is not able to make sanctity, one can at best be encompassed by clouds of glory. One can enter into holiness by eliminating the self who enters.

The entire month of Tishrei, after and during the Days of Awe, is thus a period of nullification of oneself before God, whether expressed in terms of deep religious trepidation or high spiritual joy. Its chief quality is a certain abstinence from action, more emphatically on the Day of Atonement. In ancient times, there were not even any Yom Kippur prayers; these have been added gradually over the centuries. All we are sure about is that the people and the priests all fell on their faces. They did nothing; they were passive and withdrawn. And even the very meaningful atonement sacrifices for this day, the two goats (only one a scapegoat), were chosen by lot, in sharp contrast to all the other sacrificial animals during the year. That is, the worshippers did not decide or do anything. They remained acted upon, acquiescent, and compliant, but not unresponsive. The matter of choice is here left open. It is an expression of the irrational element in human life. But the element of chance and fate behind the deliberate refraining from action is dominated by the certainty that what is best for one will be done.

Chapter eight

Speech on matters of Torah depends on the "to and fro" vibrational accumulation that precedes it. When this is lacking in holiness, the study of Torah itself can become an empty occupation or, as happens, it may turn into an elixir of death; whereas, with the right spiritual intention, Torah is an elixir of life. This elixir of life is called up by the blessing recited upon approaching Torah, just before delving into it for whatever reason. For the Torah is not like any other occupation, intellectual or emotional. The Shema prayer, "The Lord is One," itself provides us with the pattern for our response: It is accompanied by the primal exhortation "and thou shalt love the Lord thy God with all thy heart and with all thy soul and with all thy might" (Deuteronomy 6:4, 5), and is then followed by another "to and fro" vibrational sequence, enjoining the hearer to "speak of these things when sitting in thy home and walking by the way" (Deuteronomy 6:7). The point is that the love of God has to be substantiated by speech, by providing a vehicle for love to be expressed. If Divine Love remains abstract, it is impaired and useless, incapable of moving a man from here to there.

The Hebrew word for speech, "*daber*," has several variations of gradations of meaning. Amongst them is "a thing," – דבר (without the dot in the middle letter). Also it may mean to move or shift something or someone. Briefly, the word has an etymological core relating it to a substantiality beyond locution and, in the context here, it points out the direction – following the injunction to love the Lord – to do so not only by talking but also by doing. At which point, the conception widens, and the one who utters Torah with words becomes an instrument or channel for Torah to pass through, enabling spirit to penetrate reality and transform it. Such indeed is prophecy. When a man becomes an instrument, when the *Shekhina* speaks in his throat, or when an idea makes use of him, his speech is meaningful on a higher level. This is repeated most emphatically in the tradition when it is said, *"Al pi Moshe"* – according to the mouth or words of Moses.

Not every man is Moses, but in every man there is something that is of Moses in the form of a Divine Spark. And in one way or another, whether by reciting the Shema prayer with intention or by devoting one's life to God, or even by doing whatever seems worthy in the eyes of God, such a person can be said to be uttering Divine speech. The thing or word *"Hadavar"* speaks from within one. On the other hand, and possibly not in opposition, there is the saying in the Talmud: "נזרקה מפי חבורה," concerning the value of a matter that is commonly talked about, to the extent that there is no way of specifying who said what – it is simply spoken by the people.

One of the definitions of humility implies an ability to hear one's praises like hearing the praises of others. Higher even than this is the capacity to speak in praise of oneself, also in the same way that one speaks in praise of others. Following this line of reasoning, one of the Sages made the interesting comment: It is indeed written in the Talmud concerning one who flees from honor, that honor runs after him (*Eruvin* 13:6). But if a person sincerely seeks to elude the respect and esteem of his fellows, why should he be punished by being pursued by honor? And the answer to the question is that if one flees from honor, it means that he is still involved with the way others feel about him. He still has a glimmer of pride somewhere in him. Therefore he is punished by having honor pursue him. That is to say, were he indifferent to the whole matter of honor, he would not need to flee from it. He would be able to receive it with the same casual equanimity as he would receive disgrace. And that is genuine humility.

In short, humility does not lie in the denial of one's superiority, virtue, or wisdom. It rests, rather, on the absence of a personal sensitivity to what is said about oneself. It is thus an ability to accept the facts about oneself, without emotional identification of any kind, whether positive or negative. So that one will not necessarily say, "Oh no, no. Not me," in response to approbation and acclaim. Because it does not matter if one is called good or great, sagacious or beautiful, or whatever; it simply makes no difference. Moses, for instance, was able to hear terrible accusations against him without saying anything. On the other hand, he could command the earth to swallow Korah when he felt the ignominy of the lie to be such as to warrant such an action. In other words, although he was not identified with his image, he was not unresponsive; he was able to act when non-action would have been weakness; that is, he was well aware of his own power and greatness. The one who knows his worth does not have to bend or defend himself; he is correctly balanced in his own place, in his own position.

Therefore Moses could express the words of God and be completely extinguished in the process; he could be a vessel for speech; he himself did not say anything. So, too, any genuine prophecy or Divinely inspired work is based on this humility, which is selfless.

But the nullification of self has to make an impact on the world. It would not mean anything for the spirit to be closed up within itself. The Tabernacle of Testimony has to be connected with the other Tabernacle: Jerusalem is the city that is bound together, one below and one above. And this connection is a double connection – from above to below and from below to above – and it is that which makes it a place of witnessing. That is to say, the reality below receives influence and power from that which is the upper existence. Otherwise, it would be a case of divided reality, a dichotomy in human existence. A person may rise higher and higher and, under the influence of the consequent exultation, can even reach a point of self-nullification, and then, in the course of such movement, he will return below. But he will come back to precisely the same place from which he started. Since his sensitivity is now greater, the impact of the vulgar reality below has an even more terrible effect on him, and he falls from his heights often in tragicomic contrast. It is really another instance of the to-and-fro vibratory pulsation of the spirit, with the return pulsation coming back to the vessel. Otherwise the rise would indeed be continuous and the nullification final. A person returns below, exactly as he was before. The rise and descent may then be something to talk about, nothing more.

The work of the Levites in the Tabernacle (in the desert) is also such a to-and-fro action – to put the sanctuary up and take it down again. But they also sing therein; they keep raising it up from within, so to speak. Their task is thus to maintain the connection between above and below and vice versa; to enhance and sanctify His Name and to bring Divine Influence down to the reality of earth. All of which belongs to the "accounts" or "appointments" according to the mouth of Moses (Exodus 38:21) because, in essence, He is the connection between the above and below.

So, too, in relation to the mitzvot; they too are vessels, each one performing a different task. All have the capacity of bearing holiness, but they are divided in function like the organs of the body, each to its own specific time, task, and purpose. They are channels of sanctity in the world. As it is written: "And you will do all My commandments and be holy unto your God, I am the Lord your God" (Numbers 15:40).

The mitzva is thus a candle, and of course a candle is also an instrument, a vessel of light. It needs joy, like the candle needs oil, in the performance of the mitzva – a joy that is felt in the being and is understood in the mind, for *Bina* is the mother, the source. The words of the morning prayer follow this logic of love and joy from the reading of the Psalms to the Shema declaration with its exhortation to love God with all of one's being, and the instruction to "speak" of these matters, leading up to the heights of the eighteen benedictions and the concluding blessings. All of which is also a rising and descending in the pattern of the Tabernacle of Testimony, serving in the same way as a vehicle of holiness for the worshipper.

Although we have not mentioned the role of Aaron the Priest in the Tabernacle, it is clear that he represents the Great Love. That is, his essential task is "to bless His people Israel with love." The role of the Levite, on the other hand, is connected with awe, the work of Divine fear. All of which is an expression of the concept of the seven "shepherds" (the Biblical figures corresponding to the seven lower *Sefirot*), according to which people are constructed along certain lines, not necessarily biological, which are soul paths. Every person is thus bound up with these lines connecting him with the seven shepherds. The difference between souls is a matter of proportion. That is, not only is it a matter of levels of being, it is also a question of degree or emphasis on one attribute or another. It may be compared to the common tendency to trace characteristics along lines of visible, genetically inherited qualities. This child's hair is like his mother's, another resembles his grandfather, and so on. Every child of Israel thus has something of Moses in him and something of Aaron. The spark of Moses enables one to have the *Shekhina* speak in his throat, extinguishing oneself in the process. The aspect of Aaron provides one with the capacity for the Great Love, from which it follows that a person can perform in two ways: he has the potential to nullify himself completely, and he also has the driving power to go ahead and do whatever has to be done. The "doing," whether as Divine worship or routine functioning, is in its totality a ritual of love. All doing is an act of giving, a work of offering; and, in this respect, the worship of the Levites is also dominated by Aaron. Love and fear, that is, only seem to be going in different directions. Divine Awe or fear of God, as practiced by the Levites, becomes both a way of praising and of extricating a human being from the reality of the world.

It may be in place to note that later, in the Holy Temple in Jerusalem – as distinguished from the Tabernacle in the desert – the work of the Levites took on even greater degrees of spirituality. The kohanim, or priests, were involved in the sordid and practical tasks of the sacrifice. They were responsible for the sacred slaughter of animals and all that had to do with the physical aspects of the sacrifice, to ensure its purity and to eat of it. The priests' holy labor included eating at least part of the flesh of the sacrifice, while the Levites' work included singing and beautifying the Temple, and care of the implements and raiments. They had separate functions: the priests were primary, and directly concerned with offering up the sacrifice; the Levites served in secondary roles of maintenance and praise in song, the work of extension or continuance.

In brief, the Temple was oriented to a definite view of the function of man – to add sanctity to earthly reality. Indeed, there was no way of avoiding it. For the self-development of humanity was only a stage in this way of man to God; it was the stage of bringing the Divine down to this world. To be sure, man can never bring God down without himself rising significantly, even though spiritual elevation is not his essential goal, and he is totally engrossed with what he is doing on earth. As the Ḥasidic story depicts it: One learned Sage asked another, "What is the ultimate purpose of man?" "To be sure," the other answered, "it is to improve himself and rise to a higher level of being." "No," replied the first, "you have forgotten what we have learned from our teachers, that the function of man is to raise the heavens."

These are two separate concepts of humanity, one denying self-development as the ultimate purpose, claiming that it is only a stage, that the real aim is precisely what man is doing within the reality of the world, not what he raises up beyond this reality. The flight to whatever is beyond may be something wonderful, but it is the actuality of the present that is humanity's purpose and ultimate end.

This "reality of the world" view is now considered as corresponding to the last two letters (*Vav* and *Heh*) of the Tetragrammaton (lower Jerusalem), but in the ultimate future, it will correspond to the first two letters (*Yod* and *Heh*), which is heavenly Jerusalem, the Tabernacle of Testimony. Indeed, it may be said that at this ultimate time, the Divine Name will be transformed to double *Yod Heh* – יהיה – and the *Vav* (descent from above to below) will be no more. Lower Jerusalem will become heavenly Jerusalem, the Tabernacle of Testimony. That which is now inconceivable to the human mind will, at the end of time, be manifest. That is, the Divine dwelling place will be below, which is the purpose of Creation. And this will be ultimate wholeness – the perfection of the world will be when the stones cry out "Holy." It is not when the angels declare the holiness of the Lord, or even when man learns it (although that is already something), or even when the sheep call out "Holy Holy." It is when the very stones speak the name of God.

All these concepts about the Tabernacle which have here been discussed are based on the dichotomy of the revealed and the hidden *Mishkan*. The Tabernacle or *Mishkan* that can be made manifest by action, by positive utterance, and the hidden *Mishkan* that may somehow be arrived at, but since "He made darkness His secret place" (Psalms 18:11), actually seems beyond reach. The hidden *Mishkan* lies in the negation, the eternal "no," those things that cannot be said because they are above the revealed things.

To sum up, one part of our discussion was about the relation between the "yes" and the "no," the *Mishkan* and the *Mishkan HaEdut*. Afterwards, the ideas revolved around the Jerusalem that was bound together, the manifest and the hidden city, the lower Jerusalem and the heavenly Jerusalem, and the point of the bond or connection between them – how lower Jerusalem, on the one hand, is the place where the tribes went up (Psalms 122:4), while on the other hand, it is a bridge to reach the upper Jerusalem. But this bridge is not completed in the above. The bridge returns afterwards from the upper Jerusalem to the lower Jerusalem. If it does not do so, the process is actually without meaning, because the essence of the matter is that there is a manifest Tabernacle (*Mishkan*) that can be entered and seen, and a hidden Tabernacle (which is the Tabernacle of Testimony) that may be experienced occasionally, making us aware of its existence. Through the manifest *Mishkan* one reaches the hidden *Mishkan*. But ultimately one's task is not only to go up to the hidden *Mishkan* but in practice bring it down to the world point by point. The objective is to bring the two together; the bridge is only the first stage – afterward there is need for upper Jerusalem to descend to the lower Jerusalem, which is a definite flow. After which there is a binding together; the two cities become a single unit and the lower Jerusalem turns into a "heavenly" city. They now form a single essence.

Beyond all this is still another culminating stage, at which the (redeemed) lower Jerusalem rises to meet the upper Jerusalem. The whole thing is turned upside down, as in the Talmud and certain *midrashim*, which speak of the future Jerusalem as being raised up above the earth, so that one does not go to Jerusalem but flies up to it. The new Jerusalem, existing as a result of the Heavenly Jerusalem descending to the lower, itself rises up; without ceasing to be the earthly Jerusalem below, it becomes another essence. This transformation and elevation is elsewhere called the "paradox of matter." It is a perfecting of substance; at a certain stage matter, which had been engaged in the desperate struggle of spirit versus matter, animal soul versus human soul, finally reaches its own ultimate, becoming something else, light and luminous. Among the expressions used to describe this is the "crown with which his mother crowned him" (Song of Songs 3:11). In other words, the King wears on his head a crown and at the top of the crown is a precious stone. This stone has to be dug up out of the depths of the earth, crushed, and polished. It has to be treated with brutal force to become a jewel. And even then, only after considerable rubbing and polishing, is it a diadem worthy of being set in the crown. The person who does the polishing or any of the labor required to create the precious stone is not raised up; it is the jeweled diadem that is elevated, set in the highest place. Heavenly Jerusalem becomes the instrument for lower Jerusalem, the manifest *Mishkan* becomes higher than the Tabernacle of Testimony, which was its previous ultimate stage.

The Trials of Life

Chapter one

In the endeavor to understand the injunction to "follow the Lord your God, to fear Him and to keep His commandments, to worship Him and cleave unto Him" (Deuteronomy 13:5), we should read the preceding statement to the effect that God seeks to test you, to know what is in your hearts, whether you love the Lord. That is, first there is the matter of testing and afterwards comes the injunction to follow after God. As though to indicate that a person has to pass a certain trial procedure before he can be commanded to follow the Lord.

What could be the meaning of such a test? After all, God knows the end as well as the beginning of all things; nothing is hidden from Him and He does not need to experiment with people to know what they are. At the same time, the choice is freely given to man to do what he wishes. Nevertheless, as said, the Holy One, Blessed be He, knows beforehand what a man will choose. The problem is thus complex, but it is a matter of considerable moral importance. To begin, then, we will touch on only one aspect of it. Does the Divine knowledge of what will happen determine the human choice or is man genuinely free to decide for himself?

There have been many allegorical explanations to answer this question, but we may point to more familiar examples from contemporary science. A clinical psychologist performing an experiment may ask certain questions of his subjects and, although he is quite sure of what the answer will be, knowing his subject's personality, he will refrain from exerting any influence. Hence the answer, even if known beforehand by the scientist, is freely chosen and therefore valid in terms of the experiment.

In terms of Divine providence, however, what is the purpose of testing someone if the results are already known? A medieval Sage, the Ramban, has ventured the opinion that it is necessary in order for an action to emerge from the realm of the potential to the manifest; a person has to earn the reward for a good deed and not for a good intention. The trials and tests a man is made to undergo are not meant to provide God with information that He already knows; they are meant to help a person realize the greater potential in him, to reinforce his capacity to overcome difficulties and to create something new. It is a way of letting spiritual powers become expressed in practice. The emphasis is not on God's knowing but on knowing as a human experience. It may be compared to the "knowing" which the soul has before descending to life in the world and which is lost at birth. There is a sudden and total concealment of Divine Light. The soul's entry into the world below is thus the greatest of all the trials of existence.

After which there is what the Marxists have called the superstructure, the accumulation of worldly experiences, and the attachment to the physical base of existence. As in the story of Job, beyond the other terrible experiences of loss that he is made to undergo, Job is given an unendurable sickness of body and this brings him to a halt. Grief and penury can bring a person closer to God, but the irritations and pains of the body are very great obstacles. The suffering one is justified in complaining to Providence that "the ways of the wicked are successful" while the righteous seem to get punished. And this leads to the worship of other gods. The false prophet does not have to speak untruths to show how cruel life can be even for those who serve the Lord. And comparison is of no avail; one cannot prove anything by a particular series of events in the world.

The trials of life are given in order for a person to overcome them.

The experience of a test is a means for bringing a person to greater capacity to endure and to eventually defeat and go beyond an obstacle to his growth. He can thus rise to a higher level of being. Of course, there are those who simply leap over obstacles, or who avoid them. There is the story of a righteous man who served the community in some official capacity and was given a large sum of money to keep in custody. The money was stolen and when it was told to this man, he fainted. They restored him and gave him time to pull himself together and again he fainted. This time it was almost impossible to revive him. They then called on the local *tzaddik* to help them. When he learned the facts, he said that the money would soon be returned, and they should inform the man who had fallen ill. Later, when the matter was indeed cleared up, the stolen money returned, and everyone was able to breathe easily, they asked the *tzaddik* how he knew that this would happen. He answered: I was certain of only one thing: that a person is never confronted by a test that he is unable to stand up to. When it was apparent that this righteous man could not endure the test, it meant that the money would be returned.

The point is that God knows the person whom He is testing and is confident that the outcome will be for the good. As a certain Midrash teaches: just as the potter knocks on the newly completed vessel to ascertain if it is sound, so does God knock on a man. A potter will refrain from knocking on an obviously cracked vessel, it would only break; he tests the pots that are whole. It is men who are relatively unblemished and complete who are tested, and this in order to bring them to a greater knowledge of Divine presence. Before the test a person does not always have the assurance of his worth; the test of suffering enables one to see more clearly. The struggle to overcome deepens the inner forces of life and augments the capacity to understand. The *Sefira Da'at*, or Knowledge, is raised to a higher level, in the Biblical sense of "from my flesh shall I see God" (Job 19:26). Seeing is here the result of being shown, enabling one to know.

Da'at or Knowledge in Biblical terminology distinguishes between that which is wholly apprehended from within, as a direct knowledge, and the knowing which is the result of discrimination or explanation, the mental grasp of something as a particular object or idea distinct from, or in contrast to, another. Pure knowledge, *Da'at*, is the result of clear and simple cognition without intellectualization; it is the basic awareness or knowledge of Divine presence. Hence the meaning of the phrase that God tests you (the people) to know whether you love Him is that, in the testing, Israel will rise up to the level of knowledge (of the Divine). Thus, it is not merely a matter of being lovers of God but also to know Him as that which is beyond all conception and sensibility, to know in spite of apprehended reality. It is related to knowing that something is good or bad or fearful or repulsive. There is a profoundly subjective element in *Da'at*, inexorably distinct. This is in contrast to the many vague and indistinct apprehensions and fears man experiences, the realms of semiconscious awareness, which does not negate the fact that all manner of creative thought may emerge from the latter indistinct "knowing." But knowing as Divine consciousness, as an awareness of God, is a clear and fully awake experience, which is also an opening up of love. It is being cognizant of the fact that the soul gives life to the body and that without it the body has no existence; it is as though one sees with a new and authentic vision: "from my flesh shall I see God."

The awareness of the Divine as Knowledge, as a Certainty, is of the same order as the conviction one has of one's own existence. Knowledge in this sense is inclusive, containing all the various meanings of the word "to know": mental and intellectual cognition, emotional experience, physical sensation, and so on. Man, thus, comes down to this earth not to suffer but to know God. That is to say, not to suffer for suffering's sake or for any other reason, but to know His Creator. All the experiences of life, heaps of particular happenings piled on top of one another, are directed only to this one goal. The more successfully a man stands up to these experiences the more clear and complete his consciousness of the Divine.

To be sure, a human life may be lived quietly and decently, without great demands, trials, or problems. But it is not necessarily a sign of a good life or a creative life; it is merely a sign of the fact that the person cannot bear too heavy a trial. Life then simply flows along. Whereas test and hardship serve as a dam on the river, causing pressure and power to accumulate. The resultant energy and force may be sufficient to light a whole city. But the power on this lazily flowing river has to be harnessed by the existence of an obstacle to its natural course; life needs problems.

In our day there are very many persons, growing up in a religious or non-religious world, carrying on without much concern about the meaning of it all and then, all at once, besieged by troubles. A process is begun, a soul movement, which, if it is not bogged down by the search for consolation, may stir up a dramatic change in life itself. If the person does not falter and sink beneath the sheer heaviness of the trial, if he can emerge from it, he will have become more sensitive to higher things and open to genuine achievement.

The explanation for this possibly fruitful result of being tested lies in the hiddenness of the Divine vitality. The hardships that are so often the lot of man hold within them an elemental source energy, a profound and fundamental life force. In all violent upheaval there is Divine vitality, without which it could never do anything. It is concealed, or at least indirect and seemingly destructive in a chaotic manner. As certain Sages have declared: The *Shekhina* went into the Exile of Babylon (on the destruction of the First Temple) or the Exile of Rome (on the destruction of the Second Temple), not to accompany the banished Jews, but as that which was the hidden essence that gave power to Babylon, whose purpose was to try the Jews. The *Shekhina* comes down from great heights of holiness and hides itself in the overwhelming tyranny of an earthly sovereignty that provides a certain creative pressure on the people of God. Thus the concealment of the *Shekhina* is not just a metaphor; it betokens the actual presence of Divinity within the Exile situation as a redeeming force that has to be found. Just as when a great wall falls, the highest stones get thrown the furthest and the lower stones remain close by. The Shattering of the Vessels, a kabbalistic description of original Chaos and Creation, thus describes the crumbling of the wall of Divine Sanctity – the highest sparks of holiness were hurled furthest away from the center of holiness, so that the spark hidden in the trial situation is greater than the spark exposed to the one who is being tried. This holy spark of Divine vitality that tests the exiled one comes from a higher source, but having been thrown down and away, it seems to be strange and removed, whereas, in fact, it is only another mode of concealment.

It may come in many forms – as a curse or a sickness, a loss of wealth, bereavement, or anything that betokens misfortune.

When a person bears up to a test situation, the trial does not serve to hinder him; in overcoming, he goes beyond it. Then, all the masks and obstructions to light and life are torn asunder and the Divine vitality manifests and continues to affect him as genuine knowledge of God's presence. It is a totally personal confrontation, one stands alone before the adversary, in darkness and apparently without support. That is the essence of trial; one has to find the light for oneself, by oneself, the light that is hidden in the severity of the test and waits to be discovered and made manifest.

There are all sorts of tests, varying in level and phase of harshness. The emergence and uplifting are usually proportionate to the difficulty. Once the trial ceases to be a trial or a hindrance, one's self becomes strong and a feeling of release prevails. One can see oneself as he was and as he now is. The trial hid the Divine Spark only for a while; the overcoming acts to awaken something new in him and to raise him to a higher degree of being. He has managed to break the shell and extricate the hitherto hidden contents.

Therefore, he can be said to be ready for an ascent to a higher level of being. Having availed himself of the power locked in the shell of the trial experience, which is the same as the darkness containing the force of evil, he can bring it forward into holiness. Because the origins of all the fierce antagonism to good are really themselves very high powers, the act of overcoming them enables one to subordinate them, even though they are of a greater order than oneself. It is in this sense that the word *nisayon* – נסיון (test or trial or ordeal) – has in it also the word *nes* – נס (which means miracle or banner or flag). The Hebrew concept of being tried and to be uplifted points to a process of breaking through to something higher. A person climbs on the back of the trial experience as on a mountain path. At the same time, the power locked in the mountain of the ordeal is added to the climber. There is a hidden light in the darkness of the test that is of a higher level than that which was previously known, and having extricated it, the person enhances his knowledge – דעת – of the Divine. A certain degree of holiness is added, just as food nourishes the body because, in their origin, the food substances are higher in potential, containing elemental life forces that, when transformed by human consumption, are released as a higher level of existence.

Obviously there are different ways of being tried and tested. Human ordeals are varied in their levels of spiritual demand and their personal relation to a particular kind of experience. Some people, like the Patriarch Abraham, are tested on such high levels of spiritual conquest of self that we cannot really follow them. Abraham's very first trial is traditionally counted as being thrown into a burning furnace in the city of Ur of the Chaldees. It was a physical martyrdom; only his flesh was threatened. Later tests in his long life became more intense in their inward significance; they kept transcending one another in difficulty and in their stress on the mind and the soul. There were trials of ideas, of faith, and of love. They involved his relationships with other people and the ordeal of inflicting suffering on others, which, in many ways, is more demanding than physical martyrdom. There are many ways of giving oneself.

In the case of ordinary mortals, the nature of trial and testing usually follows the unique pattern of each one's individuality. For some, it is a religious confrontation, either in terms of an expression of gratitude for good or evil, or in terms of distinguishing the source of good or evil in one's experience, or in the temptation to worship other gods. For others, it may be an uncontrollable vital drive, or a psychological need of some kind that the person recognizes as inferior. For many, the common ordeals of sickness and poverty and the raising of children are enough and more than enough. At the same time, there are individuals who are tried by an absence of suffering, whose inauspicious existence, without peak experiences of any kind, is itself a test of faith. Can one know ardor and sincerity without being forced into it by loss and pain? Tranquility can thus also be a subtle and yet no less terrible trial, for the soul tends to sink into sloth and the mind has to fight against the deep urge for sleep. The crux of all Divine testing seems to be a position in which a person gets stuck, when one cannot move out and away. No matter where or how urgent the situation or how trivial, the fact of an inability to emerge and do, to think or feel what has to be done, is often a sign of genuine trial. Faith is that which often lies hidden as the decisive factor.

The manna given to the Children of Israel in the desert was one such testing experience – for each individual as well as for the people as a whole. And it was not a matter of getting used to the unusual taste and the sustenance contained in the food from heaven, it was a matter of believing that it would keep coming. The test was to eat all of it and save none for the morrow; it was a test of faith. After all, how can one be sure that God's mercy extends into the future. Many persons rely totally on the army for their safety and on the bank for their savings. Few can rely on manna for their daily nourishment and not exhibit fear and apprehension. Everyone receives a full portion of life each day that cannot really be extended till tomorrow. The test is to live this with complete faith. And from this test a person extricates the spark of holiness which lifts him to a higher level.

Chapter two

From what has been said, it may be gathered that the trials and tribulations of life are for the good. This does not mean that they are pleasant; there does exist a certain gap between the two. The point is that God tests a person in order to bring him to a higher level of knowledge.

There may be said to be five aspects of being tested: the trial of sorrow and pain, the trial of disappointment, the trial of faith, the trial of hope, and the trial of expectation. Each one of these is a testing experience of its own kind.

But before proceeding further with this division, it may be pertinent to restate the fact that all genuine life trial functions as a testing experience by extricating the good that is hidden in the formless, by redeeming the spark or good that fell from the world of *Tohu* or primordial chaos. The very essence of trial is a process of releasing the holy spark in harsh reality. One begins to crack open the meaning of the concealment, to reveal that which is in one's heart, and to bring forth the Divine Light that is thereby made manifest. The test thereby alters the essence of the self; that which was hidden becomes the source of light and revelation. The shell is cracked. The inner contents appear, and they are (astonishingly) of a greater degree of holiness.

For there are three unclean shells underneath the *noga* shell. The *noga* shell itself is a neutral sort of covering, a secular wrapping that can be removed easily by a certain action in the realm of holiness. To be sure, when a person bears up in the throes of severe trial and the demands on one are great because of the evil therein, the redemption comes when the evil is released, when the person releases the holy spark from its enslavement to the shell. Thus one can understand what the Sages meant when they spoke of "the martyrs of Lod," supreme examples of people who stood up to a great test and who, by overcoming the evil in themselves, were considered superior to the saintly people. The explanation lies in the fact that there was a removal and extrication from three unclean shells, whereas genuine saints only have to remove the *noga* shell. The complete saint or *tzaddik gamur*, as elsewhere described, is one who repairs the world by transforming the common into the holy. He takes an object of neutral ordinariness and makes of it a mitzva, such as raising food and drink from their animal function in the *noga* shell and using them to sustain spiritual expression. A penitent performs a similar reparation out of love (and pain), which is a far more complex action. To be sure, merely dressing up in religious garments does not make a penitent holy. There is nothing easier than putting a *kipa* on the head or lengthening the sleeves of a dress; the outward gesture certainly does not make one a saint. The *ba'al teshuva*, or returning one, is a penitent only when he does *Tikkun* or reparation for the sins he lived in and performed. When he does this out of love (and not fear of punishment), his transgressions are made into forces working in the opposite direction; what was once sinful is transformed into sanctity.

Similarly, the person who goes through a trial experience raises the thing that was once a shell and transforms its essence, raising it up by overcoming it and crushing its antagonism. There is a power in relationship, which is what trial really is – a confrontation and conflict. One who has never had much to struggle against, in war or life or inner conflict, does not have much opportunity to repair the evil in him. Incidentally, the many *mitzvot lo ta'aseh*, the commandments to refrain from certain things, may allow a person room to feel virtuous simply by desisting from actions he never even wanted to do. Obviously, there is no transforming action in such outward righteousness; the shell is not even touched, much less shattered. The realm of the shell is approached only in genuine conflict. Repentance is real only when evil is totally overturned and uncleanliness is transmuted into holiness.

To be sure, there is the injunction to turn away from evil and to do good. This may mean that evil is to be avoided, left outside of one's attention entirely. But thereby, of course, the evil is not changed; one has done nothing about its stubborn existence. Only the person who penetrates into the shell of evil and manages not only to get out safely, but to take away at least a portion of the pollution, can be said to have done something in the way of *Tikkun* or reparation. This is possible also in the realm of the negative commandments to abstain from certain actions. *Tikkun* occurs when there is a temptation or confrontation, a struggle, and a victory. That is, when a negative mitzva becomes a test situation and a trial. When a transgression does not exist for a person, when there is no desire to do some particular wrong, there is no reward either. But when there is struggle and war against an evil in oneself, an evil that causes pain because it exists as a desire, and if one does not succumb but manages to endure and perhaps to conquer, then the anguish becomes a light and a power for joy. It is not a matter of two different processes in the same person but of two processes that are structured, one on the other. When a person suffers temptation, when he is afflicted by desire for the forbidden, the power that accumulates and is ultimately released in victory over the temptation is proportionate to the suffering. For someone who is indifferent, it does not matter much and the spiritual gain is proportionate. For someone who is in affliction, where the spiritual contest is deep and painful, the holiness can be drawn forth out of the depths of evil. In other words, it is the inner struggle that makes the difference.

For evil is a parasitic force that lusts after a person's soul. Evil then has no real power, it sucks on the life of a man and in the struggle between the two essences – the holy and the shell – the trial situation takes shape. If the person conquers, he then draws from the shell the power locked inside it and releases it as light and enhanced life, a degree of enlightenment.

To be sure, there are different conditions of such struggle: there are the trials of survival and the temptations of power, there are subtle issues of idol worship and of discrimination between truth and falsehood. When a person has to decide between life and holiness, when it is not just a matter of one pleasure or another but rather a cruel choice of renouncing life itself, the test can be terrible and redemptive. As a result, all of life can be restituted in a moment, as in extreme martyrdom. In those known instances of lingering death in martyrdom, it has been demonstrated that there was an inexplicable release from pain, the person passed the borderline of affliction by an influx of vast spiritual life.

Upon reviewing the various positive reactions to trial, such as those demonstrated by Abraham, Job, Aaron, David, Chana, and others in the scriptural narrative, we may put them into three categories: those who accept their suffering with cries of protest, those who accept suffering in silence, and those who accept their suffering with song. The latter instance is an extreme in the struggle against evil as such, against the essence of the satanic forces, and is exemplified by Abraham's victory of faith.

As we know from the kabbalistic interpretation of the seven kings of Edom who fell (Genesis 36:31), they symbolize the seven aspects of revelation: *Ḥesed, Gevura, Tiferet, Netzaḥ, Hod, Yesod,* and *Malkhut.* And the ordeals experienced by these seven lower *Sefirot,* or aspects of Divine Manifestation, serve to enhance the *Sefira* of *Da'at* or Knowledge, providing for its growth and development. This happens in two ways. One is in the manner of the general consequences of triumph over spiritual obstacles: a certain enlightenment, a knowing that the Lord is God. That which may have been shadowy or unclear in one's mind assumes a luminous certainty that was not there before. As a result of passing the test of suffering, knowledge becomes more of an experience of truth instead of a concept about truth.

The other consequence of ordeal is specifically related to the category or level of the experience itself. If the trial was in the aspect of love, for instance, the reward, so to speak, or result of successful emergence, is in the realm of Divine love. Overcoming a distortion of desire or affection (manifesting as excess, jealousy, or any of the misrepresentations of love) augments the essential core of love, which is *Ḥesed,* the *Sefira* of Divine Grace and Loving-kindness. The esoteric power of correspondence works with definite, even if unseen, accuracy. When a person overcomes fear, he will gain an added dimension of Divine Awe or Trepidation – in the domain of *Gevura*. Similarly, in the other various and mixed domains of engagement; overcoming an ordeal in any one field enhances one's power in that sphere of life. There are ordeals in every sphere of human life, even in compassion or beauty, the *Sefira* of *Tiferet*. There can be confusion about the behavior required in situations of strong positive feeling and serious mistakes can be made. This can be seen, for example, in the destructive effects of certain kinds of "mothering." This, too, is a test not unlike the temptation to slip into idolatry as an expression of great admiration. The point is that the result of overcoming the temptation is an enhancement of one's spiritual potential in that area. The root of the soul's connection to that particular item or feeling has been touched.

To be sure, most of the mistakes in judgment and the trials of existence are in terms of emotion. There is a need, then, to go beyond, to bring the test to the level of intellectual awareness, for ultimately the matter of proving the worth of something by submitting it to an experiment is really an effort of the mind; it belongs to *Da'at* or Knowledge. The aspect of consciousness as *Da'at* is therefore crucial. *Tikkun*, or spiritual correction, requires a certain degree of awareness, even in the most obscure of emotional struggles. For example, one of the trials of the Children of Israel wandering in the desert was the urge to put away some of the manna for the morrow, fearing starvation, which is certainly a deep inner drive. The faith or power to overcome the fear of hunger and death was a definite knowledge or *Da'at*, an intellectual conviction born of faith.

As with Abraham, to whom it was said (after the binding of Isaac), "Now I know that you are God-fearing," it was a matter of the test making it absolutely clear as Knowledge or *Da'at*. So too, all trials that come to such a level of consciousness rise to a higher and more complete intellectual certainty. The Divine Light is hidden in that which seems to threaten, and by standing firm in the terror and dread, it becomes revealed and the soul is elevated.

The Kabbalistic idea of the Shattering of the Vessels points to a total shattering. Not only is the primordial evil shattered, whether as an emotional problem or a temptation, but also certain elements of consciousness, even clarity of conviction, may have to be offered up in the course of a spiritual ordeal. And since a person can be put to the test at any time, in any unprepared situation, the reaction is spontaneous. Surprised by sudden pain or a blow of fate, a person has to respond without thinking. But confusion and bewilderment make a person behave in ways far beneath him. He forgets himself, he stands naked and unprotected in his primal self. The struggle takes place in darkness, in utter solitude, without the aid of what one is ordinarily armed with in terms of high thoughts and moral perspective. One feels abandoned by one's own knowledge of love and fear. Whatever happens is of the nature of the unexpected. The light concealed in the trial experience comes forth of itself; one could not find this particular light in any other time or place in the world. It is the unique gift bestowed by Divine trial. One may worship God in the ordinary way and never arrive at such an opportunity – to be given the richness locked in an ordeal of the soul.

As the Rambam put it in *Hilkhot Teshuva*: How does a person know that he has been forgiven for a particular transgression? How can he be sure about his repentance? It happens by the recurrence of the same situation, and by his overcoming it this time. The very same people may even be involved; his struggle may be fierce and profound. But the special gift received by passing the trial is now a reassurance from God that he has been granted not only forgiveness but also enhanced light. The same situation was created for the person in order for him to finally overcome that which previously defeated him.

Chapter three

We have mentioned that there are all sorts of trials, such as those of poverty and those of wealth, and that the trial of faith is perhaps the most difficult. The purpose of them all, however, is to "know," in the sense of gaining a certain enlightenment beyond what the ordinary course of life could supply. This enlightenment is a result not only of overcoming some inner obstacle in oneself, but also of shattering the shell itself that holds the light in concealment. The darkness or mystery qualifying a particular situation, which is one of the marks of an ordeal, is seen to contain a spark that can be ignited and that can illumine the soul. So that when a person passes a life test, he is granted a particular enlightenment related to the nature of the ordeal, whether in the realm of love, fear, patience, forbearance, or whatever, as well as a general enhancement of his knowledge of the Divine.

Nevertheless, as the Sages have said: without understanding (*Bina*) there is no knowledge (*Da'at*). That is, even for the one who stands up successfully to a test, knowledge of God comes only if he strives to reach it by some contemplation of the Divine. Trial and suffering do not necessarily bring light; they generally bring pain and affliction of soul. There has to be some preparation in the understanding to grasp the significance of what is happening. The ordeal does not work as a trial experience if the conscious mind has not developed such a capacity to perceive anything more than affliction. A person can get lost in suffering, just as there are those who, lacking intellectual comprehension but possessing a certain innocence of heart, are able to pass through great distress of body and soul and acquire a gleam of enlightenment.

Moreover, this enlightenment can come in disguise or be concealed for a time, emerging at another stressful confrontation. In any case, the illumination, or expansion of awareness, resulting from a trial experience requires the active participation of the soul, its turning to Divine Contemplation in accordance with one's capacities. To be sure, when a person contemplates the greatness of the Infinite, Blessed be He, there is no fence defining the limits; each to his capacities. What is for one a vast disclosure is for another self-evident. Everyone has his own spiritual scope and range of understanding. The important point is that Divine contemplation of some kind is a vehicle for getting to knowledge of God. As previously mentioned, when a person passes a trial experience, he shatters the shell of the suffering, which is also an obstacle; the Divine spark locked in the shell is released and floods the person's being. But this is possible only with the help of *Bina* (Understanding), the conscious participation of the sufferer; he has to be aware and even contemplate the Divine in some fashion.

It may be compared to the benediction that is often given by one person to another: may you be blessed in all that you do. What is insinuated is that the blessing comes from above and that the doing either receives it or doesn't. Much of human activity proceeds without much to show for it; men toil and die in darkness, there are perhaps more failures in life, in business, in transactions, than we ever admit. Even to become rich or successful is not necessarily a sign of blessing. And yet the doing is necessary for the blessing to manifest. If a person does nothing and just waits for Divine favor to descend on him, there is little likelihood that anything of significance will occur. It does not have to be an action of any great proportion. The blessed rain descends on all, and sometimes the result is absurdly disproportionate to the effort made to receive it. The important factor is the existence of some receptacle to receive the blessedness. A person has to know how to react; one has to know what to do with a beneficial influence. The Divine giving needs a channel in order to become a blessing. A musician needs his violin; talent is not enough. True there is a relation between the instrument and the content, but that is a matter of a different dimension.

Within the scope of our present discussion, we see that it is necessary to contemplate God in order to gain more knowledge of Him; a rational receptacle, a degree of understanding has to be available to receive the light or the Divine offering of spiritual life remains somewhere above, encompassing one's being yet unable to penetrate. One may well protest and say, as was expressed in Hasidic doctrine (*Tanya*), that all Jews are given the capacity to love and fear God, that it is not a matter of education and conscious effort, that it is an intrinsic quality of the Jewish soul, even if hidden.

The answer to this is that the hidden love of God is only a point, a potential. It has to be expanded by a sincere contemplative effort of the mind. Love is something that needs to grow, become larger and stronger. There is the need to extricate the light from its concealment and manifest it. This is done gradually, in stages, each stage connected to the larger structure as intimated in the verse: "*Aharei*," "Thou shalt go after me, the Lord your God."

What is meant by this conceptual structure, "after me," the injunction to follow after God? It is connected with the familiar phrase repeated daily in the prayers: "Who, in His Goodness, renews each day the act of creation." That is, creation happens anew every day, from nothing to the fullness of that which is, just as it occurred in the beginning, so that it is not a single action; nor is it a continuous (evolutionary) process; it is an ongoing renewal of creation each day and all the time. That is to say, at every point in time there is a new creation of the world. This is elsewhere explained as the constant "*Ratzo Vashov*" (Running and Returning) pulsation, like the heartbeat of life. If the pulsation should cease for any reason, all life comes to an end. In this sense, there is an oscillation of the creation of the world. At every moment in time it is renewed; there is no existence without the creative force that continues to fashion all that has come out of nothing.

This, however, should be modified by the statement "From You comes everything (that exists)" (1 Chronicles 29:14). This declares that all of existence is not derived from nothing, it is derived from God. The life of Divinity takes on the life of creation like putting on a garment. That which is something does not come from nothing, it comes from God. The word "creation" may delude us into thinking of an act of forming something outside oneself, but the original creation by God is an extension or an emanation of God Himself. That which exists as world, exists by virtue of the Divine Essence – "From You comes everything." The concept of a vacuum that is filled by a created world does not describe the reality of being, the mystery of existence. It is the reality of God that makes for the reality of the world.

From this we may relate to the command to follow after God. For the world was created from God, and lives from the life force of the Divine that is within the world. The concept of "nothing," therefore, cannot be said to be that which preceded Creation. If God is the fundamental reality out of which the world was created, then "nothing," as distinct from this reality, is in the world itself as that which constantly changes, which has no permanence in truth. The "nothing" in the universe is that which considers itself to be "something," existing in the creaturely illusion of being separate from God.

There is no descent of God, even in terms of cause and effect, no coming down of Divine Selfhood layer upon layer with the physical world as the end result. The Kabbala describes a certain nothingness between man and God, a space between the beingness of the world and the Divine Beingness. Our world is, thus, not created directly from the Divine Essence but derived from within the Vacated Space – הפנוי החלל – the dimension that was made precisely in order for the world to be able to exist.

As an aside, this means that man cannot become God by elevating himself, no matter how high. There is no ladder to God; at best man may reach some significant point in the Vacated Space (where a certain communion is possible). To be sure, men throughout the ages have sought to strip themselves of physicality and climb into angelhood and beyond. And, indeed, this does not mean that man cannot rise through many degrees of being to a superior spiritual reality. The question is, how far? All creation is limited, surrounded by the abyss of nothingness which is the absolute reality of the Vacated Space.

It is from this point of view that the world was formed from a "nothing," which is the dimension carved out by the Divine to allow something to exist. The source of its life is from God but there is also nothing but God. All of that which is may be said to be His splendor, for the emanations and extensions of the worlds are only means of illuminating Him. Like the light of the moon, which merely reflects the sun, so are all things reflections of His light; all the celestial and the earthly evolutions of being are only such radiations of the Divine. Therefore, the created worlds are considered nothing in themselves; they are the consequences of His light in movement. They are of the aspects of His kingdom so to speak, for once God decided to have a world over which His dominion could proceed to have something work out, the possibility of the working out was provided. This kingdom is not a direct emanation of His essence, with no relation to source. It is a constant and dynamic relation of true sovereignty, a Divine ruler and a realm over which His Sovereignty prevails. The name of God is that which the reality of the world can relate to; each kingdom calls itself after its own king. That is, when we say that the reality of the world stems from the sovereignty of the Divine, we imply that it does not originate from its own essence, but is derived from the fact that there is an aspect of sovereignty which is not really a relationship. It does not have an aspect of giving (and taking) but only a status relation between two things, a result of the fact that the sovereign has to rule over a kingdom. The whole country is formed only from this potential of that which a king is called upon to manifest. The kingdom, or the being of all the worlds, is created only as a shadow, only because God said "I shall rule." And within this kingdom is created the being of a nation; the nation is fashioned; it does not exist of itself; it exists as a projection from this point of kingship. In more metaphysical terms, it may be likened to a person who imagines himself to be a king. A country has to be imagined over which he rules, full of people, cities, streets, and houses. But now all these are not necessarily products of the dreamer, they are determined by his dream. In this sense, an impression of reality is a vital experience that is fixed from the Divine will of "I shall rule," from which power all created things are formed; their being is the aspect of a transient dream.

All of which does not solve the problem of creation from nothing.

Since the *Ein Sof*, the Endless and Eternal Reality, is the only reality and there is nothing besides Him, the creation can be viewed as another version of Divine being. For God's vital life force is within all created things; it is not a something fashioned out of nothing; it is a change of form, a degradation perhaps of Divine essence but it still belongs to this essence.

Of course, there is the matter of cause and effect, in which a certain phenomenon of existence is related directly to another on a single plane of reality. They belong to the same level of existence – just as when we speak of the attributes of the mind acting on the emotions, which seem to be something else. Basically, however, they are of the same dimension of reality. In spite of the distance between them and the difference in functioning, a feeling needs a certain amount of mental awareness in order to exist, while, from another viewpoint, there is a distinct relation of cause and effect between them. Mind and emotion are connected both in essence (one needs the other to be and develop itself) and in substance (they function as cause and effect on one another), even though they occupy different spheres of consciousness.

This, however, is not so true or obvious in the relationship between the physical and the spiritual. They are not on the same level of existence. Not only are their attributes of a different order (one cannot weigh or measure a spiritual quality), they cannot merge into or become the other no matter how much time and effort is exerted to transform a physical object into something spiritual. At best, one can take a certain kind of tangible substance and transform it into another kind of substance – physical matter into gaseous matter and vice versa. One can even give form to the formless, make a cube of oxygen, for example, by sufficient cooling, or one can change matter into energy by sufficient heating. The elements involved are of the same dimension, so to speak. Whereas, when it comes to spirituality, we are in another domain of existence. One cannot bring the spirit down to an ever-lower level until one can say that it becomes tangible.

The fact that men do make all sorts of transferences of this nature – such as thought becoming the basis for action and for the formation of new substances – is due to our complexity of structure. Man is a miracle of combinations. We live in two worlds at once and move freely between them. Indeed, all genuine philosophic thinking from

Aristotle to today has been concerned with this passage and the weird combination within man of matter and spirit. It remains the miraculous essence of man, although it has been turned into a search for better understanding and used to manipulate. Still, we cannot fathom the passage; we cannot raise anything in the ladder of evolution and fashion a spiritual reality. We cannot conceivably make an angelic being out of a living creature, animal or man.

As certain benedictions have expressed it, the only means of effecting this passage or transformation from matter to spirit is by Divine intervention. The spiritual quickening of physical substance, as in human life, is called creation from nothing, from nonbeing. On the other hand, we have creation from something, transformation of one substance into another. And this not only in terms of cause and effect. Gold is sifted out from great quantities of earth, precious chemicals may be extracted from compounds, figures are sculpted from stone, and the like. That is, a new existence is derived from something available. But, of course, the new is actually still the same substance as the source material.

The problem of creating something physical out of the spiritual is of a different nature. True, spiritual vitality can be invested in a physical object, giving it a life it did not have before; nevertheless, there is no direct transformation; in the same way as with material substances, one substance is merely extracted from another. Hence the combination of body and soul is an unusual phenomenon; it requires a constant miracle to keep them together. Indeed the two parts are often incompatible and dissatisfied – only a persistent Divine force sustains the union. The two are not of the same dimension; they do not belong to each other. They cannot be compared or measured against one another. Of course, there are categories of spiritual substance as well; the human soul, angels, and celestial entities are so different, they cannot be compared. So, too, the body and the soul do not belong to the same scale or category of existence.

To be more precise, it is not a matter of being more or less spiritual. It is a matter of entirely different dimensions. If we say that God is not material, it does not mean that He is necessarily spiritual; He is neither one nor the other, He is everything, just as He is never this or something else, never specifically spiritual or material, abstract or rational, never more of any one aspect or less of another. This is to imply that whatever we do know of the spiritual is still not enough to enable us to declare that it is of the same order of things as the Divine. Our discernment is very limited. Just as we do not see color beyond the infrared, or detect most electromagnetic rays, which we measure but cannot really observe, most of reality remains in darkness as far as human perception is concerned.

And in that darkness, we cannot make comparisons. What kind of darkness are x-rays? How can they be compared to the darkness of gamma rays? So, too, we claim that beyond the observable physical world there are spiritual realities which belong to another world outside our perception. We cannot measure them, however; we cannot estimate the quantity of wisdom like we measure the weight of material things. And we cannot, in the same way, say that wisdom, or any spiritual reality (such as angels), is in the category of the Supernal God. All created entities are thus similarly part of the one world, even with all the great differences between men and angels, body and spirit, green stones and brown stones. All are creations out of the nothing. Even the *Sefirot*, inclusive as they are, do not include the Divine. The world of *Atzilut*, the highest dimension of being, is also called the world of Action, the lowest dimension in terms of the scope of the great worlds. It is also the world of *Bri'a* and the world of *Yetzira*. All the dimensions as well as worlds, therefore, are similarly "something out of nothing."

Even Wisdom, which is the source of all creation, leaps forth out of the nothingness. True, there is also the mystery of the fertilizing union of two to create another. As it is explained elsewhere, all created things have their origin in two kinds of life force. One is that which clothes itself in its inwardness and is called That-Which-Fills-All-Worlds – ממלא כל עלמין; it is the Divine force within the worlds in the form of the soul of existential reality, and acts as the vital-being force that sustains an entity in its particularity, in its own specific essence. The other is the life force or (omnipotent) Divine "Existence" that does not clothe itself or impose itself on the created thing, and is of the aspect of that which Encompasses-All-Worlds – סובב כל עלמין. It is a power that does not enter into reality, does not vitalize it like a soul of being; it is a sustaining power by its very existence outside. God as Infinite Being created the world by commanding specific existences outside Himself;

there is thus a certain distance between them. There is also a profound relation of dependence – unlike the relation of human creativity and the product of this creativity. The gap between God and world is that which is called an "encompassing," the primary life force from which every something comes into being.

This is not the case from the aspect of that which Fills-All-Worlds – ממלא כל עלמין, which is the particular light that gives something its uniqueness, providing the sustaining power from within. With man, existence is composed of two dimensions. One is his soul life which we call his inner self; the other is the experiential life. The human body is not formed from the soul. The soul resides in the human body. This body exists of itself; it has its own mind and special essence. And its driving force, the activating power, is that which Fills-All-Worlds. But this is not the foundation and the root of the body and soul's existence together. Their existence is derived from something that is beyond the individual body and soul and comes from the essence that extends without end as that which Encompasses-All-Worlds. And it is from this essence that the being of anything persists within the already existing life of creation.

Beyond all this, there are combinations of the Light that illuminate all things from within. Encompasses-All-Worlds only surrounds from above, beyond all our intellectual grasp and understanding, beyond all that connects with reality in the sense that even Wisdom cannot avail. The reality that comes from the nothing does not live from within itself but from the very distance beyond space, as a result of the fact of emanation from God that leaves a great gap between Creator and created. In the physical world, the only metaphor that comes to mind is the emanations of radium that result from the disintegration of the nucleus. That is to say, there is a certain gap beyond which something else is formed. Within the gap that exists between Divine Essence and the reality of all the worlds; there is created the worlds. From this aspect, the world is created from nothing because it indeed suckles directly from that. Although directly bound to its source, nevertheless, there is this great distance and greater encompassing.

All these things and more are part of what is termed contemplating the greatness of the Holy One, Blessed be He. Not every person can relate to these things as clearly ascertainable ideas or conceptions.

What a child can grasp is very different from adult comprehension, and many people indeed remain tied to immature notions of Divinity. But, of course, every person grasps something of Divine greatness according to his ever-maturing abilities.

The tragedy of man is that every individual has his own little God, fitted to his size. In order to gain ever-more illumination, a person has to strain to his maximum capacity. The intellectual may be able to embrace a wider scope of knowledge. But awareness of God is connected with the essence of the fact that man can meditate. When a person meditates in this matter and learns to become familiar with the contemplative thoughts of the Divine, and expands his scope continually, he can thereby make room for clarity and some higher degree of understanding. Thus, too, a person may have a great intellect and yet fail to gain clarity of comprehension; the quality of his meditations is such that he remains small and limited in these respects. But if one does prepare space, makes room in himself for God to enter, no matter what his intellectual capacities, then the light finds its way in.

Chapter four

It has been mentioned that the act of creation is a constant process of creation from God. What is more, it is not a direct cause and effect relation; there remains an abysmal gap which is the Vacated Space in which creation takes place. This gap, for the creature, is that which is simply beyond his scope. For the Creator, it is beneath His realm of Absolute Being. Therefore, we have the impression of creation as "something from nothing" and there is the need to introduce the concept of wisdom as the source. This brings us to an apprehension of what the Sages term "Encompassing-All-Worlds" as the life source which does not impose itself on reality. While the concept "Fills-all-Worlds" is that which gives every individual thing its own life and form.

There is thus a seemingly infinite distance between the physical existence of a created object and the vital spiritual uniqueness of the object. They appear to be in two different dimensions at once. Even the superiority of an angel cannot cross the boundary between its own realm and the higher, towards God.

Indeed, there can be said to be three main levels in the relation between material and Divine. One is the level of the physical (as opposed to the spiritual), which is a measurable quality that cannot be defined in any other terms but itself. The second is that which Fills-All-Worlds, the "direct" linear quality that gives each particular item its form and purpose, its place in the hierarchy of existence and its unique being. Because the third level, Encompasses-All-Worlds, does not make distinctions between things sustained by Divine light, it, in turn, provides life and being to the reality of all the worlds. In other words, even Encompasses-All-Worlds is an aspect of Divine Power and Splendor, serving to express "from Thee is the source of all."

That which we call Fills-All-Worlds may thus be said to be the imminent in things, while Encompasses-All-Worlds is transcendent. And as we have said, even the transcendent Encompasses-All-Worlds remains separate from the essence of the Divine. God is beyond anything we can conceive, even though by His Light everything is sustained. He is holy in the sense of being infinitely exclusive, separate, and total in Himself.

Nevertheless, it is maintained that we do know God, that we can meditate on Him and receive some degree of revelation of His essence. But a minimum understanding is necessary; without *Bina*, there is no *Da'at*. There is the well-known metaphor of a person who successfully passes a trial and gets a great treasure as a reward. But the treasure is inside him, and he will not find it outside. Meditation is the means of discovering it within oneself. This search is essential; contemplation is a way of directing the search for the Divine reality within. And it is one of the ways of interpreting the command "*Aḥarei*" – "Ye shall go after the Lord your God."

Among the discoveries made by this kind of meditation is an awareness of the infinite distance between God and man. Once this is realized, it is possible to understand the enormous gift one is granted in knowing Him. At the same time, the whole process of ignorance and great longing has to be experienced in depth, and the wonder of being able to cross the gap has to be felt in all its splendor.

Chapter five

In pursuing the subject of meditation on the Divine, there arises an existential aspect, beyond any mental imagery. "After me" implies that one beholds the back and not the front. The face of God is revelation, the back of God is an apprehension of the great distance and abysmal difference between us. The injunction to "go after Me" is, however, a continuation of the command to love the Lord; there is a strong Biblical relation between "go forth" (the repeated command to Abraham) and the Divine Love that gives this command its special meaning. Meditation on God makes this love meaningful in the sense that it makes going towards or after God possible. Therefore, it cannot be theoretical – a meditation that reaches ungraspable truths becomes meaningless. Meditation on God has to remain within the existentially real in order for one to be able to pick oneself up and "go after" Him. Indeed the whole frustrating contemplation of creation from nothing is meaningful only as a source of life and light; it implants itself as a radiance in the soul. Similarly, thinking about God and about the Encompassing-All-Worlds is beyond the human sense of proportion and out of one's human range – it is therefore a part of the "going after Me" and seeing the back of God. But the concealing of His Face is not an absolute truth in the sense that it cannot change for an individual person. Even a small thing can hide a landscape from view; anything that blocks one's perception, whether internal or external, serves to conceal. The purpose of meditation on God is thus to strengthen perception by getting rid of the barriers to knowing Him. This also requires a proper arrangement of our concepts of spiritual worlds, giving them their proportionate size as well as place. One's conceptions have to be ordered to build an edifice of love that is able to overcome the factors in life that hide the light of God. These factors are not necessarily walls or hills that block one's view of a vaster landscape; they can be vital forces, leaping about, and singing, and filling the world of one's consciousness; they may be a blot on one's spectacles; they may also be the closest and most treasured of one's possessions, physical, cultural, psychological.

This brings one to the matter of nullification of self. Beyond all appreciation of His Greatness or explanations of His Attributes, there is the love that desires nothing else but the Divine – not the next world or eternal life in Paradise, but God Himself. In certain respects, it is like the games we play, whether as children or adults – one can win vast sums or even power but it remains a game. In fact, it may be hard to tell when the game has reached its limits; it is not necessarily in the amount of wealth, land, or power involved. When does it all become real? When do we realize what it means to go after Him completely? And it is a matter of getting to the source of life, of saying that one wishes to "see" His Face, to be with God – to go to Him out of love.

To be sure, there are levels of approaching Him. Every person is uniquely different and at every stage of life the situation is new. This is one of the explanations, incidentally, for such expressions as "to be close to God" or "My people, My close ones," etc. Closeness becomes intimacy, like a family matter, and the quality of its appearance is delight in love, a delight of the soul in contemplation of the spiritual reality of God. And it is quite distinguishable from the happiness of physical contentment, the satisfactions of human life.

It is in this sense that it is said: "Happy is the people for whom this is so" (Psalms 144:15), for whom the Lord is God. Everything may be taken from a person – his possessions, his loved ones, his very life – but God cannot be taken from someone who loves the Lord in this way.

Every person knows trial and tribulation, but the way a person relates to them makes all the difference; for some it is suffering, for the true lover of God it becomes another mode of being connected. This allows for the feeling of great bounty, of a limitless inheritance.

Thus, the ultimate significance of Divine testing of a person may be considered to be connected to the command to "go after Me." By standing up to a trial, the knowledge of God is made manifest in the soul. The meditation that is thereby begun makes the going after God possible. The intellectual aspect of the process itself is a sorting out, a distinguishing between that which fell in the primordial Shattering of the Holy Vessels and that which is inconsequential. Soul testing raises the sparks (of spiritual life) and gives them direction. More specifically, the direction is to "go after Me." The selection process, which comes after the shattering, serves to bring about another wholeness. Meditation makes understanding possible.

Meditation on God as a form of exploration into that which is behind the Shattering and inquiry into that which is reality is a selection process. It sorts out the meaningful. The world we live in, the world that is the result of the Shattering of the Vessels, is a confused jumble of facts and directions. There are very many paths leading in all directions (up, down, north, south, east, west), most of them not going anywhere. The task of man is a work of selection, to choose properly the way he shall go. It is usually accompanied by a certain amount of error; what seems to be leading up may be going down; what gives the impression of being a correct orientation may prove to be an illusion. Life is full of steps and pathways that delude us into following them as though they were true.

The action of *Tikkun*, or reparation, is, to a degree, to correct these mistaken courses one has pursued. It's like recognizing suddenly that the life one has been living is a performance in a theoretical setting. The selection that is consequential to such a recognition is a sorting out of the sparks, giving the right name to relations and forms, putting things in their place. A fragmented world is restored to wholeness; the path to follow is the "going after Me."

This way of "going after Me" can be followed all the days of our lives because the choice merely sets one on a different level. There is a first choice and another choice after that, and then there is something that seems like a solution, and then that is seen to be a temporary solution or a mistaken solution. One passes from one stage to another along the way of "going after Me." The significance of things change constantly; what is considered happiness at one point is superseded by something else; what seems necessary becomes a matter of circumstance. New forms of behavior and new relations to people keep appearing. God seems to be ascertainable, then becomes more elusive than ever. True, the formula "Without knowledge there is no understanding" is followed by the formula "Without understanding there is no knowledge." Essentially however, the matter of higher knowledge is a profound subject of inner contemplation. It alone leads to genuine understanding.

This genuine understanding is far more comprehensive than what was previously grasped as comprehending the nature of things. It starts with the effect of the experience of love and fear of God. This experience comes in the form of the trial. How shall one's love of God be tested? Because love can be a very many-sided feeling, shallow or deep, more intellectual or more spiritual. It is certainly a great achievement in itself, but it is on a level of enthusiasm about getting closer to the truth of the Divine. To get to a higher level of love, a certain tangent has to be taken, a going off in a different direction from the circular path of adoration. This is the fear of God, or awe. As a mode of recognition of the Divine, it is a development in two stages.

The first is a more or less external fear of the majesty and splendor of God, a natural reaction to His infinite greatness and omnipotence. The second is a result of the overwhelming love for the Divine and it appears as a profound shyness. After making the effort to come near to God, the closeness itself becomes almost an unbearably wondrous and overwhelming experience. It is not fear anymore or even awe in the sense of cringing before the strange and unknowable; it is a standing still and grateful before a sublimity that is at the other end of an immensity of love.

Chapter six

As it has been said, the fear of God is an aspect of "return," while love of God is "running toward" in terms of the *Ratzo VaShov* (Running and Returning), to and fro, movement of the soul. The "return" is a withdrawing action (fear) from the thrust to the Divine (love) and has its own levels. There is the (simple) external fear that comes from a participation in the general awe of God's might and majesty, the greatness of the King, which makes all men, in their multitudes, stand in terror and wonder before Him. The result is a need to worship together with all men, responding in trepidation to the call of the celestial beings "Holy, Holy, Holy," as we do in the morning prayer *Yotzer*, preceding the Shema.

One may ask, how does man in his smallness come to such a realization of Divine greatness? And the answer, in terms of this external fear, is that it proceeds from a person's seeing all other men around him offering reverence and respect to their Sovereign, and thus influenced, he also bows down in fear and trembling. It is external in that it is in imitation of what is prevalent and is reasonably acceptable. This, in turn, leads to God's love of us, as expressed in the benediction of the morning prayers, *Ahava Raba*. Following is the Shema declaration itself, which calls out the love of God in us.

There is also the reference to the resemblance of angels to trees, in that they live vertically and do not shift positions, growing in one place or task, they reach upward to the Divine, whereas men move among the standing trees. The idea seems to be that the delight of Divine Union is a matter of this combination of fear and love.

The culmination of these benedictions is in the Shema declaration and the subsequent prayer: "And thou shalt love the Lord thy God with all thy heart, and with all thy soul and with all thy might" (Deuteronomy 6:4). To love "with all thy heart" is a definite charge to love with the totality of one's being and not with any chamber or corner of the heart. So many persons tend to give God only a certain part of themselves, a corner of the heart, a special room in their minds. The hidden love in all human hearts, however, strives to burst out and occupy all of the heart, becoming a manifest love as expressed by "with all thy soul" – with all of one's attention and thoughts. Thereafter, the love with all of one's might is a boundlessness of love, a bliss beyond measure. There is no limit in any dimension, time, space, feeling, or thought; Divine Love in delights can never be replete; there can never be enough.

In another context, the same intimate relation to God is divided by the author into the love of yearning, which is also boundless, and the love of fulfillment, or realization in God, which, in its own way, is no less boundless. In other words, there are different ways to the desired goal of fulfillment in the love of God. The fact is, men can spend all their lives in aspiration toward, or longing for, a Divine love that will fill their souls, leaving them satisfied and somehow at rest. But like so many romantic motifs in human life, the yearning for love's fulfillment often ends with disappointment in its finitude. The true love has to be without end; everything genuine has to be beyond possible satiety. Hence, the renewal each day of the whole world; nothing in creation is ever repeated. Hence, too, the (external) fear preceding the heartful love of God, and then the infinite love of God that precedes the great awe, the deep shyness or self-nullification before God as expressed in the standing prayer of *Shemoneh Esreh.*

This self-nullification is thus very different from the external fear that, at first, comes from doing as others do – participating in the general fearfulness of the people around one. It is external in the sense that one has no direct contact with the source of the dread, no real knowledge of the essence of the Divine Power and Greatness. If even the angels in Heaven cry out in trepidation, "Holy, Holy, Holy," how much more is the little man on earth inclined to be scared? It is a kind of general panic in which one is eliminated as a person.

It is in this frame of reference that we have these two kinds of self-nullification. The first is a matter of accepting some authoritative presentation outside oneself – like acknowledging that someone is a great mathematician on the basis of the opinion of experts. If everyone is in awe of God, then I, too, concur and stand in awe. The other is a result of one's own encounter with God. The latter self-nullification is of course far more profound. Previously, it was an approximation of a possible relation; now, it becomes the beginning of an endless progression. Even if this beginning is a nullification of self, one finally knows what it is all about.

To be sure, one can also expect too much; what one learns or achieves in mystical experience may or may not live up to the grandeur of the imagined ultimate realization. The question then arises whether it is not all a subjective matter; maybe everyone sees something else and there is no common denominator, no common scale of valuation. On the other hand, there is the optimal situation in which one's meeting with God exceeds anything that one has ever conceived possible. The great awe or "fear," in this case, is also recognition of the measureless distance between. It is like a child seeing the ocean for the first time. All that was ever described to one before is inadequate; the vast stretch of water is confounding in its reach beyond the horizon. The greater awe before God comes only when finally beholding Him for oneself so to speak. The greater love comes from recognizing the infinite gap between us and His Infinite compassion in letting us cross it and approach Him.

To sum up, this Divine love is thus an overwhelming abundance. And, as mentioned before, it is the result of a process. At first, it seems quite simple – as though God gets something from one's performance of a mitzva. Following this, as we have seen, the meditation on God brings out His remoteness and the recognition that the revelation is an act of Divine grace. In the play of "Running and Returning" thereafter, we witness the growth of love and fear. At first there is the lower fear, the external awe of standing before Him. When one begins to "go after" Him in love, the higher delights of Divine Union become apparent and we experience the never-to-be-satisfied yearning for these delights. At the same time one knows a love that is replete with its own joyousness, needing nothing else. If God is with me, it is everything. Nevertheless, there is possible a still-higher state of blissful fear and trembling, the Divine shyness and awe that comes from approaching the Infinite Light. Once again the effect is that of standing, not "going after," but being with Him.

Chapter seven

The soul's desire is for God and the more thoroughly this is expressed as a mitzva, the more is the mitzva felt as a gift. God has given the people of Israel many mitzvot as a Divine offering, as a sign of His Love. To be sure, the very plentifulness of mitzvot as expressions of Divine Love may well arouse the opposite reaction; one can become impervious to their value and dulled to their effect. On the other hand, those who are able to constantly revive the love they invoke, and accept them as a Divine gift, can experience an accelerated growth of the heart and feel a light within. Each mitzva then becomes another candle, lighting one's way. As it is said of Rabbi Eliezer, he used to illumine his prayers by giving a coin to a beggar on his way to the synagogue; the mitzva provided light and love for his soul and all that he did afterwards was uplifted.

It may be added that just as the world rests on three things – Torah, Work, and Human Kindness – so can the mitzvot be divided into these three categories. Human kindness is of the nature of Ḥesed and fits into the right side of the Tree of Life (chart of the Sefirot); Worship can be seen as the left side, corresponding to Gevura; and the center line of Tiferet is also Torah. Every single mitzva is a revelation of the Divine Essence along one of these lines of emanation. Thus, it sheds light in a particular sphere of existence. And all together the mitzvot burst through life in all directions. They fulfill the commandment "to love the Lord this day" (Deuteronomy 11:13).

It is written that transgression extinguishes the light of a mitzva, but transgression does not extinguish Torah. The light of the mitzva is like a candle that can be snuffed out, while Torah is a universal (spiritual) light that cannot be extinguished. The mitzva, therefore, has to be watched over; it needs to be "kept" as well as performed, lest there be some divergence or sin. The mitzva, then, requires care. For, although the mitzva itself cannot be wiped out, the light that comes from it can be extinguished. That is to say, in the balance between good and evil, the mitzvot themselves are not canceled out by sinful actions, as in a financial accounting of profit and loss. They are two different categories independent of each other. If a person has performed a mitzva, he gains a whole world; his transgressions comprise another register of accounts and have no effect on the fact of the mitzva itself. But the light that comes from the mitzva, the uplifting effect, is dampened, and even obliterated, by sin.

The conclusion to be drawn is that there is no arithmetic total of moral action; there is only a sum of mitzvot and an adding up of transgressions, each in a separate category. The evil does not cancel out the good, the good does not cancel out the evil. The problem – if so it can be termed – is that of mutual encroachment and the tendency of sin to thrust the good aside with brutal disdain. The advice of the Sages is to grab at the mitzva in all circumstances, never to be entirely overwhelmed by a wave of evil. As a story about Rabbi Ḥaim of Tsanz indicates: A good woman was selling apples in the market. A Cossack passed by and began to snatch at the apples and to fill his pouch. The woman thereupon wailed aloud in helpless mortification. The Rabbi, who happened to witness the incident, cried out, "Foolish woman, grab what you can of the apples. Just as he is doing!" For although one may not always be able to restrain the wicked, that does not mean that I myself have to succumb and lose whatever chance I have for doing a mitzva. If one were to wait for the evil impulse to leave one in a suitable frame of mind, one might well be deprived of most of the opportunities for good deeds. Because the evil impulse changes its form constantly, its very nature is insidious;

it assumes a different aspect at every stage of life. The idea is to be aware of it and to act accordingly.

Wisdom and enlightenment do not come of themselves in the passage of time. When a person performs a mitzva, there is light shed on the soul; when he transgresses, the light is extinguished and there is darkness in the soul. And this continues so that it is said that one has to keep watch and retain what one can of the light.

How is this best accomplished? By resorting to the light of Torah study. The mitzva is steeped in life, in the actuality of time and space; and its light is therefore easily extinguishable by the negative actualities of the same dimension. But the Torah is beyond human life and beyond time and space; its light is not affected by the lower dimension of existence. Therefore, by reinforcing one's soul with the light of Torah, one can better withstand the darkening power of evil in all its disguises. For the Torah is the source light of the mitzva, and being of a higher level it cannot be extinguished by sin.

It has been pointed out by the Sages that the thirteen ways of studying Torah (Midrash) are somehow congruous with the thirteen aspects of Divine Compassion. The implication is that the engagement of one's mind with Torah releases Divine Light and Love into the soul. Hence, too, the image of the thirteen petals on the stem of the rose, which is Israel.

Chapter eight

Having mentioned the Thirteen Aspects of Divine Compassion, it may be fitting to add that the month of Elul (before the New Year) is a period of drawing upon this compassion. It is a favorable time for receiving grace from above and for the light of Torah to enter the soul. Hence, the intensification of study at this time and special prayers of penance (*sliḥot*). For as we have said, while a transgression can extinguish the light of a mitzva, it cannot extinguish the light of Torah. And when God is being supplicated for mercy, the light of Torah may be a decisive factor.

What is the essence of this supplication in entreaty? Is it not a request for a free gift from God, a gift that comes without a mitzva or a deserving deed, without reason, so to speak. Ordinarily, the mitzva is a holy act that a person performs – and he does not necessarily have to be inspired to do so – in the course of which, and afterwards, light is drawn down from above. In Torah study, the light comes of itself, from the Torah, as a free gift, irrespective of what one does. It is in the nature of *raḥamim* or compassion. Whereas love or *Ḥesed* is a mutual connection in relation, *raḥamim* is primarily a matter of giving, and the receiver only accepts; compassion bestows itself and seeks no return or even response.

It is in this sense that the statement should be understood: "To keep His mitzvot and to listen to His Voice" (Deuteronomy 13:5). Keeping the mitzvot is an act of love; listening to His Voice, or to His Torah, is an act of compassion. The Divine Voice is a streaming down or evocation of wisdom through Torah, written or oral. And the one who is thus engaged in Torah also attracts the light. He becomes an instrument or a channel, listening and understanding and giving utterance (or expression) to this wisdom. Listening to His Voice is thus much more than hearing, more than an act of comprehension leading to obedience; it is a sequence in *raḥamim*, Divine Compassion.

Every individual is enjoined to perform mitzvot; it is what one does as a servant of God and is called "worship." The *kavana*, or heart's intention, is not that of toilsome labor, of course; one works with love and joy, with a willingness, an eagerness to approach God, or at least to do something for Him. Thereby, too, one aspires to add holiness to the world, saying, with the usual formula of the blessing: "Who sanctifies us with His Commandments."

As we are aware, worship is not only a matter of doing the right thing. The particular joy in doing something for God is just as meaningful. As the Maggid of Mezritch said, it is like the music played by the inspired musician, the player himself becomes the instrument; he is obliterated in the "message." So is the prophet, who does not even become caught up in love or fear of God or any noble emotion, for he has no space in himself for anything but the testimony, the Divine Message, the prophecy which he has to bear. In every man there is this capacity, albeit, at one's own level, and one can always rise to a higher level. What is required is a certain sincere devotion and a feeling that this could be clearer, more genuine, more inward. Those who are unable to feel this strongly can nevertheless learn to raise themselves to a higher level of worship by application of whatever forces they can muster, whether intellectual, physical, or emotional. The important factors are the elimination of one's self to whatever degree possible and the penetration of whatever light comes from above into the depths of the being, so that the realm of action is illuminated.

For most, the great difficulty comes at the crisis of transition, when one has to move on to a higher level of being. It is fairly simple to progress within a given framework; agreeable satisfaction is gained with every overcoming of an obstacle, solving of a problem, whether in the mental sphere or the practical world or the emotional life. But when the rules are changed and the situation demands something more than what has already been mastered, when one has to make a leap into a wider range of values, there is a crisis. For someone who is competently familiar with Euclidean geometry, adjustment to non-Euclidean geometry requires an effort of some kind. It is not easy to accept that the sum of the angles of a triangle is not what one has learned, that the circle is not a circle, and that a line is not necessarily straight. One has to rise to an understanding of the fact that what one has been convinced to be true is only a part of a more comprehensive truth; that it was only an incidental fragment, something that was correct within a limited scope.

The passage from one intrinsic level of existence to a more whole yet different level, from where one is now to where one could be, is a constant challenge. It is the very essence of the Divine Instruction to "come after Me." In Kabbalistic terms, it is in the nature of *Malkhut* (Kingdom), which receives all the qualities of life, to become the source of all the world's thrust and vital drive to fulfillment. "After Me" is an aspect of "behind," in contrast to the "front" or the face of a thing. The "front" is the use or specific meaning of a vessel, like a pot; the "behind" is the physical structure and substance that makes it possible for the pot to contain whatever is put into it. The existence of all the worlds is not of the aspect of the front or face of God, it is of the aspect of the behind, the substance that has to hold the light of God and contain His holiness. As it is written, "For with You is the source of life" (Psalms 36:9). And the whole of creation is thus a "something from nothing" in relation to His Essence and Divine Being.

Thus, too, the dance of existence is a constant swirling and delicate movement from behind to behind and to front, ultimately to reach the glory of Divine confrontation, face-to-face. And in many different cultures of the world, variations of this dance are repeated with strange fervor, whether as a wedding celebration or a religious ritual. The point is that the statement "going after Me in the wilderness in a land not sown" (Jeremiah 2:2), is a testing, a trial experience, a movement into unknown territory, where the Divine Light is hidden. When one goes in front, in the glory of His Countenance, the going is straightforward, if not easy; one seems to go on the clear path of His Torah. When one goes behind, "after Me," the going is difficult indeed, because one does not see anything clearly; it is a trial experience full of trepidation and uncertainty.

As many Sages have said, the Divine testing is a situation in which all of one's accumulated cleverness and wisdom is of no avail and a person simply does not know what to do. If one knew how to react, it would not really be a test. One cannot apprehend what lies behind the screen; the next step is totally indiscernible and the implication remains concealed. This is what is meant by "going after Me" into a desolate wilderness.

And it is this trial experience which makes one "know" the Lord, thy God. The examination is not necessarily a battle against evil; it is perhaps more a matter of persistence, of keeping on going "after Me," in spite of the obscurity and in spite of despair, even though it seems an eternal going in darkness. Because this is the way the Divine light bursts through to one. The trial is, in a certain sense, the way to help a person make the leap to a higher level of spiritual being. And it consists largely of trust, of allowing God to test one. If the vessel is sound, knocking on it will produce the right sound. If one has faith that God tests only those whom he knows are able to respond and make the leap, then one can keep on going "after Me" with courage and confidence.

Chapter nine

Briefly, the conclusion to be drawn from our previous inquiry is that the reason for the descent of the soul to earthly existence is to experience the trials of life. The soul of man has to be strengthened by test, ordeal, and confrontation with physical reality. As it has been remarked, "to know trouble" so that the soul may be impelled to rise to an emotionally higher plane of knowing God. It is very difficult, if not impossible, to make progress any other way.

The trials and severities of a human life are thus not accidental and unfortunate contingencies that simply have to be endured; they are part of the very purpose of a life. In between, there are periods of rest and relaxation, and these provide the strength to stand up to the trials. The ultimate purpose of it all, however, is to know God within.

What is indicated is a knowing that is not only intellectual, but is total, including the entire spectrum of the emotions and other aspects of one's being. It is a knowing that is an encompassing grasp, or at least a wider perception, resulting from the fact that a person has passed through an experience that brought him to the extreme edge of his capacities.

For, through ordeal, a person learns, by way of insight, to get beyond mental notions or feelings, beyond the words that fix one's likes and dislikes. That is to say, one surmounts the sentimental and transient aspects of oneself and realizes a "knowing" that leads directly to a firm love of God. Life has to impress itself on one with a profound stamp of harsh reality to enable all of one's being to respond with an act of total offering – deeply emotional as well as intellectual. This is, perhaps, what is meant by the command to love God with all your heart.

The esoteric meaning here is that, amongst other things, there is a Divine life-force hidden within the test. From a certain aspect, the Divine life-force seems predominant there because it appears as an opposition, a barrier to the human effort. For instance, in sin, one is confronted with that which is not of God, which is even against Him, and the person who is being tested has to distinguish and choose the Divine Essence hidden in the trial. He has to discriminate, pick out the fragments of Divinity that fell upon the Shattering of the Vessels at the beginning of time, and this correct choosing makes him worthy of, and entitles him to, the enlightenment which is knowledge of God.

Notwithstanding, without understanding there is no knowledge. The testing may provide some light, but in order for the person to grasp this light, he has to have achieved a corresponding level of intellectual understanding. Otherwise, without clearly distinguishing what he has been granted, he does not understand what he now knows, so that his knowledge is somewhat unreal, vague, and unsubstantial, and can scarcely be called enlightenment.

The first step, upon recognizing one's inability to understand, is to meditate on the matter of the huge gap between God and one's self. Upon which, the light that entered in the trial experience assumes a new significance; it becomes a radiance that alters the relation. A subtle, heart-lifting happiness now makes it possible for the meditation to be illuminating. And indeed, very often a whole system of values has to be reassessed. Because, if a person should come upon a treasure, it is a joyful surprise only if he is able to recognize something of its worth; if he is unlearned, he may very well see nothing more than odd-looking stones. And it is the ever-renewed contemplation of Divine Essence (through study and meditation), and of one's basic love of God, that enhances the capacity to distinguish the value of inner experience.

Nevertheless, the privilege of contacting the Divine is something that is above and beyond all levels of existence. I can tell someone that he holds a great treasure in his hands, but in order to understand it, he has to be on a certain level. It's like very large numbers that have no meaning for anyone who does not live with them. One has to assume the scale of values that comes from familiarization with the field of observation. This, in turn, is a matter of "running towards," the *ratzo*, to God with love, and is followed by "returning," a fear of God, as a result of discovering Him. For there are different grades of fear: the lower and the higher, in proportion to one's knowledge of God's greatness. On one hand, one's heart rejoices at His approach, on the other hand, there is, simultaneously, a trepidation before that which one is daring to glimpse. And it is the very same contemplation. When I am here and God is there, nothing much is happening. But when one feels an exhilarating touch and recognizes its essence, there is a certain collapse, a dread of what one is experiencing, precisely because one recognizes its incalculably precious quality. It is a fear beyond terror of mind or body. This higher fear is in contrast to the lower fear of God, which is an awareness of the Creator as King of the universe, overwhelming in His greatness.

The daily morning prayer carries one from the lower fear to the higher fear. And it brings one to a certain readiness to make one's will harmonize with His Will, to make them one action, which is the mitzva.

When one performs a mitzva, making His will one's own will, a certain merit is produced, and a corresponding reward. However, a transgression extinguishes the light of mitzva. It is not the mitzva that is obliterated; there is no canceling out of good by evil or vice versa, but the transgression does blot out the soul light of the mitzva. Therefore, we are urged to keep vigilant watch over the mitzva. How is this done?

It is accomplished by Torah. Because transgression cannot extinguish Torah; the Torah is too huge; no transgression can harm it. Indeed the Torah belongs to that which is beyond all the worlds, more specifically to the world of atonement and forgiveness. One has to listen carefully when one relates to Torah. What results from the complete coming to God through love and fear is a great humility, a totally listening attitude, like that of an obedient servant.

The root of the matter concerning the injunction "to go after God" is an aspect of both an endless going and of a going "after," or behind, God. Even the vision granted to Moses was limited to this seeing the back of the Divine and not the face. As for the endless going, in the Kabbala the Divine emanation continues through the worlds of *Atzilut, Bri'a, Yetzira,* and *Asiya* along a certain line which goes through the Vacated Space – החלל הפנוי.

The rest of the reality which is God cannot be known at all or considered as existence. According to most kabbalists, however, the Vacated Space is not objective. They claim that it is, in actuality, subjective; that there is such a space only in terms of revelation. Just as a person who does not talk to others but talks aloud to himself can be heard and even understood. Let us assume that there is a lull in his articulation while his thoughts continue. This would constitute for the listener an empty space until he started talking aloud again. It is not really an objective vacuum. The unspoken thoughts continue; the essential reality persists and develops. There is merely an interruption in our grasp of Divine speech, a vacuum born of a gap in revelation. For example, if we picture a ray of light in the darkness, as in a cinema, the reality that it reveals when it passes through air-filled space to the screen is a lovely world unto itself. But I, the observer, do not participate in this show. It is a world that comes from the ray of light; it is an aspect of *Malkhut* or Kingdom – מלכות – in the kabbalistic sense of our world being only a final reflection of Divine reality. Only the light source is Divine; the play on the screen is a parade of life forms, an aspect of "going after God." One can keep going in this way from this world to the next world on all levels of being.

Concerning the many levels of being, in this life and beyond, it is, of course, not a matter of going from one level or plane to another but of states of being, of a difference within oneself in comparison to what existed before. Thus, there is the lower Paradise to which one goes directly from this earthly existence, and there is the upper Paradise, which is not a prize given to one for good behavior in the lower. The passage consists of immersion in the waters of the River Dinur to completely forget all that was in the lower Paradise.

We have no description of the after-death experience. There is no meaning there to our ordinary sense of place. Paradise is not somewhere else. The next world is simply that which I do not as yet have any concept about. It does not even interest me. As some *tzaddik* once asked: If someone were to get to Paradise, how would he recognize it? One has to have an idea of what the place looks like to recognize it. And this follows from the principle that one cannot see something other than what one is already seeing; one cannot even have two thoughts at the same time. Just as there are cleverly contrived paintings where foreground and background can change and one sees different pictures with each, but it is not possible to see both simultaneously.

Our inability to perceive the passage to the next world may thus be due to the same kind of barrier. We are too firmly grounded in our human thoughts, memories, and conceptualizations; any other kind of existence is utterly beyond our grasp. Something has to break. Not only does the body have to discontinue its life functions, the vitality of which certainly contributes to one's inability to see anything beyond, the soul itself must undergo a severe change, because our ideas of what is and should be are also limited by life. Even if the soul does make certain abstractions out of the physical, there is almost always a need to shatter the whole of the being by death. Few indeed are they of whom it can be said that they did not really die, that their bodies decayed but their souls rose up in all their power; because their souls had already undergone the transformative process, making them ready for the next world. Such souls do not have to be broken by death in order to learn to live in the next world; they do not have to learn a new language.

Thus, we speak of persons who, in their lives, knew Paradise; they had transformed their essential humanity. The next passage, to the upper Paradise, requires a total forgetting of still another nature. There seems to be a need to renew one's view of life entirely in order to really make progress into a new mode of existence. The lower Paradise belongs to the world of *Yetzira*, of which we know a little; the upper Paradise is of the world of *Bri'a* of which we know much less; while the world of *Atzilut* is almost totally beyond us. The passage from one to another is at first through a forgetting in the River Dinur; thereafter, the passage to the highest level of being is a matter of utter self-nullification. One has to keep "going after God," therefore, without cessation; there is no end anywhere.

Chapter ten

The tests and trials which we are discussing are part of the process of selection and restitution of the holy sparks that fell in the primordial Shattering of the Vessels. More specifically, we are relating to the fragments that became part of the worlds of *Bri'a, Yetzira,* and *Asiya* and manifest as shells. That is to say, the holy sparks (Divine Effulgence) are embedded in the shells which fill the universe, and these shells may thus be said to be derived from a sublime source, higher even than the world of restitution or *Tikkun.* Because the sparks that fell in the original shattering are indeed of Divine origin, the vessels could not contain such a degree of light. The combination of Infinite Light and Shattered Vessel that were consequently hurled in all directions became fixed in earthly matter and life, the higher aspects being thrown and scattered the furthest. Their fall from the heights was thus great and terrible, because, in their original source, they were so much higher, like the stones from the top of a bursting wall that are hurled far from the place where they belong, while the stones at the bottom remain close. All these fragments, as said, in their isolated and scattered state, become part of what is known as "shells." And, as the word indicates, this is a hard covering, like the protective, tough exterior of a nut. The shell is, in this sense, the structure of most of reality; it is the hard exterior that serves to guard the inner fruit from injury. At first sight, the shell is a rather worthless object; only if it is broken into pieces and the edible fruit within is disclosed does the shell have meaning.

From which one may gather that the shell's ultimate purpose is to be demolished. The seed itself has to be separated from the husk and to lie in the ground for growth to ensue. The shell is only a temporary device to shelter the fruit within. If it is not broken, the life-giving seed cannot emerge. In terms of Kabbalistic cosmology, the holy sparks (or life-giving elements), which were thrown in all directions by the primordial Shattering of the Vessels, are kept in light shells (*klipa noga*) to protect them; sometimes they are said to be in a state of exile like the Jewish people when the Temple was destroyed. In any case, in order to extricate the holy sparks (or the edible fruit) and restore them to their original state, to redeem it, the shell must be broken.

One of the ways the shell is broken in the course of life is by the trial experience. When a person is tested by some confrontation that comes from the hard outer covering of life and he struggles to release the truth, he is shattering the shell. He has overcome the *klipa*, broken through to the inner core of that which is needful for him. Usually, the essence of the *klipa* is an evil of some sort, whether physical or metaphysical, and the confrontation is in the nature of a test or trial. It is an ordeal, more or less conscious, and within it there is a spark of holiness that is hardly ever revealed to one's gaze. The nut does not show what it contains within. Indeed, the trial may often be without serious significance, and the breaking of the shell may not provide much of a reward for the effort. But there is no way of knowing.

For there are shells that are empty; they somehow have no content and are *klipa gemura* – completely external. They constitute a very severe problem for many people; at least for those who undergo a trial and crack the shell only to discover that it was all rather meaningless. For them, the trial is a double trial and testing. Besides the effort of breaking the shell, they have to confront disappointment and dismay. Often for such individuals, there is a reaction of shrinking from a certain kind of experience. "I'll never again eat nuts." And the whole domain of that kind of "nut" is closed to that person forever.

The problem lies in the fact that what is desired is not the search or the effort to crack the nut, but the fruit within. One wants to eat the gratifyingly edible contents. Sometimes a person will throw away the whole nut, not even trying to break it and pick out the fruit; he does not bother to take the trouble, to struggle with the test situation. He has not even succumbed to the trial; he has simply evaded it, throwing it aside. At the same time, there may indeed be a situation of suffering which the proffered trial could have alleviated. But only too often, people seek to circumvent the test, afraid of the ordeal. The bitter herb of the Passover ritual has to be chewed in order to be tasted; if it is swallowed without chewing one has not solved anything. One can so easily evade a trial, neither facing it or surrendering to it.

Nevertheless, as we know, there is no evasion. A person has to live in his clothes – the covering and the shell. He himself is the holy spark within. The question is: How do I relate? True, one sees only the external shell of life and of selfhood; one is in the exile of being. And in sinning, a person goes further into that which is the refuse of exile. But sin is not only of the body, or even of the soul; it is such an entirety of being that one compels the innate God to go along with one, to be a partner in crime, so to speak.

As a result, one can ask forgiveness for one's transgression – after all, one is only a frail creature. But why must God be forced to be an accomplice? This is the double-sidedness of the Divine Spark in man. It helps to explain the absence of remorse in the wicked and the afflictions of the saintly, both of which are certainly troubling to the orderly mind.

The Divine Spark is like the ray of light that, in its origin in the sun, cannot be perceived; in order for us to get to know it, the light has to go through the intervening darkness and be refracted and reflected by substance. The fruit has to be protected by the shell; and to redeem it, the shell must be shattered. The Divine Spark cannot redeem itself; it has to come into contact with man – which contact is, for man, a traumatic experience, a confrontation he would rather avoid, with all its breaking of comfortable shells and suffering of mind and body. But the Divine Spark seeks thus to be released; it strives for redemption in the responsiveness of man to trial. If the man sees only the shell, the trial is scarcely likely to succeed; he will not try to break it in order to get to the hidden contents. There is thus a need to see what is within, on the other side of obvious circumstance.

To be sure, it is easier to see the concealed truth in someone else's trouble; God's ways seem more discernible when it is not oneself that is being tested. But it is one's own experience that is crucial, even though the temptation is to evade or pacify, to react only on the surface. One very frequently does not confront the trial; or else there are various levels of testing, with each appearing to be the ultimate one. The final test, however, is far beyond most; it is the test of faith itself. What is behind the evil? Because as soon as one accepts evil as evil, one has surrendered to it. Only when one sees the afflictions of body or soul as something other than evil is one grappling with it. To have a bellyache and survive is hardly an example of trial. The trial comes when one is prepared to see it as a relationship between me and God in all its aspects. And there can be many sides to the experience. One may see it as a punishment for something he has done; another may view it as a very limited testing of his virtue or strength, to show how well he can overcome an obstacle of one kind or another. Mostly, men will put aside the ultimate level of trial, the standing before God and the thinking of the sacred aspect of the experience. Indeed, this is frequently left for taxed moments when it is possible to indulge in theological speculation at ease, when one has nothing more urgent to do. But what is a person to do when he is in torment of body or anguish of soul? When others, dependent on him, weep in his arms? That is indeed the moment of supreme testing. He has to tear aside the veil and perceive the Divine presence. The sufferings are thrust aside; one refuses to accept them as evil.

In other words, the trial confrontation involves a change of values; it requires a restructuring of relations, or at least a deepening of existing values. And the issue is often a matter of degree: to what extent can a new or improved system of relations be built? Every situation is different, of course. There are those who meet with trouble and do not begin to revile fate or complain, and there are those who curse God at every frustration. Each category has its own trial. There are those who never seem to be tested, claiming gloomily that it is only what they deserve. And there are the few who can always see the Divine Light beyond all circumstances. The testing is complete and unique for each. The common feature is that genuine trial demands a clear perception of values; one does not relate to the apparent look of things, their externality; one suddenly begins to relate to the phenomenon in depth, with a new grasp of its significance.

Thus, a person who does not sin may simply not be in the mood; it does not mean he has overcome temptation or withstood anything; while the one who accepts suffering with an attitude of reconciliation also has frequently not really confronted the test. (The test may well be in the very nature of the affliction.)

Suffering, it has been claimed, can cleanse sin; it is able to wipe out the ugly stain of evildoing. And, in a way, there is an objective purification of this sort and a subjective cleansing. The objective comes in the wake of facts. The subjective takes place at the moment when one wishes it to happen. If one does not relate to the causes of affliction, refusing to see them as purifiers, the purification acts only partially. When a person who is dirty gets doused with water, much depends on whether he is washing or not; even though a certain amount of dirt is removed, his active participation in the process is a significant factor. So, too, the acceptance of suffering with love is not a matter of nodding one's head and muttering, "What can I do?" There is a level beyond this.

In short, the nature of standing up to a trial is such that there is a seeing beyond the circumstantial phenomenon, which is a *klipa* shell. So long as the shell exists in its seemingly resilient completeness, it's hard to break its resistance. But when one can see something further, beyond it, one has already begun to shatter it. Enough to realize that it is not something as objectively real and totally confounding as it seems, enough to detect a tiny crack in the tough covering – the peeling or cracking is then simple.

True there are fruits like the pomegranate with a hard rind and very many seeds, and one cannot always distinguish the point when the fruit is exposed. Much then is a matter of knowing the kind of fruit or situation one is dealing with. And in each case, the structure dictates the process. Some fruits (coconut) have to be knocked hard; others have to be peeled carefully (banana). There are situations when it is necessary to shout and be aggressive, others when only profound inner struggle can avail.

Nevertheless, the truth that may be drawn from our inquiry is that the shell does not really matter. The important thing is to neutralize it, get beyond it. Once the maze is traversed, no matter with what amount of frustrating error, it has no further function. Once any problem is solved, it has achieved its purpose; there is no need to dwell on it. If a person proves that he can endure and overcome a trial, that phase of life is put behind him. If he does not do so, he will in all likelihood be confronted with it again and again.

For the most part, a test experience has to be gone through on one's own; nobody stands by to direct you at a crucial intersection; there is often no help forthcoming to deal with seemingly impossible dilemmas. The trial is wholly within one's own life structure and it is full of choices; what do I sincerely desire, what is forbidden, what is it that is inevitably the result of my own actions? Indeed, there is something humiliating about it. No message in gilt letters is made available to us telling us that it is only a trial experience and that, if we only wait a bit, then in a longer or shorter while, the solution will come and we will be amply rewarded by some splendid insight. In the crude reality of the ordeal, one cannot know that the situation is a stone fallen far from the shattered wall and contains holy sparks seeking to return to their source. That the greater the trial, the greater the enlightenment it can bring and so on. It is simply very difficult to get any perspective at all, the varying distance of the lights making for distortion. That which is far away seems small; that which is close seems huge. Only when the shell is broken is perspective restored; the test puts things in place; a person finds himself.

The awfulness of sensing that evil rules over the good, that injustice prevails, and that one is being dominated by circumstances beyond control makes for an accumulation of inner power to assert the holiness. So, too, Israel may be said to have grown in adversity. In other words, there is a hint here at an extension to the truth of the shell and the breaking of the shell by trial. There seems to be a strong attraction of evil towards the good. And it is a double attraction. On one hand, evil needs the good in order to survive, to feed off it, to become whatever it has to become, and it clings to whatever goodness comes its way in desperation. The other characteristic of all the sparks of existence, including evil, is the urge to return to source, to be redeemed in God, and this impulse requires some other sparks of a higher level to rise up. Often this is done by mischievous persecution or trouble-making. The shell cannot, of itself, be delivered from its crusty inability to change; it needs the holy sparks that exist in the very force which will try to exterminate it. Evil thus can be viewed as a nuisance factor, a trouble-maker who only wants attention. Once the Divine Light is revealed behind all of it, the play is seen for what it is.

One may maintain that it is a rather childish game of hide-and-seek. But the problem is that it is not only a matter of the sparks seeking their Divine source. There is the problem of having a proper vessel for holiness. And the vessel has to be large enough and strong enough to contain the sparks. They have already fallen into unworthy vessels and the result was the bursting and a remorseless spreading of uncleanness. How shall they now be redeemed? Just by removing them from the corruption into which they have fallen, by breaking the shell, we are freeing a certain fragment. In order to restore the world as a whole, we have to strive to extinguish all the evil. One can pass through the ordeal by oneself, and that is perhaps as much as can be expected of one. One has thereby effected a *Tikkun*, a reparation of injury and correction of wrong. Holy sparks have been released. The other, greater task of man is to refuse to receive evil anymore, to bar admittance to all evil – to be occupied only with light, with that which is beyond the grasp of darkness, beyond one's own capacities to understand.

In such a development of the soul, there is a thrust that allows a person to realize his love for God. And this includes two aspects. One is the redemption of the spark that is able to encompass much more and the other is the redemption that is thereby added to man. As the Rambam said, we are in a great darkness, not knowing before or behind, and then there is a flash of lightning, which, for a moment, shows us where we are and makes it possible to move ahead.

The trial experience of a person adds the light necessary for progress. He may not be able to hold on to it for long and often it eludes him completely. Nevertheless, this light can raise a person to a much higher level, if only because he touched it and became involved for a critical moment.

Chapter eleven

As indicated, the trial experience is thus the way a person confronts evil as it appears in the *klipa* or shell. The splendor of the Divine Light in the enclosed core is not yet apparent; only the shell is there before one and the struggle expresses itself as a breaking process, a violent shattering of this visible outer form. Thereupon the fruit appears, which reward is also restitution for the broken shell. The standing up to trial is not a matter of repairing the shell, of altering anything in the external world of appearances; the shell remains a hard covering that has to be broken into fragments, and it is this shattering that is *Tikkun*, correction or reparation. So long as the nut remains as it is given, as a shell, swallowing it whole may be disastrous; it has to be smashed and/ or discarded and only what remains within it can be safely absorbed.

In order to purge the land of evil and for the darkness of Divine Hiddenness to be removed from the lives of the people, to overcome suffering, that is, there seems to be a need to undergo such trials or testing of one's own being. To do it successfully, however, there has to be some intimation of the Hidden Light; one should have an idea that there is something worthwhile awaiting one. And indeed, there is almost always such an occasional glimpse available; everyone has known a glimmer of light, hinting at what is covered over and concealed. This glimpse is of the possible restitution of the world at the end of time, the final *Tikkun*. The little private glimpses of truth simply aid us in the struggle. But, of course, the complete illumination, the real light, the redemption, can only come as a total experience of the race of man. Everything is interrelated, in this sense; nothing and no one can be isolated.

Of course, we each deal with one shell at a time, each to his own trial. The knowledge, however, of the fact that one is a small part of the vast human testing, which is reality as we know it, adds proportion. We are able to manage with partial enlightenment; we can wait for the greater once we know that it exists. We get only a glimpse of the great structure that is being built; but it enables us to take note of the possibility of something greater than what we are able to understand.

Passing a test adds to a person's capacity to rise to a higher degree of soul. The reason for this is that this spark, which is an aspect of chaos, *Tohu*, is higher than the soul in terms of *Tikkun*, or restitution, and therefore, it can penetrate one's soul, in the aspect of *Da'at*, knowledge, as it is written, "for God tests you to know." If a person is privileged to make contact with the inner spark that exists in the shell, this spark, as said, is an aspect of *tohu*, and as such it is of a higher level than *Tikkun*. This means that *tohu*, in every place, is higher than *Tikkun*, and when a man reveals the inner spark that exists in evil, he thereby reveals what was in *tohu*; and when this holiness is revealed and comes forth, there is created another enlightenment altogether, because then a person is connected with holiness of a very high level, and by its power, a person comes to be on a higher level than previously. Therefore, he links up with very high powers that formerly were distorted, that used to be hidden, and when he succeeds in making contact with them, he is elevated to a higher consciousness of an entirely different order.

Hence the trial experience brings a person to *Da'at* or Knowledge, not because one learns something from the experience; sometimes one does, sometimes one does not – generally not. But the standing up to the test is a process of shattering evil, and this breaking of the covering and revealing the spark of light within enhances a person unconsciously and raises him to a higher level, which is also a matter of *Da'at*. "Thereby shall a person grow into an awareness of the greatness of *Da'at*," of know-ing God, which was not so before the experience of the trial.

To know God is here not a matter of being cognizant of some-thing outside one's own experience by being informed about it; it is not merely an intellectual knowledge acquired by mental effort. It is a knowl-edge of inner feeling or certainty, like the feeling of one's own self. And this certainty, of an inner reality that is beyond sensual apprehension, is perhaps a greater certainty than anything else. Thus, too, one is able to love God with all one's heart and soul, and also to fear Him. Because God is then a reality beyond mental doubt.

When one has undergone a trial experience and has emerged undamaged and more whole, there is a certain awakening of the soul that does not come from directly learning from the experience and does not even seem to be associated with the trial. In a trial of poverty or riches, it does not matter if the person stood up to the test. Whereas in a trial of suffering, there is a more definite awareness of standing up to it and passing through the adversity. It is not an intellectual challenge or situation in which one learns something new. The trial ordeal is a shat-tering of the shell that had arisen and demanded a certain alteration of self. And when the outer shell was broken, its evil aspect was also bro-ken and thereupon the Divine spark was connected with the inner me. Whereupon there was a light shed within this "me" and something was added that did not before exist as part of my essence.

It is, in a way, like the process that occurs when a person swal-lows a medicinal pill. Whatever it is that is in the pill has to be ingested, its covering dissolved, and the contents must work on one and effect changes in one without one's awareness. Similarly, the trial experience with its breaking of the shell, emergence of the redeeming path, and freeing of the sparks allows *Da'at* to emerge. As the Sages said, "if there is no understanding there is no knowledge" – "אם אין בינה אין דעת." We have claimed that experience brings knowledge of God and spiritual enlightenment. For it is known that the *Sefirot* in the *tohu* that was shat-tered were an aspect of *Nekudot*. They came from the aspect of 63 or סג, which aspect, as described in the *Kabbala of Etz Ḥaim* is one of the different ways of writing out the name of God, with its specific choice of consonants adding up, arithmetically, to 63. In this aspect of the broken Chaos, there are no *partzufim* (countenances), only *Nekudot* (points). The *partzuf* emerges from a certain combination of parts of the various *Sefirot*, and their consequent containment or transmission of information. This information creates in itself the *partzuf* or recognizable countenance, an image or level of definite being containing parts that are in some orderly relation to one another. The world of *tohu* or Chaos however has many lights and few vessels. The lights are very much greater. In the world of *tohu*, there are no combinations because each *Sefira* exists in its own absolute independence. It cannot be included or become a part of anything else. There is a power of chaos in *tohu* that is almost infinite and it stands as only a point. Because it cannot make contact, standing as it does, alone in all its power and all the fullness of its own purity. Therefore, when there is some attribute of the aspect of מ"ב present, this attribute cannot include or relate to another, it stands in its own absolute wholeness and is unable to attain to anything else beyond itself.

Consequently, the human emotions generally are not pure emotions, if one speaks in terms of the *Sefirot*; they are combined emotions. We have entities like *Ḥesed* of *Gevura* and *Gevura* of *Ḥesed*; and there are much more complex combinations in the category of *Gevura* of *Ḥesed* of *Gevura*.

Gevura of *Ḥesed*, for instance, is that state in which, for the sake of, and in the name of, love (*Ḥesed*), actions are done that are the very opposite of love, as in the maxim "spare the rod and spoil the child." The idea is that love is not absolute; it knows that there are other things in the world, and can allow itself to blend into something else. It's as though love makes room for its opposite, and does so for the sake of the beloved. To be sure, this sort of action can take place with any of the *Sefirot*. Out of fear or any other emotion, one can step aside and make room for a different attribute to take over. But for this there has to be a certain mental control over the attributes, a matter of discipline. When this is absent, there is no possibility for the attribute to adjust itself. The attribute simply reaches its extreme – when one loves, one loves completely; when one hates, it is the same. There can be no compromise or combination – the mind does not have control in such cases.

Among men, therefore, as we know, it is necessary for the attributes to be more plastic and for a person to refrain from extremism. An attribute stretched to the utmost will burst. Everyone learns that love, hatred, anger, and the like can lead to Hell if not curbed at some point. If the mind does not assume control, the attribute becomes a part of *tohu*, the world of Chaos. And, in *tohu*, the attributes are normally without limit, in their unadulterated pure state, and they cannot integrate with anything else; they cannot cooperate or blend. Each one exists in its own completeness and essence. Each one says, "I will rule."

In life, too, this occurs. When a person is grieving, he cannot be joyous; when someone gets angry, he finds it impossible to feel sympathy or to smile. And this is an aspect of *tohu* in existence. Every attribute tends to hold on to its own integral self and thereby to approach a breaking point. It is that which we call the world of *Nekudot*. And their *berur* – the resolution of the broken attributes of the world of *tohu* – is an aspect of *Bina* of *Atzilut*. That is where the resolution occurs, and a *partzuf* takes shape. The task of the world of *tohu* is not to build a better *tohu*. It is to destroy and demolish, and then to organize the substance of *tohu* in a new form. That is, the *tohu* is needed to build in terms of *partzuf*. *Tikkun*, then, is a concomitant factor in the process. The *partzuf* (countenance) of man is a wholeness, a level of existence based on an organic assembly of coherent parts that is connected to a wider reality. Thus, the difference between a human being and an animal is not much more than that. Man is not as strong as the lion or swift as the deer, but he can be brave and agile; he can do all sorts of specialized things, even though he is not, like an animal, built that way. The creatures derive much of their power from *tohu*, from a single capacity, a special aptitude for something or other. Thus, specialization can be said to belong to *tohu*; the one who has a certain capacity has to use it. The spider will spin its web with perfection in all circumstances, but it cannot make honey. Each to its own point of perfection. Man is the inclusive *partzuf* of all the attributes; no one attribute has complete predominance; he has his own countenance. When these sparks of chaos become ordered into an aspect of a *partzuf*, that which they were formerly – isolated and withdrawn each unto itself – become integrated in creative fashion into another kind of wholeness and unity. This is the *Tikkun* of the sparks of *tohu* – that after they are sorted out and released from evil, they are set in holy order and are able to become a *partzuf*, a countenance.

Therefore, sorting out and restitution (*Tikkun*) are aspects of *Bina* (Understanding). This sorting and developing is primary in the making of the *partzuf*. It is called Mother, as the one who carries the embryo. The concept father is the source of the seed, which is no more than a point. And only as the seed, the point (*Nekuda*), rests in the womb of the mother does it assume human form. The task of the mother concept is to develop the single, individual, point-like seed (*Nekuda* or *tohu* – self-sufficiency) into a *partzuf* or the wholeness of a particular child. The development of a living form is a result of countless relationships and interaction between biological, chemical, and other systems. A *partzuf* is not merely a consequence of enlargement or of growth; it is part of a complex creative process of mutually harmonizing forces molding a distinct whole. That which is called *Partzuf* or countenance is necessarily a unique and perfectly proportional oneness born of amazing complexity. The original point contained all this as a kernel that had to be opened, unraveled, and allowed to proliferate.

Like all creations – physical, literary, or intellectual – the essence of the result is in the development of the various aspects, possibilities, and relationships. When some more or less vital detail is missing, the final result is damaged, distorted, and impaired from the start; a child is born crippled. The task of this containment wherein the development takes place is that of the mother or *Bina*, which is the essence of the creation of the *partzuf*, of synthesis. It is similar to the earth's role of containment in the development of the seed into a plant, a tree.

Bina is thus called the Higher Mother, the constant source and nourishment of the other attributes or *Sefirot*. Its mode is not that of intellectual conception or emotional thrust; it is slow embryonic growth and development. The attributes themselves, like love or severity, *Gevura*, function by virtue of their innate attractions or repulsions, toward something and against something else. But for this impulse to become expressed in action requires a certain process which is connected with *Bina*. The mind (*Bina*) has to contemplate and give form to the initial impression. If that which is fearful approaches, its recognition and the imaginary conceptualization of consequences make the fear real. Without some such conscious development (*Bina*) no attribute can function (whether Ḥesed or *Gevura*, *Tiferet* or *Yesod*, etc.). All are thus constantly being nourished by *Bina*. The emotions draw their being from *Bina*, through contemplation, by nature of the creation of a *partzuf* from a single impression; a recognizable entirety has to become available to consciousness. When a person is suddenly startled, it takes a little while to determine what caused fear to take possession of the individual; when there's a sudden irresistible attraction, there has to be an awareness of the quality of the attraction. People without imagination are less inclined to emotional pleasures and stresses. The mind's role is crucial; the mother *Bina* creates a certain wholeness that works existentially in the attributes. Even a childish terror requires something to feed the imagination.

The exception of course, is the higher attribute of Ḥokhma or wisdom. As the "father," which nourishes the *Sefira* of *Bina* with the primordial seed, or *Nekuda*, it is complete in itself.

The contemplative action of *Bina* is not emotional; it is the basis for emotion – it does not create it. True, a person who contemplates a triangle may never reach any emotional heights, either of love or fear. The triangle may be analyzed but when any kernel of feeling is contemplated by *Bina*, it grows from a point to a unique form that makes the feeling wide and powerful. In this way, it is said, "If there is no *Bina*, there is no knowledge." After all *Da'at* is the inwardness of the attributes; it is itself the point (*Nekuda*) where contact of an emotional sort is made with the thing; *Da'at* is the root of all the attributes because it is that which transforms awareness to emotion, to feeling. This system we call *Da'at* is necessary if the soul is to participate. It is not enough just to see something objectively – so to say, without feeling anything for or against. A fact can be contemplated, even understood, but only *Da'at* supplies it with value, meaning, and emotional content. So reality only assumes emotional value when "known" by *Da'at*. One sees many objects, confronts many facts in the course of the day; only those that impinge themselves emotionally on the self become reality.

Thus *Bina* and *Da'at* are not the same at all. There can be *Bina* without *Da'at* even though there cannot be *Da'at* without *Bina*.

The kabbalistic insight into this matter reverts to the view that all the *Nekudot* of *tohu* are an aspect of the Seven Attributes that fell at the Shattering of the Vessels. And these seven are the seven kings of Edom who ruled before there was any king in Israel. It is a certain kind of soul world that never had a mother and therefore, was never absorbed or developed to become a *partzuf*. The inner essence of these lights was beyond the power of the Attributes. The essence of the *tohu* could not cultivate or accept these *Nekudot* and therefore, they continue to fall and shatter. These broken sparks have to be repaired anew, reconstructed by the aspect of *Bina*. Except that this is impossible. They are not born whole, only fragmented. Every such spark, which was once a single *Nekuda*, is shattered into pieces and each of these fragments is now a beginning and it is necessary for each fragment to be put in its proper place in the primordial pattern. That is to say, Ḥesed of *tohu* is now broken into a great many thousands, billions of kinds of Ḥesed. And this Ḥesed of the shell has to undergo the stage of *Tikkun* so that each one of its fragments becomes transformed into a total image. And all these images afterwards are combined, woven together into a complete weave of a single essence.

Therefore, if there is no *Bina*, there is no *Da'at*. And if there is no *Bina*, the *Da'at* cannot be formed. This matter of "knowing God" comes from the spark, and this spark is entirely emotion. The broken sparks are all of them pure emotions, vast in their comprehensiveness, and very strong. Therefore, this world and the *klipa*, or shell, are so aggressively assertive; everything in them is exaggeratedly prominent and overbearing.

In order for the spark to become something definite, it has to pass through the passage of the aspect of *Da'at*, to reach its own *Tikkun* and its greater structure. Actually, the trial experience wants to know God, but one cannot know God without the instrument of *Bina*. Therefore, what happens, as we have said, if a person stands up to the test and he has no *Bina*, he is then still incapable of response. He has released the holy spark, but he cannot do anything with it because this spark has no place to plant itself – it is not on my own level; it is not my size and I cannot relate to it because it is created beyond my reality. In order to get planted in my own private reality in entirety, or even partially, it has to pass through the medium of *Bina*.

Incidentally, it has been noted here that if there is no *Da'at*, there is no *Bina*. This is an aspect of Higher *Da'at* that unites Ḥokhma and *Bina*. There are two levels of *Da'at*. The lower is *Da'at* that is the connection between *Bina* and the emotions. In which order of things, there in Ḥokhma, *Bina*, and *Da'at*. We have Ḥokhma and then *Bina* and then *Da'at*. The aspect of *Da'at* is the conclusion of *Bina* that makes the connection between the emotions and *Bina*, and this is called *Da'at*, to know. The more there is of this level of *Bina*, the more whole, complete, and comprehensive *Da'at* becomes. Before this, there is this matter of *Da'at Elyon*, Higher *Da'at*, because Ḥokhma and *Bina* by themselves also need some kind of connection.

Again, if we consider Ḥokhma in its most elemental state, the *Nekuda* is the spark of brilliant awareness. This is the quality of those people whose power is to create ideas. They can create brilliant notions, flashes of ideas, but they cannot develop them. Just as there are people whose ability is chiefly to develop ideas and not to create them. Thus, there can be a situation where there is no proper connection between Ḥokhma and *Bina*. It's as though a person has ideas and can understand and explain them, but by himself he cannot bring them to a point of application. There is some impairment, damage, in the *Nekuda* of transfer, the points of translation that are called the paths of wisdom. For some reason or other, it is considered a damage in *Da'at*. And this impairment of *Da'at* is the factor that makes Ḥokhma, the idea, unable to express itself. What happens is that a person cannot understand himself, and he cannot do so because there is a *Tikkun* needed in the process itself. There is this aspect of "if there is no *Da'at*, there is no *Bina*." If there is no *Da'at*, in the sense of a connection between Ḥokhma and *Bina*, there is no *Bina*. A person finds himself with ideas and brilliant insights, but these flashes (of wisdom) cannot create *Bina* because the essence of *Bina* is that it cannot create, of itself, the primary objects of thought.

What we are here considering is "if there is no *Bina*, there is no *Da'at*." In order to grasp it – in spite of the statement that God tries you to know whether you love Him or not – if there is no *Bina* that can receive this *Da'at*, the *Da'at* cannot accomplish anything. Therefore, it is necessary to bring *Bina* forward to absorb the *Da'at* that is created in the trial experience, thus enabling the person to receive it in some fashion or other. Even in pragmatic terms of an experiment, tools are needed to absorb or receive. No matter what happens – whether it's an external action or reading a text, the equipment for apprehending it is crucial. It's true in every experiment, test, or trial. One needs the proper means, tools, instruments to make sense of it all. If there is no *Bina*, there is no *Da'at*. Knowledge needs understanding to absorb these experiences and to develop them.

Chapter twelve

Carrying our inquiry further, there is the matter of the love hidden in all human souls that is manifest only as a *Nekuda*, an aspect of concentrated pointedness. It is a *Nekuda* in the sense that it is a self-sufficient essence, not dependent on the consciousness of a person, nor on what he knows or comprehends. It belongs to one's essential being, indeed like any other aspect that is not a *Nekuda* (such as biochemical processes or feelings of self), except that it remains a self-contained center of the being, hidden away, independent of awareness or thought.

In particular, this concealed love, especially when it is a love of God, is of the nature of a *Nekuda*, in as much as it lies concentrated in the depths of the heart and has no size or expansion as yet. It is also *Nekuda* because, at its essential source, it is a hidden point of love, unable to include a reason or a method, a why or how, and it has no form, only a single center of communication, for connection, for relation. It is like those *Nekudot* of which we have spoken that remain forever a single wholeness or self-sufficient entity. As such a perfect entity it is also very aggressively itself, jealous of its independence.

In the *Tanya*, mention is made of a situation in which this secret love is made manifest. A person reaches a state of sudden decision and then, even though in his previous life there did not appear to be any awareness of such love, no signs of it having been evident, suddenly, it all comes to a head and ignites. Everything that the person had been previously conscious of changes; he is now ready to die for God with a love that bursts forth from its concealment.

It appears that this *Nekuda* of hidden love can be uncovered and made manifest, at which time it can also become a continuous thing. That which was a point can become a flame that spreads to all of one's being and beyond. The concealment of this love may thus be seen as a concentration, a potential. How can it become a *partzuf* (a recognizable entity)? It is a matter of *Tikkun*, a development of certain attributes that is also a growth, as mentioned: How is this done?

First of all the process of growing has to be done within the aspect of Mother *Bina*. This is true also of the human soul, incidentally. The soul grows by contemplation on the greatness of the Divine, insofar as one's mind can do so. Hence, too, contemplation and probing are the means that enable the hidden love, the single *Nekuda*, to become manifest. This isolated *Nekuda* simply needs a place where it can grow. And this place, like the mother's womb, is *Bina*, the contemplation and deepening of "knowing." It is necessary to absorb the essence of the concealed love by letting it grow in the congenial surroundings of understanding.

From which it may be gathered that from *Bina* comes *Da'at* (knowledge), which is the inwardness of the emotions. Indeed, without *Bina* there can be no *Da'at*. The point of deep feeling, in itself, does not become manifest. It does so only when there is the influence of *Bina*, just as, when a person gets angry, or falls in love, more is needed than a point of provocation; there is a certain amount of thinking, imagining, and turning the feeling this way and that before the sensation becomes a passionate rage or uncontrollable desire. Without this incubation in *Bina*, the matter remains – as with children – a passing upsurge, a flash of reactivity with no development.

It may be compared to a situation in which a certain practical problem is faced and an expert is called in to render advice – whether to give the problem more thought and effort or whether to drop it. If the problem is indeed important enough, it is worth taking a risk and making the effort. If one does not bother to make the effort and to think about the problem – like contemplating the greatness of God – nothing much can be gained. The contemplation here is an exploration in depth to get to genuine understanding. To be sure there are grades of understanding, and no matter how much one understands any matter, there is always more; the essential thing is to attain a level of understanding that is meaningful for oneself. And this, too, requires a certain persistence, a minimal penetration beyond the externally given.

For example: a person may have learned something well enough to be able to talk about it. Nevertheless, he doesn't really understand what he is saying. He has become acquainted with the forms, the external, visible structure, but nothing more, and he does not grasp its purpose or meaning or even its function. When one asks such a person a question in a different context than that in which he spoke, he will be unable to answer. That is, he has not absorbed the truth of the matter. He knows only the outer aspect; he has acquired information about the subject but no comprehension. Real understanding is also a matter of the heart's participation; indeed, in most human situations, the secret love in the heart has to be awakened as well.

All of which is to shed light on the fact that the *Nekuda* of love, of fear, and of faith exist in the essential soul. But they exist only as concentrated *Nekuda* potential; they are not yet manifest because they have no space, no soil in which to sprout and to grow. Many people thus remain only possible persons of any significance; they never had the chance to develop. For instance, it is said that Jews are intrinsically shy, compassionate, and kind. But if there is a social framework that does not allow for natural kindness to express itself, the capacity may be stifled; it remains in the root of the soul only as a potential. Kindness, without space for development or structure for giving it expression, is suppressed, crushed at the start. Thus, without *Bina*, there is no *Da'at*; without a place in which to flourish, *Da'at* cannot exist.

From which it may be gathered that the *galut*, the exile of the Jews, and indeed much of what is considered misfortune, may be considered in another light. The exile is also known as *hester panim* – a concealment of the Divine countenance. And, as it is written (Deuteronomy 31:18), many evils follow upon such a hiding of God's Light. If God does not pay special attention to His people or to a person, evil penetrates the defensive mechanism and tends to gain control.

This is where the trial experience enters. The trial is the human confrontation with that which is evil in one form or another. For evil can appear in any number of disguises: as bad luck, human malevolence, or wickedness. There is evil that only seems to be bad for one, like a toothache, and there is evil that only seems to be good. There are bitter evils and there are sweet evils. In this sense, the trials of life are of all sorts, such as the test of poverty and the test of riches. In which case, a trial experience could be a relatively pleasant affair, a relatively painless procedure, so to speak, but in terms of being tested, the standards are just as rigid.

The concealment of the Divine countenance is that which happens when the guiding hand ceases to guide and seems to vanish altogether, when the reality of the world, the circumstances of life strike at one in a cruel fashion and one feels without support, like a driven leaf, and the misfortunes keep coming. The trial comes to sort out the sparks that are integrated in the *klipa* or shell that confronts one. Its task, as we have said, is twofold. First, the person is tested in his capacity to rise above the situation. It consists of the ability to put up a barrier between oneself and the assaulting evil. Then, he is tested in his power to raise the level of reality itself. The procedure is thus a double action, upon the person and upon the experience itself. It acts to elevate the person and it acts on the reality of the circumstance, to raise it to a "higher" level. (The shell of the nut has to be cracked and the kernel eaten. The situation has to be given a life-enhancing quality.) In other words, the trial experience, as we have said, is so constituted that a certain smashing is necessary in order to raise up the "fragments," the sparks of holiness that are contained within it. Sorting out the life enhancing or the holy in this manner is also called an embryonic process, an incubation within the mother womb, as a result of which *Da'at* is formed and eventually manifested. So, too, the exile and all the misfortunes of human banishment from God are periods of transition, of inner growth and ultimate birth, of manifestation in truth.

Amongst the ancient prophets, like Isaiah and Jeremiah, the image often used to represent redemption was the birth process, the coming into life. And the period before birth is a time of gestation, a time of pregnancy, of preparation, and inner transmutation. There is also a clear difference here between the revealed and the hidden. The embryonic growth takes place within covered recesses, in a certain protective darkness. In order to reach the aspect of *Da'at*, there has to be a breaking out, in the nature of a trial experience. Certain types of knowledge demand that the knower stands up to a test. The challenge is part of the learning. The experience of trial and overcoming is a necessary part of attaining to knowing God.

The attributes in the tree of the *Sefirot* that follow after *Da'at* get their inwardness, their vital meaning, from *Da'at*. Thus the manifestation of love as a prevailing quality comes as a result of contemplation; it is also a birth process out of a gestation situation. So, too, is the coming out (exodus) from Egypt a redemptive process of this nature.

It may be summarized, therefore, from the aforesaid that the trials of life serve two purposes: to give birth to *Da'at* (through the womb or *klipa* and the breaking out) and then to understand (through the development of inwardness) what has emerged from the experience. As it is written in the Scriptures, a person can receive a scroll in the ordeal of a test, but if he cannot read it, there is not much gained. One has to comprehend that which has been brought to one's attention by the trial.

This introduces another question. Why does one have to pass through an ordeal at all? Why cannot this ordering of life, the sorting out of the Divine sparks and putting them in their proper place (*Tikkun*), be accomplished by some other means, such as the positive mitzva, the simple performance of a Torah commandment like the *etrog* or *tefillin*? By doing the mitzva, with blessing and proper action, the holy sparks in material substance are released. Prayer, too, raises the level of reality. That is to say, there are other ways of releasing sanctity, of going from one level of being to another, besides the trial experience. Why the anguish of the test?

The matter involves a certain amount of probing into the nature of the *klipa* shell. As we know from the esoteric wisdom, there are two kinds of shell: the *klipat noga* and *klipa temaya* (unclean). The first includes much of the world around us – inanimate things and living creatures, plants and people. *Klipat noga* is simply that which is not either distinctly good or bad in itself; it is the ordinary world of varying and undefined degrees of importance for man. For the most part, it belongs to the permitted and not the forbidden, but on the whole it is such a mixture of good and bad that it may be considered neutral. That is to say, it is *klipa* or shell, insofar as it is not holy. The other *klipa* is a total unclean category of shell and is itself divided into three grades. On the whole, however, this unclean *klipa* consists of that which is absolutely forbidden in the Torah. For instance, all trees belong to the *klipa noga* but the first fruit for the first three years of any tree is considered *orla*, absolutely forbidden. The fruit from the same tree in the fourth year becomes *klipa noga*, permitted, that which is given to *Tikkun*. The unclean shells are not given to any kind of *Tikkun*.

This brings us to the root of the matter concerning the difference between the mitzva "to do" and the mitzva "not to do." By performing the positive mitzva, to do something, the *klipat noga* is sorted out. It is a line of holiness directed to a secular object. The positive mitzva can include action on anything in the universe; indeed, the secular object to which it relates may be the person himself, the body of the performer. A mitzva is done on the body, a certain selection takes place in which the *klipat noga* is sorted out and raised up; the essence of the object is transformed by means of holiness.

The prohibited things, however, in their three unclean *klipot*, cannot be sorted out or raised up. Hence the negative commandment, the mitzva not to do, such as "Thou shalt not eat of the blood," etc., is absolute. Whereas in the realm of the permitted, where the *klipat noga* prevails, the mitzva to do can release the holy spark. The realm of the forbidden, however, cannot even be approached; the injunction is firmly clear, to keep away. This avoidance is not necessarily to prevent the objects from joining the side of holiness; it is to safeguard the person. When a person eats forbidden fruit, he brings it into himself, he draws sustenance from the *klipa* and the *klipa* becomes a part of him, a part of his humanity. It acts upon him to his detriment. The mitzva not to do is concerned with the hygiene of the spiritual world. If something is dirty or poisonous as spiritual influence, do not touch it.

To be sure, it may be agreed that nothing in the created world can be totally unclean; nothing is altogether bad. A complete evil could not exist, it is really only an abstraction, a concept. For existence itself is holy, if only because of Divine Sanction to let anything "be." Even these *klipot* of the three categories of the unclean have sparks of holiness in them; it's just that they simply cannot be sorted out. That is to say, the difference between the holy spark in the *noga* shell, *klipat noga*, and in the unclean shell, *klipa temaya*, is that in the *klipat noga*, there is something that can be separated out. In the unclean *klipa*, there is something that cannot be separated out; the good and the evil cannot be taken apart because they are so tightly bonded.

For instance, in very crude terms, we may note that wood pulp (cellulose) has more or less the same ingredients as sugar. And, theoretically, it can be converted. But the starches and sugars are so complex that the body can receive sustenance only from bread, a special kind of substance originating from the same kind of vegetation. A person cannot swallow a piece of wood or a stalk of vegetable fiber and be nourished. It would only harm him. On the other hand, a cow can eat paper or grass and be nourished by it because its stomach is equipped to digest it and extract the energy that man cannot get at. In such manner does the unclean *klipa* have the evil so especially mixed in it that the mitzva cannot redeem it. No sanctified action can avail; man cannot extract the holy spark from the evil. Hence, a transgression cannot be made into a mitzva. (If a person were to take a forbidden object and try to do a mitzva with it, it could not be done.) And since there is no way of redeeming the spark in the shell of the unclean *klipot*, we keep the shell with the spark intact. One cannot deal with the *klipa*; it is dangerous and harmful; to take it apart would be beyond one's powers. Therefore, one throws it all away, shell and spark. In Torah, it is known as the forbidding mitzva, the "*mitzva lo ta'aseh.*"

The unclean shells are forever beyond repair; only when evil has passed from the world and death has been swallowed forever will the spirit of uncleanness pass away. The world of Torah and mitzvot, in its normal essence, cannot deal with it. The only restitution is by way of repentance and the way of the trial. These two function not only through the proper and accepted channels, but also in the opposite direction; they can work precisely by way of the forbidden. They even function best on that which is prohibited. That is, the closer the trial experience is to the realm of the forbidden, the low, and the ignominious, the more lost a spark it is in its powerful willfulness and incompliancy; the greater the test and the more meaningful the overcoming of the ordeal. As a result, the person can rise to a higher level or *madrega*.

Chapter thirteen

A s mentioned, the sorting out of the holy sparks takes place when the matter in question is of *klipat noga*, which is neutral in essence, and the action involved is in the domain of the positive mitzva, "to do." The mitzva, however, is not only an action done by a person; it is also an action done on the person himself. The body of the doer, which is also a *klipa* shell, participates in the process and is acted upon as well as acting. The process is thus a double process of selection, that of the person and that of the thing. And it all takes place within the domain of the *noga* shell, the domain of the permitted.

What about the domain of the forbidden, the unclean, which also has holy sparks bound up within it? The answer is that there is nothing to be done about it. Only at the end of days will there be a *Tikkun* (restitution) of the unclean. That which is prohibited cannot ever be raised up. Whereas in the domain of the permitted, even without intention one can raise up an object to holiness, as happens with a mechanical benediction over kosher food.

Non-kosher food can never be raised up to holiness, no matter how many benedictions are said intentionally or in error. No ordinary human action can shatter the unclean shell and release the captured sparks.

What, then, is the fate of these holy sparks that fell so far from the source precisely because they were higher (as in the metaphor of a bursting wall)? The answer is repentance – which transforms the transgressions to merit. By turning around and repenting, a person can change the nature of his past actions – the non-kosher food he ate that brought him to this state gains a certain value and can now be classed among the meritorious actions that brought his life to a higher level. The repentant thus raises the holy sparks that were in the unclean shells by transforming evil into good.

The *tzaddik*, too, can effect such a transformation of the unclean shells. His sorting-out action constitutes a process of rejection; either he casts them out entirely, or else, by thrusting them aside, he does not allow them to influence the good. Nevertheless, he is unable to raise them up. Only repentance of a high level (which the *tzaddik* can also perform, of course) can transform the lower *klipot*. Hence it is said that a repentant can stand on a higher level than a *tzaddik* who does not repent.

Probing more deeply into the pervasive problem of evil, where the disposition of the sparks is indeed an endless task, we have to refer to the negative mitzva, to the injunction to refrain from a particular action. And, it is said that the negative mitzva is higher than the positive mitzva to perform some action. The idea is that those things which can be fully understood can be given a positive definition, whereas those things that cannot be completely grasped can only be defined in negative terms. That is to say, the *mitzvot lo ta'aseh* are negative definitions of an insufficiently understood (transcendent) reality. They are thus, at root, higher, being based on our relation to ungraspable truths. Nevertheless, the negative mitzvot only thrust away the shells by a kind of avoidance; it is not really a sorting-out process. At the same time, there is a raising up of the doer. The deliberate rejection of evil (in any form) is itself a higher mode of action than compliant obedience. Because there is always the possibility that the evil sparks will not only be repulsed but that they will also be transmuted. *Tikkun* or reparation is never to be ruled out. The one who performs a negative mitzva can also be said to serve repentance; he makes a distinction and helps define the inimical. Therefore, the action of a negative mitzva may be considered to be on a higher level.

In spite of this fact – that overcoming evil brings one to a higher level – there is no denying that involvement with evil is not a way to follow. To be sure there were those who tried to pass through transgression safely by raising the sparks to holiness, such as certain followers of the Shabtai Zvi (false messiah) movement. But the notion of accomplishing a higher good through evil is both theoretically and practically unsound and leads to disaster.

Here, we come back to the issue of trial. There is a way that a *tzaddik* can sort out the unclean shell, and that is when he stands up to a test. An extreme example is the Bible story (in the Book of Daniel) of Nebuchadnezzar testing the three young friends of Daniel – Hananiah (Shadrach), Mishael (Meshach), and Azariah (Abed-nego) – by throwing them into the blazing furnace. They had been accused of refusing to bow down to the golden image. The trial of fire is the place of absolute evil, where the various layers of the shells must burn away. And, even though we do not here consider the matter of the miracle, which may be irrelevant to our argument, the fact is that when the higher man is in control over the lower man, when the shells are overcome, the ultimate good is revealed. When absolute evil is in control, the burning fire consumes. When a person stands up to Divine Trial, he is protected; the absolute evil is sorted out and made ineffectual. It is an elimination process, an excluding of the three shells of uncleanness. By passing the test, the *tzaddik* casts out the evil from the deepest shell; he simply breaks through its encompassment and raises the holy spark that was imprisoned therein to its source.

From which it may be gathered that all trial experiences are issues of sovereignty: who is in control, man or shell? Even the testing of Job can be seen as a struggle with the shell; he, too, had to sort out the evil. Like any *tzaddik*, that is, he had to sunder all contact with evil, refrain from bargaining with it, and expel it completely. And like any repentant, he had to extricate himself from the encompassing wrongness and release the holy spark caught in its net.

It may be said: every *tzaddik* to his own initiation into sainthood. It is not simply a matter of a person not being able to pass a test, then making another try and passing it. The trial experience, in its spiritual aspect, is far more complex. Its secret lies in the nature of the conflict and the manner of dealing with it. There are all sorts of temptations and inner struggles with transgression. And these are astonishingly parallel to the level of one's capacities. When a *tzaddik* is being tried, his trial has two aspects. One is the Divine grace behind the placement of the person in such a situation. The *tzaddik* so chosen has not been able to rise to a higher level; he may even be in a state of decline, he may be falling. Thus, he is given a test. But, as so many stories tell us, everything he has ever felt or known seems to leave him; his previously achieved powers of understanding are of no avail; he has to pass the test unaided, so to speak. He must draw upon the deepest resources of his soul.

The premise, of course, is that the *tzaddik* cannot rise except in the intermediate space between one rung of the ladder and another. He has to be at a point of perilous transition, unbalanced and even dangling between one stage and the next. It is a point of decline and, precisely for this reason, a proper stage for trial experience. The difference between the test of a *tzaddik* and that of a "wicked" lies in the capacity for resurgence, the ability to pull out of a crisis by rallying inner spiritual forces.

The other aspect of the trial of a *tzaddik* is even more complex, being more impersonal and profound. Not only is one confronted with a situation of one's own weakness and temporary loss of control, but there is a total crisis of faith. Divine Providence seems to be in doubt. There is a terrible crisis of faith in God, not only in the life that one has fashioned for oneself. The great figures of the Bible contend as best they can – wrestling stubbornly or arguing with God or acting the martyr. For each, it is an extreme experience from which he (or she) emerges wounded and troubled, enlightened, and elevated. And one can give examples from Abraham, Isaac, and Jacob to Moses and Job, from the prophets to the saints of all time. The test of a *tzaddik* is usually a formidable instance of critical decision, of choosing between moral alternatives at the highest level. The so-called sins of Moses, for example, were the result of a clash between his extreme devotion to God and equally extreme love of the people.

For ordinary persons, the trial is usually an encounter of one sort or another with the essence of evil. It may be at a very high level not very different in essence from the testing of a *tzaddik* or it can be at a lower level of the human struggle against the demonic. In all instances, as we have said, the struggle is a breaking of the shell that has no *Tikkun* and extricating the kernel that is life enhancing. The trial experience cannot be a compromise; the shell has to be shattered. To be sure, the Kabbala has numbered at least four layers of the shell, each with its own peculiar resistance – *noga* shell is the fourth and, in a way, the most difficult to overcome. Nevertheless, there is always help that comes from above and, therefore, the shattering blow that breaks the shell need not be altogether a result of one's own efforts. The trial is often a situation, a temptation, an ordeal that has to be accepted. That is primary, the acceptance of it as real; one must not flee from it, saying it is not real or of no concern. Then, there has to be a certain declaration within, a matter of saying "no" to the evil temptation while recognizing its power.

To be sure, as has been mentioned, the trial experience is not only a rejection of evil, it is also a sorting out of the evil and a reparation or correction (*Tikkun*) of evil. Therefore the *mitzvot lo ta'aseh*, the negative injunctions, which may not seem so vital, are actually the more important mitzvot. The difficulty in grasping this lies in the fact that these negative mitzvot are not usually accompanied by overt suffering. One simply avoids some action or thing; *avoda zara* can just be ignored – one does not bring it into one's home, and therefore, it is relatively easy to be righteous. But when an impulse of some kind takes control over one's being and one has to overcome it, there is a test situation. The shell has to be broken by non-action. For example: in the case of forbidden sexual attraction within a large family circle, the distress and torment may be a greater ordeal than anything of an external nature. In many ways, the struggle of "negative" obedience, to refrain, can be extremely demanding. For, as is fairly well known, the greater the power of the temptation or urge, the more painful the abstinence. The process of merely sorting out the bad – calling it by name – usually has little effect; there has to be a controlling action. It may involve much time and patience as well as anguish; and only *Tikkun* is the final victory. There may be no sign of change in the world, but what has been accomplished is a transformation of the unclean to holiness.

The person who thus stands up to the test really places himself, in his entirety, before the evil; he exposes his inward being in the process and smashes that which is inimical in himself. He breaks it as a result of a certain conscious effort. The *Tikkun*, or repentance, of the *ba'al teshuva* – the one who returns to the fold – does not necessarily deal with the depths of evil. Whereas the *Tikkun* of the one who stands up to a trial experience, does get to the depths. It has to reach the roots of the evil that is being confronted in order to contend with it. It's not a matter of something that was done in the past; one must wrestle with a present evil whose grip must be overcome. By so gaining a certain supremacy, one approaches sanctity; the power of the evil that was overcome becomes a seat of goodness that can be a step towards holiness. The one being tested does not struggle only against the consequences of evil, that which was done in the past; he struggles against evil as it faces him, and endeavors to extirpate its power. He has to uproot, to eliminate from himself, the very essence of evil, and thereby, he comes closer to sanctity. There is a transmutation of evil here into an instrument for the release of a spark of holiness, which transmuted spark is somehow higher and more complete than other sparks.

The work of the trial experience thus raises the holy sparks very high, more so even than does the action of the positive mitzva. It can be said to occur on an exalted level of the spiritual life, in spite of accompanying difficulties; and its *Tikkun* is correspondingly outstanding and unique. Indeed, the greater the trial and the more intense the struggle, the more profoundly does it change and rectify the essence of evil.

Although it may not be a trial experience in the usual sense, the moment of death may also be seen as a confrontation with the ultimate evil. The *tzaddik* will make the most of it – since no man may see God and live – by recognizing the moment as his supreme test and victory, wherein he shatters the last shell, which is his physical self, and thereby breaks through to the kernel of eternal life. Thus, too, the martyr who chooses death (rather than apostasy), and the one who, in devoting himself utterly to the life of goodness and the spirit, is like a martyr to the Lord in terms of renunciation, are both meeting death in this way, even when there is no actual physical exterminator.

The end of the trial ordeal is thus to learn something, to "know," as it is written, "God tests you to know." And this, in turn, needs Understanding or *Bina*, which reminds us that there is a process involved – a process of dynamic meditation or learning growth, like the development of the embryo in the womb. It is not enough for there to be a first cell of life (or knowledge); it must grow and develop in terms of *Bina*, the mother factor of Understanding.

The Kabbalistic literature mentions the need for a second aspect of growth following on the first embryonic stage. After standing up to the test, there must be adequate means or a vehicle to give the whole thing practical meaning. It must be expressed in life. With the infant, the various limbs and general attributes have to be formed from nothing. This second growth is what makes the beginning of a person into an individual human being. In the trial experience, a certain inner development is involved as well as an ordeal – an enlightenment that changes the original person.

The point is that, although all learning is rather empirical, a matter of experience, the empirical fact in itself cannot do much. It has to assume some significance; one has to understand the problem in order to grasp the solution. It is called meditative in essence because there has to be inner grasp, emotional as well as intellectual. There is a new recognition of oneself and a certain joy in ascent to a higher level. A new level consists of a new mind, a different way of seeing things.

Indeed, any rise to another level or *madrega* involves a new birth of sorts. What was effective before is no longer sufficient; the new revelation requires a new approach. On the other hand, one has not overcome suffering altogether; sometimes the very same things torment one. True, there has been a passage to a higher degree of sanctity, but it may be only the beginning of a new framework of test and trial. It's a matter of "going after God," stage upon stage, without any visible end.

Thus, the trial experience is not necessarily a single liberating process. It may well be followed very soon afterwards by another test, perhaps even more difficult, more profound, to enable the person to make even greater progress and get to the next level with the best results. The *tzaddik* is thus tested even more than ordinary men. It is the Divine Gift granted to those who can benefit by it, to make a *Tikkun* on the highest possible scale. That is to say, the *tzaddik* lives in his own closed world of perfection.

Chapter fourteen

In overcoming evil (in himself), the *ba'al teshuva*, the true repentant, manages to reach a higher level of spiritual being. The *tzaddik*, however, who does not have much to do with evil, transforms it only by the trial experience. Evil is fairly pervasive, and the need to struggle against it arises, primarily, when it threatens to become injurious. The *tzaddik*, thereupon, has to shatter the shell of evil and release the holy sparks caught in it by an act of sanctification – which is usually (as distinct from magic) also an inner test and an ordeal for him.

Such is the way of *Tikkun*. Evil is forever trying to get close to the good and to strike at it destructively. It fails by virtue of human resistance – that which is manifested in the trial experience when a person struggles within himself as well as outwardly. The result is *Tikkun*, as we have said, the curiously involuted process which indicates that the shattering of the vessels before creation was not just a primordial accident or a cataclysm, a matter of excessive force. Evil has a definite role to play in creation; it has a task in the struggle toward perfection.

Part of this task is to function as a temptation – an unavoidable enticement and contention. When a person is enduring a test, it means, quite simply, that the evil in and around him is doing what it is supposed to do from the very essence of creation; it is functioning properly as a bait, an allurement or magnet drawing a person out of his self-contentment. In the framework of holiness, evil can be transformed only if it is placed precisely where it belongs. Its purification is a process involving repentance in the widest sense, and it takes its own very special course. And this, incidentally, concerns the difference between the person who does not transgress and the one who stands up to a trial ordeal (whether he has transgressed or not). The problem here is the fact that when evil is not intrinsically a part of the process, there is no real trial.

For the trial takes place when there is some severance from the intimate relationship of one sort or another with evil. And there has to be a recognition of this relationship in order for the severance to be genuine and not merely difficult. One has to be aware of one's terrible vulnerability, of the way one is being controlled by something profoundly human and yet evil. Otherwise, there is no trial. Essentially, too, this is the basis for sincere knowing, selecting, and rising to a higher level.

All of which helps to explain the reason for suffering. And the possible benefits served by suffering. It has to be admitted that suffering often does cleanse, by discharging all manner of defilement. Evil lies deep in human existence, and it is hard, insensible, and obtuse, one layer upon another of shells. Pain and death are the gross manifestations of this pervasive evil, absolute in their detrimental potential often even beyond *Tikkun*. When a person goes through suffering – and if he can do so without inflicting too much harm upon himself – he thereby releases the holy spark hidden within the evil and redeems it.

As previously touched upon briefly, death by martyrdom is an ultimate degree of Divine test. The offering up of one's soul to God is a direct transmutation of the holy spark that was held captive in death, freeing it into a higher level of holiness. One thereby snatches from death its power over one. As soon as the mind ceases to be dominated by fear, death loses its sovereignty.

The idea that suffering comes from evil implies that pain is not holy. And indeed, pain is always a matter of the *Sitra Aḥra*, the other side, which is the dark and unholy aspect of human life. So that, when a person suffers and passes through an ordeal, the result is not only a triumph for himself, it is also a blow struck at the *Sitra Aḥra*. Pain is thereby inflicted on evil. The *Sitra Aḥra* becomes the suffering one and cries out with mortification at the loss of his despotic influence.

Thus, for example, the person who accepts a death sentence from an authorized *beit din* (court), recognizing its rightful punishment for his actions, finds himself in a dialectic relationship with death. He suffers, of course, the agonies of facing his physical mortality, but, at the same time, he is ennobled and exhilarated by the elevation of his soul to a higher level. Indeed it may be conjectured that the torments of death that come from violence, from one form or another of martyrdom, can become the factor that transforms death into something else, making a person into a saint. Someone, who, in life, was very much the opposite of holy, can so thoroughly shatter the shell at the last that what dies is the outer shell and not the soul. Death as punishment or complete repentance is also *Tikkun*; it amends the evil as well as the person. The shell is able to release the holy sparks held captive in it while it is being shattered. Death is transmuted; from being absolute evil, it becomes a door to sanctity.

As it is written, when a person is normally suffering evil the *Shekhina* weeps. Nevertheless, no attempt is made to ease the situation for the suffering one. It is as though a person contains his own wickedness, and the wicked have to suffer, and the *Shekhina* has to weep. If the *Shekhina* strove to avoid suffering to save itself from weeping, it would be doing the person an injustice. The suffering one needs his suffering; he should not be relieved of it. There is no other way, it seems. And, of course, there is no joy in it, in the giving or enduring of pain. But sometimes the living flesh has to be cut into, when the wound is fatal.

Suffering is consequently a complex structure in which purification, *Tikkun*, and pain work their dynamic action on the shell. The *klipa* covering, or shell, thereby undergoes transformation. It is a process of compulsion; the shell has to be forced to change through suffering. Hence, evil is a factor that cannot be dispensed with. Good cannot serve the purpose. Pain does it by freeing the person and freeing the shell that causes suffering. Sin is what happens when a person enhances his holiness by surreptitiously adding it to his shell, when he nourishes the shell with his own holiness. He gives the shell life by cooperating with it.

How then can the shell be amended? Can evil be corrected, and how? Is it only by suffering, it is only by releasing the sparks from the *klipa*? The procedure that is opposed to the action of sin is the understanding of the *klipa*; when the sovereignty of the *klipa* is overthrown by recognizing it for what it is, man becomes free of it.

A person can raise *klipat noga* by performing the positive mitzvot or even by relating properly to the whole world of profane action, by regarding it as action for the sake of heaven. (Although, to be sure, complete evil itself cannot be redeemed by doing it for the sake of heaven.) But when the shell rules over the holy and man suffers, when evil reigns over the good, no matter to what degree, what then? The *Shekhina* weeps. Nevertheless, this happens only when God hides His Countenance, when He permits time and history to work itself out. When a person or a people transgress, the holy spark within the thing or situation is thrust more deeply under the weight of the evil. The potential evil becomes active evil, which evil – bigger and more manifest – soon becomes sin and corruption.

Similarly, the soul that in sinning helps to nourish the *Sitra Aḥra* loses both itself and that which was desired. It is like the original sin of Adam, who missed out on the fruits of both the Tree of Knowledge and the Tree of Life. How much like the child who could not wait for his birthday and ate the chocolate cake, thereby losing holiday and cake together. The whole process of transgression is a double loss, one's own soul and the thing mistakenly clutched at.

And there is no *Tikkun*, or restitution, for this loss. Therefore, it may be preferable for man to be in distress and remain exploited by other men rather than commit crime to free himself. The suffering of evil can be a process of purification in which not only the suffering one, but also the evil itself, undergoes cleansing. It is a cleansing by pain and as it is said, the *Shekhina* weeps.

The *Shekhina* weeps over this situation of double pain – the dominion of evil over good – which situation must be repaired to prevent its getting deeper and more permanent. The *Tikkun* of such matters of simple suffering is one of reversing the phenomenon. One brings the phenomenon back through reality, through all that preceded; one restores all that one was before having given the shell its power over the will. Because the shell usurped one's joy and became an instrument of suffering.

That is to say, the *Tikkun* of sin is accomplished by reversing the dominion of evil over the good, by revealing the true nature of the evil. When a person sins, it is generally not because of the evilness of evil but because of the good in evil. As Baudelaire discovered, a person sins because of the spark of beauty, of pleasure, of magic in a certain temptation. One surrenders to the holy spark hidden in that which is forbidden. However, when one suffers affliction, it is the very opposite. The suffering comes only from the evil in evil. One does not receive anything of the hidden good in the evil; one receives from the overt evil that catches one in a net. The holiness that can give the evil its attractiveness, its pleasurable lure, is reversed and one knows only the absence of joy and the pain of loss.

In other words, just as, in sin, one meets the pleasure in evil, so, too, in genuine suffering, one meets the affliction in evil and thereby, one calls out for reversal; there is a crying need to repent.

The point is that the positive mitzva is an act of choosing to do something in the realm of *klipa noga*, the shell of light which is permitted; all that is needed is a certain amount of good will. There is no need for greatness of soul or martyrdom. Whereas in the realm of the negative mitzva, there is no other way of dealing with the sorting out and choosing except by a certain extraordinary soul effort, such as martyrdom at one level or another. There is no way of easily undoing a sinful action; that which is forbidden in terms of a negative mitzva cannot simply be erased by a feeling of regret. Damage has been done, to oneself or to others.

Repentance out of love that reverses the past is valid of course. But more effectively and profoundly true is the trial experience, which involves suffering. Then the real significance and essence of the repentance process comes out. The greater the consciousness of the act, the greater the *Tikkun*. For there are many levels of offering one's soul, from overcoming temptation to martyrdom itself.

Not every trial experience results automatically in *Tikkun*. There are times of extremity when a person is helpless and the Divine has to interfere, to help the process. This may even reach the level of miracle, as in the case of Daniel's three friends who were cast into the burning furnace. This does not necessarily mean that they failed to go through their test of faith. The miracle was not the significant part of the trial. To be sure, almost always there is a hidden miracle in the Divine trial. But the one who relies on the miracle is not utterly sincere and generally fails to pass the test. A person cannot offer up his soul in martyrdom in order to invite a miracle. True devotion does not expect any reward or return, much less a miraculous intervention. In fact, the miracle is likely to occur precisely because, in the deadlock of misery, one has already suffered the pangs of death.

To return to our starting point, which was the command to go after the Lord, the trial seems to be the way God brings a person to know Him. The going after is not a mechanical action; it requires a "knowing" of the Lord. There are many grades of trial, as we have seen; there is the trial of poverty and the trial of wealth, the trials of suffering, of faith, or self-satisfaction, of loss, of temptation, and the like, whether originating from within or without.

We have delved into the way the trial experience creates knowledge of God by bringing one to a point of revelation that could not be reached any other way: the point where the spark of holiness in evil is made manifest and released by one's inner capacities. The trial experience is thus a process through which a person reaches a higher level of being and of knowledge.

The enhancement of being, or a certain enlightenment, is granted as a result of the test, but it still has to be received. This requires understanding; there has to be work in the realm of *Bina*.

The *tzaddik* also needs the trial because that is the only way he can restitute evil. He may be able to cast it from him; he cannot make *Tikkun* or repair the evil except as he, himself, goes through some ordeal. In the process of trial, he can achieve more because it is beyond the normal process of suffering as punishment for sin or as warning to be good. For the *tzaddik*, the trial is a chance to effect a higher *Tikkun*, to transform evil and cause it to lose its power and meaning as evil, to bring out the essence of sanctity held captive in it.

The purification through suffering is thus a kind of miracle. It is not something that man can do of himself. The *Tikkun* happens, it is not made by a person; it is the indirect result of the human effort to break the shell. It happens – just as at the end of days, when death shall be swallowed forever. But in the continuity of earthly existence, the capacity to endure suffering with love, the acceptance of trial with faith, is a process of bringing out the holy spark from the defilement in which it is held captive.

Implications of the Menora

Chapter one

I t is written (Zechariah 4:2–7): "I saw, and behold a lamp stand (menora) all of gold, with a bowl above it. The lamps on it are seven in number, and the lamps above it have seven pipes. And by it are two olives, one on the right of the bowl and one on the left…" "Do you not know what those things mean?" asked the angel who talked with me, and I said, "No, my Lord." Then he explained to me as follows: "This is the word of the Lord to Zerubbabel: Not by might, nor by power, but by My spirit, said the Lord of Hosts. Whoever you are, O great mountains on the path of Zerubbabel, turn into level ground! For he shall produce that excellent stone; it shall be greeted with shouts of 'Beautiful! Beautiful!'"

This is part of the *haftara* reading for the weekly Torah portion of *Beha'alotekha* and related to a variety of ideas. Amongst them is the concept that the candle, or lamp, of God is the soul of man. And that the seven lamps of the menora are the souls of the seven shepherds, those central figures in Jewish tradition who are reputed to exert influence on the spiritual lives of the people for all time: Abraham, Isaac, Jacob, Moses, Aaron, Joseph, and David.

These seven shepherds appear on different occasions, such as in the *sukka*. They represent the seven chief pathways through which the

Divine influence is transmitted to every Jew. Or, to put it in another context, each of the shepherds opens up a way to know God. Usually it is in the field of emotional or intellectual comprehension, such as a new idea or a revolutionary insight. After a certain amount of study and adjustment, the new way seems to be so self-evident that one wonders how it could ever have been otherwise. One follows without knowing that, like all the roads on the face of the earth, it was cut out of the wilderness by someone; first, as a single path; then, as a thoroughfare. The knowledge of God and Torah, the ways to achievement, have been made available to us by the shepherds.

Even if one does not know anything about the patriarch or prophet, the pathway that was opened up by him is there, and the seven lamps or candles of the menora represent each of their contributions. Also, in a general, symbolic manner, each of the seven lower attributes of the kabbalistic Tree of Life is represented.

Thus, too, the menora is an emblem of the whole of the souls of Israel. And, according to the Torah, it is all beauty, entirely of gold. As the phrase in the Song of Songs puts it, "Thou art all fair, my love." The original menora was cast in one piece of gold; the menoras in following generations were mixed with other ingredients, made of alloys, and pieces of different metals that were joined together. Even a stone menora is incomplete in that it has to be carved, fragments must be cast off. It is not of one piece. The idea is that Israel has to be a wholeness; each member is responsible and liable for the others in a singleness of essence.

Concerning this concept of mutual responsibility, there is no denying the obvious fact that Jews do tend to be contentious and argumentative with one another; antagonisms and conflicts within the community have always been all too prevalent. Nevertheless, the sense of spiritual unity has usually been present, the knowledge that there is a basic connection. Each Jew is a part of an organic whole, like a limb or an eye of a single human body, and even if there is a lack of harmony or an illness in the body, the organic unity remains. The whole is a molten menora, all of gold.

Thus, there is a certain basic understanding among the people, each type nourishing the other. To be sure the golden mold of the menora may become covered with dust, and the dirt may accumulate into such a considerable layer that the gold will be completely invisible. The task, then, of the teacher is not necessarily to devise some new system of thought or to provide the people with a new head and a new heart – which cannot be done in any case – but to dig strenuously into the covering layer of dirt to reveal the gold beneath.

All of Israel is of one mold then, and each individual receives inspiration from the seven branches of the menora. These, as said, are the seven shepherds and mark the availability of different pathways to the Divine. There is a division of essence; there are people who are more inclined to the soul of Abraham and others who favor the line of Isaac. Each receives a certain quality from source that determines the structure of his personality. The greater the receptivity, the more one is able to get from any one branch of the menora.

The word "*ner*," ordinarily translated as candle, is of biblical origin and denotes a vessel containing oil and wick, or that which we now call a lamp. The metaphor of the candle of God and the soul of man refers to this lamp of ancient times, the vessel. Thus, too, the saying that man is a candle or a lamp of God indicates that he is something that can be illuminated; his body is the vessel and his soul is the burning wick.

At the same time, it is also claimed that the mitzva is a candle of God. That is to say, the mitzva has only theoretical meaning; its value rests with its performers, just as the oil and the wick cannot give light without the vessel that contains them. The instrument of performance, the vessel, is that which makes the light possible, even though it is only a technical device. Without the vessel, the oil and the kindled wick could not be a lamp. So too the mitzva has to be located in the vessel of the human soul, otherwise it has no meaning. The soul here can also be considered an instrument, or means, for the mitzva to happen.

So, too, is Torah called light, and it also needs to be kindled by means of oil and wick; the more oil and wick, the greater the light. If the wick is of more refined quality, the more splendid the illumination; if the oil is of greater quantity, the longer the light will last. Thus, one speaks of the candle of mitzva as supplying the light of Torah. The oil and the wick create the light. How much oil is there? How much wick? What is the quality of the wick? This determines the nature of the light, just as in the case of the soul of man.

That is, just as impure oil and poor quality wick make for inadequate illumination, so too, man's capacities must be constantly refined if he is to be a proper light of Torah, a candle of God. And where there is a fault in the human soul, the effect is immediately made visible. Thus, we are only too well aware of people who are supplied with all that is necessary in terms of substance and learning, oil and wick, yet when kindled there is a poor flame, or smell of burning, or excess of smoke. There is a fault somewhere.

In this sense, the light of Torah may be considered a function of the way one interprets the mitzvot. The Torah is thus the result of performing mitzvot; or on the other hand, it may be seen as the meaning behind the mitzvot. There is a scriptural correspondence to every mitzva – and yet the connection between Torah and mitzvot is not at all that simple. The question asked by the ancients, for example, was: Which precedes? Is the Torah the instruction and means of the mitzvot or are the mitzvot instruments enabling us to reveal the Torah? The idea, of course, is to bring light; it is not only a theoretical question of principle and practice. What, after all, is the role of theory; what is its importance against the actuality of practice? To illustrate: There are instruments that perform complex operations; sometimes the operations are so complicated that they can make conclusions in the realm of theory. In fact, laboratory equipment exists not for its own sake, but to help gain conclusive evidence for the theory at the basis of knowledge. Some cyclotrons of research are not only huge and very expensive toys intended to provide information about the tiniest of particles; they also help to create theoretical conclusions about the nature of matter. Similarly, one could say that there is a great mitzva with lots of details, such as Shabbat. The tractate *Shabbat* (theory) is thus the principal instrument to gain knowledge of the mitzva (practice). It is only theory – the mitzva is what counts. The Torah is only an accompaniment, that which comes to surround and explain the mitzva. Or else, one could say that the mitzva is the essence and the Torah is that which flows from it, giving it a certain form.

There is a saying to the effect: As with the material, so with the spiritual; as below, so above. The mitzvot are commandments, expressions of Divine will. God wishes that certain actions should be performed in a certain way. The Torah is only a framework, a means of conveying this instruction. Whereas the mitzva is qualified by the gratification, and even great happiness, of doing God's will, and it does not matter whether it is a positive or a negative reaction, towards or away from the Divine harmony. With a musical instrument (as with the mitzva) one can produce delightful sounds or terrible dissonance. And this is very much what a person does with his life; he can create happiness or its opposite, discontent. For it is written that God is pleased when men do His will.

That which a person desires gives him pleasure and even delight. That which is against his desire causes sorrow and suffering. Wishing or will is a function of the desire for happiness. Why this should be so is not given to explanation; one does whatever one does because it brings one further to the heart's desire and, eventually, this is rather final. It is not unlike the theological inquiry: Why did God create the world? And the answer is that He wished it and we cannot know anything more than that.

Will and delight are thus bound together in a mutuality of many-sided kabbalistic meanings: *Keter* is both will and delight, both *Atik yomin* and *Arich anpin*, encompassing a great variety of inner and outer expressions of delight. To be concise, the mitzva, which is an action of nullifying the personal will, is connected with the highest level of *Atik yomin*, a superior grade of delight. So that, it is commanded that a person should perform the mitzva with joy, for joy is the expression of delight.

The Torah is wisdom, and delight is higher than wisdom. Wisdom is an instrument that makes delight possible, that expresses the will. One wants something; a way must be found to obtain it, and this way is wisdom. At the same time, we have the recognition of the delight that is in wisdom. For delight penetrates everything. This is not true of any other attribute: love, or *Ḥesed*, for example, is not relevant in certain situations, whereas delight does apply to every level and every aspect of reality. Anything can give pleasure and be enjoyed.

Therefore, the Torah is only an envelope or an encompassing that enables delight to be manifested. It is a framework and a dynamic means, inducing the highest satisfaction; wisdom is one of its instruments. The purpose of this inquiry – what is primary, Torah study or the action of mitzva? – is not an academic exercise. It has its own repercussions in life.

For example, when a new Jewish community of immigrants is started somewhere, there is the problem of what comes first? Some will arrange for a Talmud Torah school, another will build a synagogue, yet another will set up a kosher restaurant. The automatic response to what is felt to be most urgent is significant. To be sure, there is the rather obvious argument that Torah study as first priority is only to enable the people to do mitzvot, while mitzvot or correct action does not always lead to study. It is thus an operative argument. The real problem is where the priority rests within a person inwardly. What is the fulcrum point of his life? Is it in the intellectual pursuit of Torah (and study, after all, is largely intellectual), or is it in the action of performing a mitzva (which is essentially not intellectual)?

A partial answer to the dilemma lies in the fact that the mitzva is the expression of Divine Will and therefore a higher delight. The mitzva is also that which must be done. And Torah is the instrument for the performance, in the sense that it instructs one what to do and how to do it. The important thing is the action. The significant aspect of this self-evident truth is connected with the candle and its light, with the menora and the Holy Temple.

The menora in the Holy Temple was lit every night. Why? It was situated in a part of the Temple that no one entered; it had no practical use. The closed chamber where it stood was visited only once in the morning and once in the evening to kindle the light. Or else it was entered once a week to change the shew bread. The menora was out of proportion, far too huge and imposing for such a simple purpose. Unlike the holy altar, which was carefully constructed to be functional, the menora had many features, structural and decorative, that were not functional. What was its meaning? Was it only to provide light? Why did it have to be all of one piece and all of it gold?

Chapter two

We have mentioned that the candles of the menora have two symbolic meanings: one is related to the soul of man, the other is called *ner* mitzva or the light of Torah. For the mitzvot are instruments expressing the Divine Will. And this Divine Will is enveloped by, or clothed with, the higher delight, the *oneg elyon*. Therefore man has to perform the mitzva with joy, for joy is a revelation of the highest delight or bliss. Indeed, it cannot be otherwise; the heart cannot but be joyful when the heavenly delight is made manifest. And when this manifestation is more conspicuous, so is the joy that follows all the greater.

However, since the Shattering of the Vessels before Creation, all that we know of physical reality are remnants, fragmentary sparks of the Infinite Light that was broken up. To be sure, reality does contain sparks of the original delight, even if only as residue of its infinitude. We do know pleasure and happiness, but it is no more than what is left over from the immeasurable delight of Divinity at its source.

As Rabbi Akiva is reported to have said concerning the noisy enjoyments of Rome as heard from a great distance: "If, for those who transgress there can be so much joy, how much more so for those who do His Will." The Divine Plenty is available for all, and it is the source of greater gladness for those who are close to Him. The celestial beings receive from the Chariot, and the lower beings receive from above them whatever delights they are capable of absorbing.

Thus, the entry into higher bliss is evidently not open to most men who transgress, even if, as so often evidently happens, they transgress without even knowing it. Therefore, they have to be cleansed by going through the fiery River Dinur (Daniel 7:10); a kind of painful purification is necessary before receiving the higher joys of Paradise. This is a different approach to suffering and hell; it views the torments of life not as punishment but as cleansing. There are levels upon levels of heavenly bliss and of the degree of purity related to each. Some Sages have mentioned seven firmaments, or heavens, pointing out that the passage from one to another demands an ever-more intense purification. There is no rest for the Sage; he has to keep going from level to level, each with its own sanctifying fire.

This follows from the recognition that the highest delight of God, *oneg elyon*, is without purpose or aim; it is infinite. And since man is finite, and even his soul is limited in terms of the Divine, he has to be made receptive to the highest delight by some special means. Even in the realm of the spirit, man has to be prepared to receive the higher joys of being. Indeed most men are structurally unfit to absorb even the lowest manifestations of bliss. Hence, the need for worlds upon worlds of spiritual Being, beyond the physical.

The point of this emphasis on the incapacity of men to enjoy the higher delights is to draw attention to the fact that Divine mercy has made it possible to attain the bliss of *oneg elyon* through the power of the mitzva. It is said that the mitzva performed in this world gives fruit in the next world. At the same time, the mitzva has its own radiance below, in the lower world, and in the act of Divine service through the mitzva, something of this radiance is transmitted. As a matter of fact, we get the fruit itself immediately in the doing, while the radiance passes on to the higher worlds. The mitzva is a total thing in itself, that is, and through it we are vouchsafed heavenly delight.

But the joy of the mitzva is already clothed in the Divine Will, which is the higher delight. The mitzva is already superior in its contained joyfulness, beyond all reality in the worlds. It has an inner quality that cannot be expressed in words; it is beyond anything conceivable. For the mitzva belongs to the level of the highest delight, *oneg elyon*. It belongs to a different dimension of rules and natural law, manifesting a new world, a new order.

The mitzva is thus beyond any manifestation physical or spiritual, and even beyond the upper worlds themselves. It is as though God reveals Himself to one with the inner delight of His essence. In Kabbalistic terms it is expressed in the central *Sefira* of *Yesod*, which connects so vitally to all else.

This explains the apparent contradiction between the generally accepted view of the next world, with its very extraordinary paradisiacal quality, and the view that one hour of repentance and good deeds is weighed against all of the pleasures of the next life. In the next life one cannot experience the unique act of performing God's Will. The mitzva is a priceless jewel that can only be enjoyed in this life; there is nothing in terms of value in this world or the next with which it can be compared or exchanged.

Chapter three

We have mentioned the saying "Better one hour of repentance and good deeds in this world than all the life in the next world." As a figure of speech, what is being expressed is that in the performance of mitzvot, or in living a life according to Torah, a person acts as a sort of extension of the manifestation of Divine Will. He is participating, that is, in Revelation, whereas at any other level of being, even in any world above, he merely enjoys the radiance of the *Shekhina*.

The reason for this apparent exaggeration of the power of a mitzva lies in the recognition of the fact that only God encompasses both aspects of reality: that which is and that which is not, this world and the world beyond. Just as we are convinced of the substantial existence of this world, so does the world above view us as a nothing, seeing itself as the genuine reality. In illustration of which there are certain clever drawings with subtly shifting foregrounds and backgrounds; the viewer is never quite sure which is the real picture. So too, the world below and the world above can be portrayed as a cosmic optical illusion, each fitting perfectly into the other and providing us with either the real against the unreal, or the front against the back, constantly changing places in our consciousness. It is not only the old problem of subjectivity of vision, it is primarily the comprehension of the nature of reality itself, a recognition of the existence of a higher and a lower, a world of the graspable and a world of the ungraspable, being and nothing.

Since the performance of a mitzva is ultimately a matter of self-nullification – a person relinquishes his own personal momentary existence before God – it may be seen as an act affirming the higher reality. One is doing that which expresses Divine command and feels the delight of participation in the higher will, even though one may not have any concept of what this means in terms of the upper world. But the delight is there and, since it involves one's own will and understanding in the world below, a connection is made between the two worlds. The messianic salvation, the Divine Unit of above and below, is brought nearer.

What is more, God also delights in the mitzva, and this is the inexplicable factor. Bliss explains itself; the reasons may follow but they don't really count for much. Delight has its own logic and its own unreasoning ecstasy. So that when we say, "He who sanctifies us with His Commandments," we are thereby emphasizing the utter uniqueness and exclusive, blissful quality of sanctity. Holiness is completely separate from man; it cannot be put on like a garment; one can only be wrapped in it by a Divine sanction. God remains apart forever. Unlike physical substance that upon contact usually leaves a mark – a residue, such as a liquid that wets what it spills upon, or a chemical reaction of whatever sort – the holy does not make any impression. It cannot even be put on like a cloak. Yet we say that we are sanctified by His Commandments (mitzvot). God transfers something that we ourselves cannot acquire or touch. It is the higher delight. The mitzva itself is grasped and performed, of course, but it is only a vessel that contains the holiness, which is another aspect of delight. The mitzva thus has no meaning in itself; even though there may well be mitzvot that appear to have objective value, it is only so on the surface. The mitzvot are not objective in the sense of actions that should be done; they are real and have meaning only in the doing by a specific person. Whatever results from the mitzva is also only an immaterial consequence, it is not part of the ritual action that remains restricted to the individual human being's performance. The mitzva cannot be a mechanical action, therefore; it is not a matter of getting a thing done. If one were to go for a stroll on the way to town and get picked up by a vehicle, one would get to town, but the mitzva of a stroll could not be said to have been performed.

Moreover, the mitzva is not a phenomenon, something that can be said to exist independently; it is that which is accomplished within a person. And the person himself is only a vessel; he is the carrier of the mitzva, and remains a component, even if a necessary component and even when the mitzva can be considered his responsibility. Man is thus an integral part of the mitzva. So that one may divide the mitzva into three constituents: man, the Divine commandment, and the action. Each one alone is not enough. The Jewish ritual requires the active participation of the person at one level or another of consciousness. Prayer is not only a matter of getting certain words sent off to heaven; it is an interaction between a specific man, certain words, and the saying of the words.

Therefore it is maintained that the candle of God is the soul of man. If the human soul is a candle or lamp, in the sense of its being a vessel – a container for the oil and wick that provides the flame – then it is possible to insert into it the Torah and the mitzva. And precisely into this vessel and not another. For which we express our gratitude: "Who hath sanctified us with His Commandments." The expression has the same quality as the ceremonial marriage vow, "Thou art sanctified unto me." There are two things pertaining to sanctification: one is the matter of holiness as that which is essentially "separate from"; the other is the matter of "holiness for" (thou art sanctified unto me). The woman who was available to all suitors has become exclusively mine. She is separated from all others but she is sanctified to the one. Holiness is thus seen as a double-sided power of absolute otherness and of absolute connectedness.

As for the menora, the seven candles – symbolizing the seven shepherds of Israel – are primary and we kindle our light only from them. The whole of Israel is seen as a golden candlestick and is the symbol of *Malkhut*, the tenth *Sefira*. And it is the inwardness of the menora that is *Knesset Yisrael*. Its outwardness, which is the externality of *Malkhut*, is the candlestick that kindles other lights on the external plane. The inwardness, which is *Knesset Yisrael*, is the highest unity, from which the Infinite Light emanates as holiness.

The question behind this far-reaching thought is "What does it mean to bless God?" (Because all our prayers assert: Blessed art Thou,

Lord our God.) It is as though I, the one who prays, am giving something to God, as though I were wishing Him well and offering a blessing. But the question is: How is this at all possible? What does God need that I can supply with words of benediction?

The meaning of the blessing and of the mitzva that follows it lies in the wholeness of the sanctification, in the necessary inclusion of oneself, the Torah commandment, and the outward action. There is an inner connection between the *ner mitzva* – the candle of the mitzva – and the candle of God, which is the soul of man. For as we have said, the soul of man becomes the instrument for the mitzva; he is the lamp or vessel containing the components of light. For the mitzva has no significance other than as light-giving reality, and the soul of man is where this takes place.

One may thus view the human being as nothing more than a vehicle, a means for the mitzva or Divinely inspired action to occur. Or one can see the mitzva as an essence in itself, a potential reality that receives life when man touches it. What is the primary, what is secondary? The combination is one that is necessary, as we have said, and neither of the factors stand alone. The question is, Where is the light? What is the oil and the wick? For example one can take the *lulav* and recognize that, in itself, it is a branch and not a mitzva. It becomes a mitzva when a Jew waves it within a certain set of circumstances. All the components are essential – as with every mitzva.

The mitzva is thus a commandment from God; it is also an idea that can become a reality, given the right combination of factors, and then it is manifested as the light of Divine revelation. This makes it preferable to heavenly bliss, and one can declare with the Sages, "Better one hour of repentance and good deeds in this world than all the life in the next world."

Chapter four

The Torah is an emanation of Divine Wisdom and expresses the higher delight. But these two are not necessarily identical in the realm of human life. For if one just fulfills an order, even if it is a Divine Commandment, as in Torah, this does not, in itself, create delight. Whereas, if one is allowed to participate in wisdom by some inner agreement, this does make for delight. That is to say, a proper exertion of the will – merely doing the right thing – does not necessarily make one feel inordinately happy. But if it is my own desire that is thus fulfilled by making God's Will my will as an expression of genuine inclination, then is the carrying out of Divine Commandment accompanied by delight.

Delight may also come afterwards, upon comprehension of what was done, or in identification with the source of all desire, so that making His Will my will need not be confined to the action itself. It may be part of something deeper, lodged in the framework of a whole relationship in which there is delight, childlike in its innocence, in being allowed to participate in the workings of greater wisdom.

Well known, too, is the delight that comes from an intellectual attainment, when something has been grasped by the mind. Thus the Torah can be such a source of intellectual enjoyment, with or without relation to the mitzvot. At the same time, there is a spiritual delight in Divine Wisdom, as mentioned, which is of another dimension. It is in this respect that the light that comes from the lamp of mitzva is directly derived from the oil and the wick, and the oil can thus be viewed as the Infinite Source, the wisdom of Torah.

The idea is that the revelation of Infinite Light is a matter of wisdom. Why wisdom? Why not one of the other *Sefirot*, like *Bina* or *Da'at*? After all, Wisdom (*Ḥokhma*) is not active, like understanding (*Bina*). Although to be sure, it is Wisdom that provides the kernel of the idea, and understanding only receives and develops it, in which respect it would seem that Wisdom is active and understanding is passive. Nevertheless, Understanding, as *Bina*, is a matter of constant building and even reconstruction, in relation to the original idea which wisdom conceived and merely transmitted. Like the birth of a child, where the seed is given by the father and that is the end of his function; the long development and nurturing is done in the womb of the mother. The original seed had only a code of its own, it could not grow; the original idea, too, requires the act and process of Understanding. In this sense, *Bina* is active and *Ḥokhma* is nothing but a means of transmitting the kernel of a concept. There are ways and means of developing an idea, but there is no way to conceive one.

Ḥokhma can be used as an instrument for the inner inspiration of Infinite Light because it has a part, even if ever so slight, in the whole interaction (of primary forces). Just as a person cannot really hear or see anything without there being some sort of interaction, and yet the stimulus itself cannot be concocted. Indeed, one of the problems of reception (or knowing) of the world is the rather inevitable distortion that goes into the process. If we could absorb in purity, without interpretation, we would be able to know genuine inspiration. We would then gain knowledge by self-repudiation. But since this is so seldom the case, the possibilities for genuine creativity are relatively small. A new idea is rare. A flash of inspiration is a novelty, and frequently, it is lost because there was no way of developing it within a particular time, place, or circumstance. The "eureka" of Archimedes is not an experience that no one else ever had; it is simply an insight that could or could not unfold and be put to practical use.

It is in this sense that the soul of Israel is a candle of God, a point where a certain ignition takes place, the direct result of wisdom as a source of Torah and people. Therefore we see the people as the vessel for the oil and the wick of the Divine light. The problem is the relation between the (ethereal) light and the (substantial) body. After all, the Divine light of Torah does not need to be dependent on anything; it is an inner light. Nevertheless, the giving of the Torah is the result of the souls of the people being in the body. They were not abstract essences. And only as material bodies can they carry out the Torah's commandments.

As an aside, it has been maintained that in recent generations there are very few "new" souls; most people are "used" souls. One of the aspects of a new soul is that it experiences everything afresh, as a novel configuration of events. Whenever a new soul comes into the world something unprecedented is brought into being, a certain unknown. The new soul sees everything in another way, vivid and unfamiliar. Used souls cannot do this; the "first time" cannot be repeated. Which does not mean that the second time is necessarily a lesser experience; in fact, it is likely to be of greater quality, less impressionable, and more meaningful.

That is, the oil of the Torah needs a wick to hold the flame of light; it cannot burn of itself. Something has to transfer the oil in small, controllable quantities; otherwise, there is a conflagration. And it is the body of man that constitutes such a wick; the ignited flame is the mitzva, giving off a spiritual light. The body functions as a useful device; it helps to manipulate the immense things of the world so that there can be "light" without an explosion. Of course, the body also causes a lot of trouble for the soul, but it does provide the means for the soul's achievements.

The mitzvot are the essence (of spiritual life), they relate to Divine Will, which is the *Sefira* of *Keter*. Whereas Torah is related to *Hokhma*, which is the second *Sefira* and, in a sense, lower. But Torah gives vital force to the mitzvot, as the Sages said: "Great is the learning that leads to action." The problem of Torah (or consciousness) versus mitzva (or action) is very old and is not easily resolved, even by the conviction that one has to first assume the Yoke of Heaven (which is faith) and then the Yoke of mitzvot (which is works).

This points to a certain order in the education of a person and the disciplining of his life. And for everyone it is different. Some need to learn the alphabet first, others need to be inspired by the ideas of Talmud in order to have the incentive to learn to read. There are those who have to love God before they can fear Him; there are those who are built differently and need to fear God first.

The notion of acceptance (*kabbalat ol malkhut shamayim*) preceding action comes from the certainty that a relationship to God must be established before demanding anything of a person. Practical work requires direction. On the other hand, there are instances where the opposite is true. A child would better do the mitzva before understanding it, just as he is given his porridge to eat before he can choose what he prefers. An adult may well be obliged to choose first before being given spiritual nourishment. The problems that arise in the worship of God and the correct order of preparation are not only theoretical; they are very personal and vary from individual to individual, from situation to situation. The basic principle is that genuine relationship, comprehension, and acceptance must precede the act of committing oneself to the practical mitzvot – even though, as we have said, the mitzvot are primary in their being the expression of Divine Will.

Chapter five

The act of faith in Judaism is expressed by the acceptance of God's will as the way of the kingdom of Heaven. This is intimated in the declaration, "Hear, O Israel, the Lord our God is one God." The meaning of the word "hear" in this context is to apprehend, to recognize, and to understand with both heart and mind. Its essence is of the *Sefira* of *Bina,* which is the mother *Sefira* giving birth to the various other human attributes such as love, strength, beauty, etc. To have an intellectual understanding is to have an insight into the way one thing follows another, a grasp of process, of the way things come to be what they are. It follows that to contemplate has the double meaning of seeing and of comprehending at the same time, since genuine looking or seeing consists also in recognizing that which is perceived. It has to be known in order to be apprehended.

To return to the theme of the menora, which is "all of gold," and has seven candles that represent the seven lower attributes or *Sefirot,* we recall that these seven candles also symbolize the seven shepherds of Israel. A little above the menora branches there is a supply vessel that signifies meditation on the unity of God, His higher Oneness. This meditation – like all meditation in Judaism – is never systematic or available as a technique. One of the methods of this meditation is to open oneself to new strands of understanding, to be awake to a higher consciousness. It is a concentration of awareness rather than an emptying of all awareness. It focuses on a definite subject and builds on it with the soul as well as the mind; it does not exclude an aspect of wonder and emotional exaltation. It is thus more like a deep reflection, rumination, or reverie on something that has profound emotional overtones.

In a broader sense, this mode of meditation is also a nurturing of spiritual feeling, allowing it to take definite form in consciousness. Love, for example, is seldom a matter of instantaneous response to someone, although attraction at first sight is certainly common enough. But for love to grow in earnest, it needs time, repetition in memory at least, and the reiterated and accumulated excitation of wonder and beauty. The same process may be said to hold for anger and hatred as well; an emotion needs to work itself up in the imagination; otherwise, it remains a passing sensation of attraction, irritation, etc. Most resentment and lasting hatred is a product of mulling over a grievance, lingering on a real or imagined reason for believing that the other has somehow injured one's pride. It's a matter of repeating a thought, five, ten, a hundred times until it becomes a certainty. In other words, there is a dynamic function of the soul involved in almost every conviction or lasting emotion. The Hebrew language often describes this in the reflexive form of the grammatical structure of the verb, to be enraged, to be in love, enraptured, etc. A person makes his selfhood, creates his passion or his belief.

Insofar as faith is concerned, we do not set up a new system of conviction; we use that which exists; only our goal is different. The soul reaches exalted states by way of contemplation or meditation, in the sense of dwelling on the source of wonder and inner joy. Such a person may insist that he has never meditated in the customary way of removing himself from the world, but if he were made to realize that almost all of his deep feelings, ideas, and desires are a product of brooding over a thought, repeating and nurturing a sensation, the concept of meditation would become more comprehensible.

Worry, incidentally, has the same quality. One lets a fearful thought return again and again, with or without variations perhaps, but with a tendency to accumulate force until it becomes painful and a source of suffering. Imagination helps. Creative cogitation can prove disastrous. In other words, the structure of the mind is such that with meditation anything can become a powerful reality for one.

So too, the command "And thou shalt love the Lord, thy God" has to be allowed to grow in a person. It is obviously not the sort of order that one carries out automatically. It is a directive to meditate as well as to feel. The meditation involved is a matter of cogitation as well as repetition and emotional nurturing. And there are definite frameworks for doing this. One takes up a serious subject, not necessarily the greatness and glory of God – and one thinks on it, ruminates on it until a certain breakthrough takes place, even if it is only a slight emotional and intellectual shift. As with worry, an excess of imagination and strong feeling can be disastrous. Fortunately, the problem of Divine Greatness in Jewish tradition creates its own limitations to such excesses. But it remains true that a person praises God according to his capacities. There are those who are capable of greater degrees of abstraction and wonder, and there are many who are very restricted in their conceptualizations.

The central feature of this framework of meditation on the Divine Unity is that the point of departure is not the world but God. One does not begin with the experience of the external world but with the experience of the Creator of the world, and the thought that there is "nothing else." The world has to be constantly recreated in order to exist, even though it seems to be the same all the time. Like the television screen on which the picture constantly changes, the world is only a means of transmitting forms or information; the source of reality lies elsewhere. As for what reality consists of, just as creation is supposed to be a process of making something from nothing, we may ask, do the letters or pictures on the screen exist? It is perhaps a matter of what is defined as real. If one defines reality as that which can be grasped, then the pictures on the screen, like the meaning of the words on the page, are questionable. They are open to constant re-creation; forms are forever changing. The world is more like a hologram; everything depends on the direction of the light and, of course, on the very fact of light, without which there is nothing. The constant re-creation of the world demands that we focus attention on the Creator.

This brings us back to the command: "And thou shalt love." Since everything is always brought back to the source – to the one origin of all that is seen, heard, sensed, and thought – this unified source is able to concentrate one's entire being. God becomes that which is mine; He is what I am attached to in the most intimate sense, even though He dwells in heaven. I have not much choice but to be related, and to dwell on Him. This thinking of God, this meditation on the Divine as source of one's experience, leads to love.

Finally, we can view meditation on Divine Unity as a way of enhancing the emotional capacity (for love) and developing a sense of ever-increasing wonder and awe. It is represented by the supply vessel in the menora that transmits oil to the seven branches. As the source or fountain of knowledge (of God), it also creates the desire to worship God, to assume the burden of the Kingdom of Heaven. In other words, for the flame of the seven candles or lamps of the menora to keep burning, in order for the worship of God to continue unabated, it has to be kept supplied with the oil of a fundamental awareness of God, by a constant dwelling on His Presence, on His Greatness and Glory.

The question is: How shall love become embedded in the soul and heart of man? What we have here is a transformation of the emotion that was stirred up by some cause into something that is a permanent, active force in the soul of man. To give an example from life (which is possibly not very positive), let us suppose that one keeps repeating to oneself how unfair someone was, how mean and wrong he was. With the redundancy of recollection, one begins to get angrier and angrier. If and when one stops thinking about it, however, the whole thing tends to fade away. It all depends on the persistence of the exasperating thought. And this process, so inadmissible to our pride, is quite common in the emotional life. The problem is: how to make any feeling last, seeing that emotions are so dependent on continual stimulation? The other problem, in terms of the spiritual life, is how to make this emotion into a permanent feature of the soul. And to return to our disagreeable example, we may ask: at what point does one pass over from anger to hate? There is such a passage; anger or irritation with someone is fairly common, and there are those who are indeed very quick to flare up. According to the Talmud, this is akin to an act of idolatry because one is worshipping an alien god, even if it is one's own indignation or rage, by submitting to its dominion. But usually it passes – usually one does not keep holding a grudge. When it does not pass, when it is transformed into a lasting hatred, when it does not have to be stirred up anew by recollection but becomes a permanent imprint on the soul, then we have the negative side of the capacity to exercise influence on one's inner being.

It follows that the same is true of love – falling in love may be easy, but holding on to the intensity of the emotion requires a constant renewal of the feeling of affection. If the object of love is far away, it becomes difficult. The problem of the lasting power of love is a crucial one and highlights the stage of passage when that which was still taking shape becomes permanent and fixed in the soul. The original stimulus may have long been forgotten, the slender girl may well have taken on the lines of age, but the love remains firm.

To be sure, even a single event or experience can induce a permanent feeling of love or hate; it does not necessarily have to be stimulated afresh. Which only affirms the fact that lasting emotion is a result of a variety of experience; the soul has to be pressured whether at once in great intensity or over a period of time with earnestness of feeling. And to be earnest in the love of God is a matter of assuming a burden, taking on a readiness for responsibility and pain. This is what is meant by the process of repetition; it is a deepening of the original imprint, ensuring that it does not fade and keeping one's attention on it over a period of time. One has to keep engraving into the stone in order to leave a permanent mark.

This means cutting into the substance of the rock, pressing oneself into life with a certain need for salvation. The permanence of one's relation to God has to be made by effort – which pressure, although difficult, may also be viewed as a means of extracting the bitterness from life, as with the olive, which only becomes edible when its bitterness is crushed out. Even though the process is often as much as one can bear, and leaves a scar on the soul, the scar is no longer painful. The permanent mark, unlike an unfeeling scar, is not only a matter of residue, it is itself a wonderful ongoing experience of the Divine.

Chapter six

It is written that a person should be serious when he stands up to pray. The Hebrew expression for seriousness is "heavy-headed," in contrast to "light-headed," and there is a definite relation to weightiness, to being so weighed down that the head tends to sink or droop. This heaviness comes from the fact that the *Shekhina* (Divine Presence) accompanies us wherever we go, and when we sin, the *Shekhina* is there in our degradation. And since we thus have reason to feel ashamed, the head is lowered in sorrow. Subsequently, too, the head of all of Israel is heavy; a certain seriousness prevails. The world was not made with toil and trouble; it was created with the Word, lightly and without noticeable effort. Indeed, the only thing that could burden God with sorrow is the sinfulness of man. And the only thing that could separate man from God is not distance or an iron fence but transgression. There is therefore good cause to approach the Divine seriously, heavy-headed in more than one sense.

Similarly man is exiled from the Divine Presence. If God is concealed and there is a separation, it amounts to a virtual state of banishment, or exile – that which the Kabbala terms *galut haShekhina*, the exile of the *Shekhina*. The world is divided from that-which-is, from God, the only reality, and man feels dislocated, lost. It may be compared to a state of sickness. Only when an organ hurts us do we feel its existence; otherwise our hands or hearts are scarcely discerned. Man is unaware of himself in health; when there is an ailment of body or soul, however, he becomes conscious of himself. He becomes conscious of a self that is separated from the universal oneness, which separation is the exile of the *Shekhina*. That is to say, one needs to know bitterness, pain, and sorrow in order to be aware of the *Shekhina*'s absence, and thereby to learn that the *Shekhina* exists. When a finger is squeezed, the pain brings us assurance that it is there – a part of us that we ordinarily pay no attention to.

Therefore, the bent head of seriousness is not necessarily a sign of sin or grief, although there is no doubt that every person has his own portion of transgression to occupy his conscience. The point of the heart sorrow, or seriousness, is the restoration of consciousness to the exile of the *Shekhina* and to one's own particular role in this separation. Even to view the world as the real existence and not see the intrinsic Divine Presence is a reason to let the head drop with regret for the exile of the *Shekhina*. To be so absorbed in one's own body that one's love for others is impaired can be considered a state of exile. To love your neighbor as yourself is the way to overcome the locking of oneself into the darkness of the feeling that the world was created for oneself alone. To love someone without using him is one of the ways of extricating oneself from the limitations of physicality, from the error that there is an existence separate from God. Thus, the existence of the body has several spiritual advantages. But the greater the enslavement of the soul to the body and the more material the physical influence, the harder it is to speak to the body, to convince it that it is only a means to another end. It becomes so absorbed in itself that nothing else seems real to it. The problem of the density of physicality, making it almost impenetrable, is a problem of consciousness and actually limits one's capacity to make optimal use of the body.

This raises the question: Why, indeed, is one unable to see the Divine as the prophets, for example, saw? It is this same problem of one's own density of spiritual perception, for God is evidently there for all to perceive. And it is a very general problem of the whole world, the exile of the *Shekhina*.

Therefore, the Sages once added to the prayer benediction preceding *Shema Yisrael* (Hear O Israel) the sentences calling "with great mercy, have mercy on us," in order to stir Divine Compassion for our materiality. Since we cannot, of ourselves, extricate ourselves from this density, we can only ask God for His merciful intercession to help us overcome the desolation of His absence, the bitterness of not being able to be aware of the indwelling, His *Shekhina*. As a result of becoming conscious of this distress, a person could begin to ease the pain and move in the direction of the Divine Love that is called for. To love with all of one's soul, however, requires a degree of greater understanding that comes from meditation, as we have mentioned, and a certain affliction of the body, a crushing of the physical density, in terms of spiritual regeneration. It is a process and not an isolated action.

What is vital is the correct view of the process, the realization that what is meant is not an ascetic suffering imposed on the body. It is an integrated body-soul action of freedom, not compulsion. Every weakness is a combination of body and soul weakness; it includes an infirmity of will as well as muscle. A person cannot make himself into an angel by willpower; he can, however, limit the scope of his weakness and alter the range and direction of his thought. And strangely, it is precisely when the mind concentrates on fasting that food becomes an issue; it is when a person lashes his back that he becomes aware of a back that he had not noticed before. So that the ascetic practice has a function; it works directly on the weakness of body and infirmity of will. But no change is made in the relations one has to the body; one simply deprives it of something or indirectly brings a certain part of the body to one's attention.

Nevertheless, the important thing is the relation to the whole problem of matter. If one persists in seeing substantial things as big and important, then human existence becomes a matter of nurturing the body, paying tribute to it in sickness and in health, in poverty and riches. The process of "crushing" the body to extract the sweetness is thus not a matter of ascetic practice but of smashing the ideology of the body, changing its primacy in the order of life.

The change involved lies not in that which a person does, but in the way one does things: how one eats, talks, thinks, functions. The problem becomes one of dominance – body or soul. It can better be observed in a situation of spiritual awakening. As a result of this change, a person, for instance, is no longer aware of what he is eating; it has become a mechanical action, part of the routine course of his life. The difference is that the body is no longer dominant; what one eats and even the ordinary content of action lessens in importance. Something else has become paramount. And, as we have said, it can be caused by a great variety of situations that stir the emotional frame, whether it be terrible anger, fear, or sorrow; whether astonishment or great joy.

It does not matter, therefore, what the outer circumstances are; a weak and sickly body is not necessarily more spiritual. True, some of the talmudic books mention *halakhic* rulings that seem to state otherwise – for instance, that a member of the Sanhedrin must be hale and healthy; he cannot be crippled in any way. On the other hand, we have certain folk traditions that grant spiritual superiority to the blind, the bent, and the diseased, in contrast to the scriptural saying that the *Shekhina* rests on the wise, the strong, and the rich. Without attempting to draw conclusions, it is rare even for learned men to reach a genuine separation from the physical. As the Ḥasidic story relates: At a feast in honor of the installation of a new leader of the group, as everyone was eating and drinking happily, the Rabbi who was being celebrated was given a bowl of soup. After taking a spoonful, he sighed and said: "If I can still feel the taste of the soup it seems that I am not really a Rebbi."

Of course it is not a matter of being ignorant of the spices that are added to the soup, but of being so occupied with other thoughts that the soup is of little consequence. A person is changed when he is no longer dominated by the physical aspect, when the material stuff has been pulverized into something of another essence. To be sure, we do utter a benediction for every morsel of food, and a special blessing for a new fruit, and so on, but the intention here is to give thanks, to render homage to the One who has provided objects of pleasure and sustenance. There is no spiritual value in abstinence of itself. Refraining from adding salt to avoid taste does not have much point to it. On the contrary, a person has to be fully aware of where he is in the world and of all his reactions and sensations. As another Ḥasidic story goes: On the eve of Sukkot, after the Rabbi had been so very busy building the booth that he had missed his regular midday meal, he was given a plate of food. When he finished, he said ruefully: "Berl, Berl, I think you were not sitting in the *sukka* but in the plate before you." The question is always: "Where am I?"

It is not merely an exercise in the realm of thought. That is to say, so long as the world and the substantial aspects of the world are paramount and the contemplation of Divine unity is a mental exercise or even a sort of mystical experience, there remains something unreal about the spiritual aspiration. What then is to be done?

Compassion has to be aroused. It may very well be that we cannot prevent the substantiality of the world from dominating our consciousness. The world is indeed too much with us, a part of us. We find ourselves unable to avoid enjoying our dinner, and we find it hard to experience the embers of compassion. What is demanded of us then, what is demanded of all men, is seriousness. Let each one feel sorry that he is where he is.

Let a person know the sorrow and sadness of the dominion of matter. In that way, he breaks the absoluteness of this dominion; the physical reality is not thereby diminished, only its tyranny is challenged or at least questioned. As the Sephardic version of the Sabbath blessing after meals so simply puts it: "Even though we have eaten and drunk, the destruction of your great Temple we have not forgotten." Sorrow about our human condition accompanies us, not only in the synagogue or on the fast of Tisha B'Av, but also when we enjoy the Sabbath meal.

This seriousness, as recollection of the truth of oneself, is most poignantly present in the detail and trivialities of fulfilling the commandment: "And thou shalt love thy neighbor as thyself." The one who is full of himself is incapable of loving another. There are those who are so weak in this capacity for loving another person that they cannot distinguish it from the preference they have for a trinket, a sweetmeat, or a house, saying, "I love herring for breakfast." Love is essentially a very opposite feeling of separation or of release from the ego; it is a real relationship, a giving of oneself and, at the same time, the more abstract it is, the more difficult.

How does the stirring of great pity or compassion affect the bondage to physicality? It is a roundabout way of seeing the glory of God's

Kingdom, not as a sublime splendor but as that which fills all the worlds. The Divine becomes imminent as well as exalted and beyond us; He is in all directions and He is equally present in every place, in Heaven and Hell and in every human heart. With great mercy He shows Himself and hides Himself. Therefore, we can ask for clemency because, essentially, He is compassionate and merciful without end.

This is a given possibility because the Divine penetrates the world to the lowest level of existence. But what is the connection between requesting Divine Mercy as an expression of His Love and the other side of our supplication in the prayer: "And let us not be put to shame and humiliation...." For the unspeakable truth of the matter is that men do things in the privacy and concealment of their being, when they believe that they are utterly alone, which they would be terribly ashamed of doing if they were exposed to the gaze of another person or persons. When and if they feel that God is present, the shame becomes unbearable mortification and self-repugnance. To the Divine, nothing is hidden.

One of the most subtle and most desperate, perhaps, of human petitioning, therefore, is to be saved this shame and terrible humiliation. Transgression that one is ashamed of admitting can be shattering to life as well as to one's image of oneself. When a person recognizes the despicable in himself: "What have I done with my soul?" he is ready to make a profound change in his whole life. The cry: "Have mercy on us," takes on added meaning; something is added to the human request for pity. It is a realization of the falsity and pathos of concealment, of the terrifying need to live in the light, in truth.

As an aside, we may wonder at the power of this relatively secondary factor of shame. (Secondary, that is, in relation to the love and fear of God.) But just as compassion and pity often go deeper than love, so does shame, with or without the element of punishment, penetrate the being with an extraordinary force of its own. It assumes a disproportionate reality in the secret depths of the individual. Hence, too, the Thirteen Attributes of Divine Mercy have their external and internal aspects. And much has been discussed about this in the Kabbalistic writings, dividing Divine mercy into two aspects: the soft, fragrant, and felicitous action of benevolence; and the painful, crushing subjugation of the mind and body resistance. One can hardly be expected to make a chart of the workings of Divine Mercy. All we possess are hints scattered in the rituals and the sacred writings. For instance: the platter of the Passover Seder on which a number of clearly specified items are placed in prescribed order. Oddly, the bitter herbs are placed in the center. According to the logic of the Kabbalistic *Sefirot*, it perhaps should have its place to the left, on the line of severity. But the attribute of love and compassion, on the right, also demands the bitterness. Why? One could ask: If one is in a state of grace and contentment, why does one need mercy? Mercy is for those who lack something critical. And the bitterness is the beginning of Divine Mercy; if one eats of the bitterness and weeps with distaste, one is at least in that beginning state of need.

Similarly, in order to arouse the Thirteen Attributes of Mercy one has to be serious, one has to taste the bitterness in the soul that comes from being apart from God. "With Thy many mercies, have mercy on us," is a cry of great need, distress, and privation, expressing a lack of that which is essential on any level of existence – personal, moral, or spiritual. "Why don't I have what I need?" is at least a consciousness of the distress and one's inability to understand it. So that the Sages have said that this *Da'at* (Knowledge) is at least a beginning; one is not smug in one's ignorance, and mercy has a chance of being aroused.

This consciousness of need is thus the beginning of the beating and crushing process, operating on the body and the identification with the physical. And the pain and heartbreak involved in the particular individual sense of lack, irrespective of circumstance, is a part of the world problem. The cry is: "Have mercy on us and give our hearts understanding to comprehend and to know," so "that we shall not be ashamed and humiliated." Understanding, therefore, comes first; after that, the mercy can work on one through love and fear and all the other Divine Emanations.

True, this does not always operate in the same fashion. When a person gets to an awareness of some lack, he may try to find a quick solution and be satisfied with it. The distress often has to be painful – no matter in what way – to make a person pray earnestly. Then, too, the distress may pass and a person has learned the value of prayer, to a certain extent; his soul has grown accordingly. But if it is only an isolated instance, it may not have any more effect than an opening of the heart.

Nevertheless, one begins to see things differently. The pressure on one may be in its early stages, but if it continues, as it tends to do, and there is growing awareness of the distress of others, the soul stirs out of its slumber. And, although there may be added heart crushing in the process of being open to the pain of the world, it leads to growth, increased capacity to bear the sorrow, and to invite Divine Mercy.

Chapter seven

At the olive press, the hard and bitter olives are partially crushed in order to extract the oil and to sweeten the fruit. So, too, it is written, the body of man has to undergo a certain amount of pressure and adversity to enable the inner self to emerge. But where is this self? In the description of the menora in scriptural texts, there are two olives, little hollow bulbs, one to the right and the other to the left of the stem, and these provide the oil for the lamps. The right and the left, grace and severity, the two aspects of man, struggle against each other; they represent the need for friction and conflict as a part of the purification process. It represents the refinement of the self that comes from adversity, when man cries out, "Have mercy on me, Thou who art all merciful."

The man who is satisfied with himself and seeks no Divine help is perhaps more comfortable, but he will, in all likelihood, be unable to comprehend the contradictory synthesis of love and fear of God. It is this knowledge of love and fear that humbles the heart and makes the soul a vessel for the holy oil that lights the lamp.

This process may also be interpreted as the "running and returning" movement of the soul, which vibration is so necessary for the life of the spirit. When one is in great need, one runs ahead, pressed to attain that which is lacking, that which one yearns for. Afterwards, when there is nothing missing anymore, there is the necessary returning movement to one's self or to that which constituted spiritual origin. And so it continues; a constant oscillation and drive to higher achievement, to a more comprehensive spiritual selfhood.

The essential point of the process is expressed in traditional terms as a "speaking of." It is not a speaking "to" or a speaking "about." One speaks of those things that one feels strongly about and that are above one. They are even more difficult to talk about than a pure feeling. A certain different kind of identification is needed; the contents are in oneself, but not about oneself. The self is a vessel through which the contents flow. One is like a person who is being played upon to make music. The sounds are emitted by the person but he is not the speaker or the music-maker. Of course, this comes only as a result of having become humble and unobtrusive, in consequence of adversity and crushing maturation, through love and loss. A person should become a perfect channel; nothing is distorted or lost as it passes through him.

But as is known in modern technology, electric current has to be transferred by a conductor that provides a minimum of resistance – otherwise most of the energy gets lost. In physics, the best conductors of energy are of the lowest temperature where there is a minimal movement of molecules. For a man in the world, full of the thoughts of the world, the problem of being a conductor of Divine plenty raises many questions. How is one to retain or pass on the word of God in all its power and purity? The whole crushing and pounding of man in this respect is to make him more malleable, less resistant, a better conductor of Divine light. The idea is to make oneself nullified before God in order to speak His word.

The result is wondrous and miraculous, beyond all ordinary limitations. The way of prayer and self-sanctification, as exemplified by the hundred benedictions a religious Jew pronounces in the course of a single day, is a part of this continual pressure exerted on the soul. The wondrousness of the change thus inaugurated cannot be made visible. For the redemption is not by the king of the universe but by the King of Kings, the realm beyond the knowable.

The understanding of this highest realm is perhaps more accessible through the most profound and terrifying of questions. As in higher mathematics, the answer is usually lodged in the original problem – the paradoxically unanswerable question. Often, the way is through the meeting of the opposite ends – "I am the first and the last." In terms of the human soul, we realize that the heart of man is in exile, imprisoned in the creatureliness of the body, and the yearning for God can be filled only by freeing oneself from this physical bondage. Fortunately, however, it happens that within the tempestuous drives of the physical frame, there are various levels and also a number of obligations. And hidden within all of these are certain intimate longings and searchings. If we were to paint man and his physical passions only on the surface level, the picture would shame even the most bestial of animals. Beneath it all, however, there is, in every human being, something that is unique, that is not built on hunger. There is a complexity in desire.

Human desires obviously are not only physical passions. The body, in itself, is a biophysical instrument of life, experiencing what we know as desire only at a certain higher level, which is different somehow from its basic appetites and instinctual needs. We make a distinction then between the inner desires of the heart and the demands of the physical structure. When a dentist probes one's teeth, there are many disagreeable sensations, but when he touches a live nerve, one jumps. It is a different kind of pain.

In the soul, too, we can distinguish what really touches it and what is external. Called by the Sages the "inwardness of the heart," this vivid sensitivity of the soul to that which is critical to its own particular being makes it feel a stranger in the body, exiled so to speak, or imprisoned. And we therefore keep speaking of freeing the soul to enable it to soar and fulfill its desire – the desire for emancipation. But in order for this to take place, as we have said, there must be a process of crushing the structural resistance. Only then can the desires of the soul begin to sort themselves out, each to its own direction. Only then does a person recognize what is really important for him. Frameworks begin to crumble, a new outlook makes its appearance.

To be sure, we should not wish such things on anyone, but it does often happen that only in adversity do people break through to a realization of what is truly of central importance as far as their own lives are concerned. The core of the heart's desire may be so hidden away that finding it may be a startling revelation and a shock.

What is indicated by the above is also an admonition not to wait for external circumstances to afflict one so severely that one is broken open. Better by far to do the breaking by oneself. Rather than have disaster work its way, with the uncertain consequences of the crushing process, it is clearly preferable to raise up the inwardness of the heart and release it to find its fulfillment in freedom from the terrors of pain. Suddenly all that which was once so very important can be discarded; it is no longer important.

We are brought to the practical expression of this emancipatory dedication as it is formulated in the first part of the Shema declaration. The yoke of the burden of heaven is here accepted, the burden of the mitzvot as Divine Command, and also, as we have mentioned, as heavenly delight. First, there is the innermost spontaneous need to perform the mitzva out of love. It is completely self-evident that a command is best carried out in willing and enthusiastic participation. At the same time, there is an element of service involved, doing something for another, and if the other is the Divine, a note of joyful surrender enters. The performance of a mitzva includes a comprehension of the terrible seriousness of a high edict, the awe of voluntarily participating in the power and wisdom of the Almighty. In this respect, it goes against the all-too-human mania for entertainment, for the lightness and liberty of the pursuit of pleasure. Why do we need to be encumbered by a yoke – even if it is called a yoke of heaven?

Nevertheless, as tradition claims, the people of Israel assumed this yoke out of the gladness of their hearts, with genuine enthusiasm. And, in the passage of time, a certain inner discipline was developed to sustain the life of Torah. It was not a coercive system of social domination. For the most part, it remained an individual matter, left to one's own choice and degree of spiritual ardor. The self-discipline grew out of the nature of the Divine Service within daily life.

At the same time, there was no degeneration into a certain amateurish attitude of "not important to do this correctly – after all, I am not someone in authority." The strangely obligatory realization of being personally responsible – no matter how one feels (one had good days and bad days) – retained its effectiveness for many generations. Because ultimately it is discipline that makes for power in history.

It has been said that even when a person does a mitzva with great joy, out of complete identification and delight, there should be an element of seriousness in the doing, a recognition that it is the Yoke of Heaven he is bearing, even when it seems light and desirable. There is a certain difference between the Kingdom of Heaven and the Yoke of the Kingdom of Heaven. It may be compared to the enraptured love of engaged couples and the mutual obligations and duties of married couples. Love can remain magnificent and blissful throughout all the stages of a relation. Why get married? Why do we have to get mixed up with obligatory constraints and endless liabilities? Indeed, it would be wonderful, perhaps, for love to remain free of all bonds, duties, and even promises. But life seems to have decided otherwise, both in personal scope and in the national setting. The day of the giving of the Torah at Mt. Sinai was the wedding day of the Jewish people.

Chapter eight

There seems to be a rather conclusive agreement about the teaching that there are two essential aspects in accepting the Yoke of Heaven – קבלת עול שמים – love and fear of God. But there are differences of emphasis; some sources say that fear and love – דחילו ורחימו – is the correct order in assuming the religious life; others insist on love and fear – רחימו ודחילו – as the proper way to God. To be sure, it may be considered inconsequential; what difference does it make how one gets to the ultimate object of devotion? But, according to some Sages, it does matter whether one arrives from the mind to the heart, or the heart to the mind. Each is a different route and the influences are not the same. For the way, the process, or technique, is a significant part of any final product, whether it be a matter of chemical combinations or the art of painting. In holy worship, the quality of joy is a primal factor on the way to love.

One rises in the act of worship; it is a soul movement from below to that which is higher and true. As in the benediction following the Shema *Yisrael* declaration where the blessing is for that which is "True and Everlasting," *"Emet VeYatziv"* – and it proceeds to receive the descending grace as "Good and Pleasant" – *"Tov VeYafeh."* There is an act of self-nullification involved; indeed wisdom requires the removal of narrow selfhood; it demands the right-of-way, so to speak, in order to allow for right action and for joy to flow freely. (The implication here is that the mind has to surrender first so that the heart can truly rejoice and attain fulfillment.)

All of which, as we have said, confirms the fact that Torah expresses Divine wisdom and the mitzvot express Divine Will. And since Divine Will (*Keter*) is higher than Wisdom (*Ḥokhma*), it may be surmised that Divine Wisdom is a rationalization, a mode of interpreting the Supreme Will. The essence of the mitzvot is thus seen as obedience to God's Will, a merging of my will with His. And this merging and fulfilling is a source of abundant satisfaction. Indeed, it is the greatest bliss.

Subsequently, there is the difference between the one who understands what he is doing and the one who does not have any idea of the meaning of his actions. From experience, we know that the one who is actively cooperative, who thinks he understands, is more likely to make mistakes, even if with the best intentions, than the one who, out of ignorance, follows instructions blindly. The Jew who waves his *lulav* in a certain manner because that is the way his fathers did it for generations is more apt to be right than the intelligent newcomer to the mitzva who considers how he could give it a personal meaning.

To be sure, this is one of the accepted differences between Torah and mitzvot: that Torah is inward and the mitzvot are outward. One performs the mitzvot and the mitzvot do not become a part of one's existence; they remain external, like garments that one puts on; the performer is only an instrument in the performance of the mitzva, which remains something independent. The study of Torah, on the other hand, besides being a mitzva, has the added aspect of being an internalization; a degree of understanding is involved, to the point at least, of making it part of oneself, if only for a moment. The mitzva never becomes a part of oneself in the same way. The Torah is an inner light, illuminating the depths of one's being. The mitzva is an external light; it surrounds one but does not penetrate the being. When one learns something of Torah, it becomes a part of one's comprehension of self; when one does a mitzva, one is doing an action in the world. True, it may also illuminate inwardly. And this illumination by the mitzva is called doing

God's Will. But it is external, a reality outside one and not within one's being. The inwardness, when it does occur, the interiorization of the mitzva, is of another nature. It is an extension of the aspect of doing the Divine Will. And, in this respect, it no longer belongs to place, it is beyond all location, even though one says that He is the place of the world and the world is not His Place. Which, again, has to be corrected somewhat. The Divine Encompassing relates to the perimeters of the world, the Divine Containment is beyond space and time. To do His Will, to carry out a particular Divine Command, involves the aspect of place. One transfers something from one realm of existence to another, from encompassing light to inner light. It is a process of revelation. As the expression "the blood is the soul" hints, that which is in oneself and moves within the body is illuminated. From which it may also be gathered that a way of life may be considered the supreme goal, higher even than the particular mitzva. As it is said, "wisdom shall give life to its owner" (Ecclesiastes 7:12).

This brings us back to the beginning of our discussion concerning the menora, "Behold I saw a lamp stand all of gold...."

One of the symbolic features we observed in the biblical menora of the sanctuary was that it represented *Knesset Yisrael*. Why all of gold? Jeremiah and Ezekiel speak of this matter in somewhat derogatory terms – "כסף נמאס קראו לכם" (Jeremiah 6:30).

And indeed if one were to be honest about the constituent quality of the Children of Israel, one would agree that there was much that was not pure gold. Of course, there was some precious metal here and there, and this made the menora precious. But, the people could hardly be called "all of gold?" True, the prophet Zechariah did call it entirely of gold in contrast to Jeremiah's cold rejection of its intrinsic, sterling character. In the *parasha Teruma*, it is suggested that the gold descends to silver and copper, and the book of Daniel designates a great figure with a head of gold, body of iron, and feet of clay as a metaphor for the decline of empire. The point is that the fact of something being solid gold in the Bible may have different meanings. In this sense, of "all" the menora, it is parallel to the phrase in the Song of Songs, "Thou art all of you beautiful my love."

The idea is that it was only the Babylonian Exile that added this total quality to the golden menora. Because of the afflictions of their banishment, they overcame their old feelings of disappointment in the silver and gold of the sanctuary, as Jeremiah had put it, and raised their hearts in praise of what had once been theirs in Jerusalem, the menora that had been (ostensibly) all of gold. "My soul thirsteth for thee, my flesh longeth for Thee in a dry and thirsty land where no water is; to see Thy power and Thy glory, as I have seen Thee in the sanctuary" (Psalms 63:2). The idea here is a longing to see God's Holiness as once it was felt in the wilderness. The Exile of the Jews from their homeland and spiritual source, being like the desert in its afflictions, may awaken this Divine Love. For at many levels it is true that the great yearning for the Divine rises to the surface in times of distress. The problem is that there are so many things that are felt to be precious only when we do not have them; only in their absence are they cherished. When they are in abundance, they are disregarded: health, freedom, homeland, and so on. Thus, for instance, the second day of celebration of Jewish holidays expresses this emphasis on the homeland. When in *Eretz Yisrael*, we scarcely celebrated the holy times of our tradition, but in the Diaspora, we do it twice over. Exile makes it more precious. The menora, which is *Knesset Yisrael*, becomes all gold.

In more than one passage in the liturgy, God is addressed: "You are our father" and in kabbalistic terms this particular father concept is often represented by the patriarch Isaac. In the context of the *Sefira* of Severity, *Gevura*, which is Isaac, is seen as the source; even though in many respects Love, or *Ḥesed* (Abraham), is considered primary. The point is that *Gevura* or Severity, the *Sefira* of Isaac, is the reddish color of copper or gold, whereas *Ḥesed* is silver, sparkling gray and light. Also in terms of value, the *Gevura* qualities of severity, precision, awe, and power are gold; they are more rare and consequently more precious. Thus, as we have indicated, in the framework of the mitzvot, the negative commandments are more important, as opposed to the positive commandments, for that which is not revealed is more powerful. Silence is greater than speech. The esoteric is more profound and abundant than the visible.

In the menora symbolism, the little olive-shaped vessel (sign of the shell that has to be crushed in order to be eaten) is the vessel from which the oil flows to the various branches of the candlestick. Isaac shall be called "For you are our father" – he is the golden source.

Why did Jeremiah and Ezekiel call the menora a rejected gold? Why did they speak so critically of the people who were represented by the menora? Only after the exile could the menora be seen as all of gold – even if it could also be considered to be dirty and covered with dust, requiring purification and the rehabilitation of *Tikkun*.

The important aspect of the menora is that it is all of gold. And the meaning is that Israel assumes the Yoke of Heaven, as a total commitment.

About the author

Rabbi Adin Steinsaltz is a teacher, philosopher, social critic, and prolific author who has been hailed by *Time* magazine as a "once-in-a-millennium scholar." His lifelong work in Jewish education earned him the Israel Prize, his country's highest honor.

Born in Jerusalem in 1937 to secular parents, Rabbi Steinsaltz studied physics and chemistry at the Hebrew University. He established several experimental schools and, at the age of 24, became Israel's youngest school principal.

In 1965, he began his monumental Hebrew translation and commentary on the Talmud. To date, he has published 38 of the anticipated 46 volumes. The Rabbi's classic work of Kabbala, *The Thirteen Petalled Rose*, was first published in 1980 and now appears in eight languages. In all, Rabbi Steinsaltz has authored some 60 books and hundreds of articles on subjects ranging from zoology to theology to social commentary.

Continuing his work as a teacher and spiritual mentor, Rabbi Steinsaltz established a network of schools and educational institutions in Israel and the former Soviet Union. He has served as scholar in residence at the Woodrow Wilson Center for International Studies in Washington, D.C. and the Institute for Advanced Studies at Princeton

University. His honorary degrees include doctorates from Yeshiva University, Ben Gurion University of the Negev, Bar Ilan University, Brandeis University, and Florida International University.

Rabbi Steinsaltz lives in Jerusalem. He and his wife have three children and many grandchildren.

The fonts used in this book are from the Arno family

Other works by Adin Steinsaltz
available from Maggid

A Dear Son to Me

Biblical Images

The Essential Talmud

The Tales of Rabbi Nachman of Bratslav

Talmudic Images

Teshuvah

The Thirteen Petalled Rose

Maggid Books
The best of contemporary Jewish thought from
Koren Publishers Jerusalem Ltd.